5530

D0371436

PHOENIX FIRST ASSEMBLY COLLEGE
13613 N. Cave Creek Rd
Phoenix, AZ 85022

Library
Oakland S.U.M.

Eldercare
for the Christian Family

Eldercare
for the Christian Family

TIMOTHY S. SMICK
JAMES W. DUNCAN, J.P. MORELAND, JEFFREY A. WATSON

WORD PUBLISHING
Dallas·London·Vancouver·Melbourne

PHOENIX FIRST PASTORS COLLEGE
13613 N. Cave Creek Rd.
Phoenix, AZ 85022

Eldercare for the Christian Family

Copyright © 1990 by Word, Inc.

All rights reserved. No portion of this book may be reproduced in any form without the written permission of the publisher, except for brief excerpts in critical reviews. Unless otherwise indicated, authors have used their own paraphrases of Scripture. Those marked TLB are from The Living Bible, copyright 1971 by Tyndale House Publishers, Wheaton, IL. Used by permission.

*Stories of Sally and Martha in chapter 11 are adapted from *Talking with Your Aging Parents* by Mark Edinberg, © 1988. Reprinted by arrangement with Shambhala Publications, 300 Massachusetts Avenue, Boston, MA 02115.

Library of Congress Cataloging in Publication Data

Eldercare : what to do when a loved one becomes dependent / Timothy S. Smick et al.
    p.   cm.
Includes bibliographical references.
ISBN 0-8499-0719-5
    1. Aged—Care—United States. 2. Frail elderly—Care—United States. 3. Adult children—United States. 4. Caregivers—United States. I. Smick, Timothy S., 1951–
HV1461.M67 1990
362.6—dc20   89-77105
                                          CIP

Printed in the United States of America
0 1 2 3 9 BKC 9 8 7 6 5 4 3 2 1

Contents

Eldercare
for the Christian Family

1

The Sandwiched Generation
Timothy S. Smick

Carol's Story

When the phone rang I just sensed from the abrupt sound of the ring that the caller on the other end had a message of urgency and was not the bearer of good news.

"Your mother has fallen and is being rushed by ambulance to Northern Memorial Hospital." I was stunned and caught totally off guard. After calling my closest friend, Julie, with the news, I asked her to inform my husband, Tom, who was due home in about an hour from a short business trip.

While driving to the hospital my mind raced. *Would this accident disturb our long-awaited vacation plans that were only*

TIMOTHY S. SMICK, a graduate of Wheaton College, has been a long-term care professional since 1974. His experience has ranged from serving as a nursing home orderly to overseeing the operations of a division of one of the country's largest nursing home chains. Smick is one of the principals of PersonaCare, Inc., a Baltimore-based health care company with retirement and nursing home facilities throughout the United States. He serves as the company's Co-Chairman and has direct oversight of all health care and retirement management operations as well as the firm's acquisition division. He has taught health care professionals on the national level in the area of bioethics and twice appeared on James Dobson's radio program, Focus on the Family, as well as The 700 Club, to discuss the practical problems faced by those caring for the elderly. He serves as an elder at the Bay Area Community Church where he, his wife, Bobbi, and two daughters, Kim and Amy, worship.

three weeks away? I hope not. It's been so long since Tom and I have had some extended time together. Then, all of a sudden, I became overwhelmed by the sense of guilt that accompanied my self-acknowledged selfishness.

Mom, eighty years old, was as active now as she ever was. Although Dad had died of a heart attack almost twelve years ago, she seemed to have hardly aged. She still had the uncanny ability to say just the thing that would drive me crazy with guilt. Yes, we enjoyed a love-hate relationship that was not remarkably different from the relationships some of my other girlfriends had with their mothers. Yet, somehow, as much as we can get on each other's nerves, I know I love her very much and see so much of myself in her.

Was this fall a chance accident or was it caused by her advancing years? I really hadn't stopped to consider the totality of the little changes I had observed within her during the last decade: the uncontrollable shaking of her hands, the lack of fluidity in her walk, and her inability to focus on a conversation of any extended duration. All at once, Mom's sudden forgetfulness during the last two years began to make sense. I remembered the day that Tom came to pick her up for dinner and found the water running and overflowing in her bathtub, or the time a pot boiled over extinguishing the flame, allowing escaping gas to fill the apartment just before our son had come to visit her. She was Mom and always would be Mom. It was only when my daughter and I thumbed through the family photo album that I'd notice any of her physical changes.

Upon my arrival at the hospital, I was immediately faced with questions about Mom in a clerk's attempt to complete hospital admission forms. Impatiently, I answered each question, intermittently inquiring as to the status of my mom.

Finally a doctor came to answer my many questions. "Mrs. Thomas has suffered a broken hip in her fall. She was found by her landlord when she did not answer her doorbell. Apparently, she had been too weak to move from the bathroom to the phone to call for help. We would like to operate on her as soon as her blood pressure stabilizes. Within two to three weeks she should be on her feet again. Within three to four months she will be able to walk almost as independently as she did before the accident."

"May I see my mother?"

"Of course, but keep in mind she is in considerable pain."

As we walked through the double set of doors I saw Mom on the hospital gurney. When she heard my voice her eyes met mine and she began to speak with excitement. The medication she had been given caused her to slur her speech, but it was clear to me by the expression on her face that my presence was the only reassurance she had in this time of fear and pain.

As I sat holding her hand and looking into her glazed eyes, I saw the fiercely independent woman who had accomplished so much in her lifetime. Over and above raising three children, all of whom had such successful careers, she had excelled as a high school English teacher. Recognized as a "Teacher of the Year" numerous times, she had earned the respect of students, administration, parents, and fellow teachers. Articulate and captivating, she was as comfortable in a formal social setting as she was singing in the church choir or playing contract bridge.

Now, for the first time, she looked really old to me. The shaking in her hands was even more pronounced and she seemed confused as she looked at me. As she was wheeled away to be prepared for surgery, I was struck with the notion that I *won't always have Mom.*

I thought again about the toll the years had taken on her. Seeing her so dependently holding my hand caused me to recognize the gradual erosion of independence she had so reluctantly and gradually surrendered through the years. The process had been so subtle in each of its stages, starting when she asked me to drive her to appointments she was unable to schedule before sunset. Gradually, she grew dependent on me for trips on even the smallest of errands. Although financially secure due to Dad's good planning, she was now quickly overwhelmed by fear about relatively minor transactions. Last winter, she didn't eat for three days when she suffered the flu. She joined our family for dinner every night for two weeks until her dehydration and malnourished strength had become rejuvenated. And yet, dependent as she had become on her family, Mom still vigorously protected her privacy and the independence she enjoyed within her apartment. Somehow, I knew that this "independent" chapter of her life was coming to an abrupt end.

(Three weeks later . . .)

The operation a success, Mom, true to character, fought vigorously to be able to walk again. Working with the hospital physical therapist, she began to place weight on her hip within three weeks.

Mom convalesced at our house for ten weeks after her hospital stay. We took her to her physical therapist's office five days a week. Although it was stressful at times, the whole family pitched in knowing that the inconvenience caused by Mom's dependency was only temporary.

Everything about the morning of March 27th suggested that this day was going to be trying. The improperly set alarm clock combined with the dark inclement weather made the start of the day unbearable. As I went into Mom's temporary quarters in the guest room, I uttered a brief "good morning," helping her out of bed. As she stood to grab her cane, for no apparent reason, she sank to the floor. Her groans of agony immediately made me aware that something was drastically wrong. I quickly called the ambulance and did not attempt to move Mom other than to make her feel comfortable on the floor. As the medics wheeled her outside, I could see the tremendous fear in her eyes. Her look communicated an uncertainty that she could pull off another rigorous restorative program. Mom's eyes clearly communicated a physical as well as an emotional defeat.

As expected, Mom's situation was serious. She had refractured her hip and her physician was much more pessimistic about her full recovery than he had been at the time of her initial accident.

It was uncanny, but I suddenly knew that my new role of primary family caregiver was not to be a temporary position. Even in its most trying moments, caring for Mom during the last two months was emotionally manageable because of the promise of her full recovery to independence. Now, I intuitively knew my role as Mom's primary caregiver had shifted to a more permanent position.

Mom's stay in the hospital was considerably longer than her previous visit. Emotionally, she had given up in her will to regain her independence. It was clear to me that it was only a matter of time before her body would submit to its inability to foster an autonomous lifestyle.

Once Mom was discharged from the hospital to our home, I quickly became aware of her dependence on our family for just about everything. Toileting, bathing, grooming—and even eating—were now chores she had become incapable of managing by herself. It was clear that Mom could not be left unattended for any extended period of time.

As I expected, these caregiving responsibilities were taking their toll on the entire family. The novelty of participating in Mom's convalescence after her first fall had become inconvenient and tedious labor. Moreover, the front row seat we had in observing her daily physical and emotional decline had introduced another depressing reason to dread involvement in caring for her. It even seemed as if Mom resented our involvement.

One day, in the midst of a terrible fight with Tom, I reached the point of breaking down in tears. It was clear that the situation which provoked our original disagreement that day should never have elevated to the level of anger it did. Yet, neither Tom nor I could emotionally acknowledge the source of the constant low level of depression we were feeling from day to day.

It had been months since we had spent a social evening with our friends. Our son, Phil, had volunteered several different times to stay with Mom for the evening. Yet, I was too emotionally and physically drained to muster up the energy for any healthy diversion such as this.

I, more than Tom, seemed to wrestle with a feeling of guilt about the increasing resentment I was indirectly projecting toward Mom in my role as her caregiver. That resentment was more directly focused toward my brother and sister who had only made token overtures to "help when they could." They sent cards and routinely made a weekly telephone call to Mom. Mom felt so uplifted by those phone calls and expressed her appreciation to them for their thoughtfulness. Yet she seemed almost resentful toward me as I knocked myself out to make her comfortable. My brother and sister's presumption that I was the one who would care for Mom made me angry. Yes, they both had careers, but I had just begun the schooling I needed to "restart" my career in teaching. Now it seemed that my career plans were on an indefinite hold.

In the aftermath of my fight with Tom, we began to reflect on how unprepared we were for this "interruption to our dreams"— dreams that had been inaugurated from the time Tom proposed marriage to me twenty-nine years before. Our dreams included a beautiful wedding, the birth of our first child, Tom's career successes, the purchase of our new house, wonderful vacation memories, our children's graduations and weddings, our first grandchild, and even a contented retirement somewhere in the South. Nowhere had we contemplated a stage of life that was so dominated by my mother's continual need for care in almost every activity of daily life.

I felt so alone, so guilty, and so very depressed. My relationship with God seemed strained as I seemed to project some of this resentment toward him.

* * * * *

Carol's story is no longer an unusual phenomenon. In fact, it is highly likely that each and every family in our modern-day society will be impacted either directly or indirectly by the consequences of caring for an aging relative. Yet, with the increasing likelihood of encountering just such a situation, few families are physically, emotionally, or mentally prepared for the caregiving needs of an aging parent.

Today's Modern Family Is Unprepared for Its Caregiving Role

There are numerous reasons why today's families are generally unprepared for the increasingly common event of caring for a loved one.

Unlike parents of young children who anticipate each step of early childhood development, adult children of senior parents must deal with an unpredictable calendar of physical aging. Some seniors have the capacity to live engaging and active lifestyles. At age 90 they are capable of running their own lives and sometimes try to dominate their children's too. By contrast, their children at age 65 can be in a rapid physical decline with increasing dependency on others.

Many families are unaware of the "graying" of the American population. The elderly garnered little attention during the first half of this century. In fact, until recently the later stages of life have received little notice by our culture resulting in a society that is indifferent and ignorant about the special needs of the elderly. Society's recent mounting concern about life in the later years is understandable with a quick demographic review of the swelling senior population.

Throughout most of recorded history, only one in ten people could expect to live to the age of 65. Today, nearly 80 percent of Americans will live beyond that age. In the last two decades, the over-65 age group has grown more than twice as fast as the rest of the population at a rate of 5,000 per day. Each day that someone in America turns 21, two people turn 65. This increase is accompanied by a significant change in age distribution within the senior segment. The number of those 75 years old and older will increase by 74 percent by the year 2000. Even more dramatic is the increase of the very old (those 85 years of age and older) whose number will more than double to 5.1 million over the next twelve years. The elderly, who were once considered an insignificant demographic "blob" by planners of all types, are now seen as a highly segmented population with varying and specific needs.[1]

Most of us have only a vague understanding of the magnitude of this senior demographic explosion. Yet, even if we had a better understanding of the senior population's requirements, we would have emotional forces within us that would blind us to the potential needs of our parents. Our general inability to accept a parent's old age is often another reason we find ourselves unprepared to confront our parents' need for care assistance. As children, most of us viewed our parents as immortal and strong enough to protect us forever. Obviously, somewhere along the line, we learn that our parents are not quite as invulnerable as we originally thought. Yet we still retain, sometimes unknowingly, the notion that our parents are there to protect us if we need them. Intellectually, we have the ability to understand their increasing feebleness, but on the gut level we are sometimes sad, frightened, resentful, or disappointed when we are struck with the reality of their mortality.

Carol Continues

I was thirty-four years old when I rushed to the hospital to be with my dad who was brought to the emergency room one Sunday morning complaining of chest pains. As the doctors waited for test results, Dad actually began to suffer cardiac arrest while in the emergency room. Mom and I stood by helplessly as we watched the cardiac specialists try to minimize the extent of muscle damage caused by the heart attack. Although Dad survived that heart attack with only minimal muscle damage and reentered the hospital months later for successful bypass surgery, I remember the fear and helplessness I felt as I watched the strongest male image in my life reduced to tears as he fought the pain of the heart attack and the fear of death. It quickly became apparent to me that we would not always have Dad around. Although I had never stopped to think about it, Dad was a stabilizing influence on everyone in the family. The notion of his mortality had never before "sunk home" and now had caught me quite off guard. Frightened, sad, and in a way very disappointed, I began to make the emotional adjustment to the fact that someday Dad was not going to be with us.

The senior demographics highlighted above underline another force behind our uneasiness with the caregiving role—the absence of the caregiver model. Most roles are learned through modeling of behavior. Unfortunately, few of today's adults had parents who effectively modeled caregiving of their grandparents. In those days there were very few grandparents who lived long enough to need the care of their families.

Possibly, our culture's gerontophobic mindset is yet another factor that blinds us to the realities of the natural aging process. We have a fear of aging and a prejudice against the elderly that clouds all our perceptions about what it means to grow old. Billions of dollars are spent each year on plastic surgery, tummy tucks, laparotomy, hair transplants, hair coloring, and numerous other products and procedures designed to cosmetically remove the natural impact of the aging process on our bodies. In China, where significant esteem is bestowed on the elder family member, a 55-year-old might cheat a bit and claim to be 59. But an American asked the same question might likely respond with "I never tell my age" or cheat a little bit and answer, "I'm 49." It is no wonder that in a society striving so hard to repress the ugly impact of aging that we have succeeded at times in thinking that neither we nor our loved ones will ever grow "old." Indeed, admissions personnel in most retirement communities report that seniors shopping for apartments in these communities almost always subconsciously consider themselves ten years younger than their actual chronological age.

The Sandwiched Generation — The Woman in the Middle

Whether we are prepared or not, as our population ages, the need for caregivers and long-term care will continue to increase. Most likely, the reader of this book is already in the midst of caring for a parent or some other loved one. Often these caregivers feel very alone as they daily fulfill the responsibilities "bestowed" upon them. As they enviously watch their friends with schedules clear of caregiving duties, they wonder if anyone else is in the same predicament. There are many. Accurate data is not available on the precise numbers of caregivers in our country, since most caregivers go about their heroic roles in nonassuming, humble silence. However, we know that as of the 1980 census, 65 percent of fifty-year-old women in the U.S. had living mothers as opposed to only 37 percent in 1940. Since the number of three- and four-generation families has greatly increased, it can be assumed that the number of caregivers in our country has increased proportionately.

Unfortunately, some of these caregivers are not well postured to take on this critically important role. Studies indicate that over one third of these caregivers (average age 57) are poor, and roughly 25 percent of these caregivers are in poor health.[2]

Nearly seven out of every ten primary caregivers are females who spend an average of sixteen hours a week providing care. The question of who cares for Mom and Dad rarely comes down to who is capable or willing. In the past few decades the presumption that this role was the female's has been left unchallenged. Some experts believe this presumption has roots that were formed in early childhood when we learn what behaviors are appropriate to our gender identification. Caregiving happens to be one of those roles that are socially sanctioned for females. In our modern-day society the traits of nurturing, caring, sensitivity, sweetness, understanding, flexibility, compassion, self-sacrifice, gentleness, and warmth offer little reinforcement to the male esteem and are almost always associated as admirable traits exclusively attributed to females.[3] Therefore, when it is said "she lives with her son," it really means "she lives with her daughter-in-law."

Socially sanctioning the caregiver role to daughters, daughters-in-law, sisters, and nieces is a presumption that is causing tremendous family stress in this day of two-career households.

Betty works as an executive secretary to support her two college-aged children. Although her brother had demonstrated an admirable willingness to contribute time and energy to caring for their Alzheimer's-stricken father, her father almost always turned to his daughter "Liz" for the assistance that consistently interfered with her recently restarted career. Betty resented her father's traditional notion that her single brother's job was more important. Yet, feeling helpless to reverse years of determined role expectations, she assumed an increasingly larger role in her father's care that forced her to forego her career ambitions. "With the kids in college I had finally found the independence to do something, and now it's like I'm being pulled back," she says.

Betty's experience is the story of the "sandwiched generation." With no assurance that she will live to the ripe old age of her father, she knows she risks the chance of never realizing her career objectives as well as other opportunities that life has to offer. She fears that she will miss these chances because she is wedged tightly between two generations grappling for care. "Sandwiched" between her children's and her parent's needs, she has little room to pursue her own goals and desires.

Many in the "sandwiched generation" feel cheated, deprived of self-fulfillment, robbed of the opportunity to indulge in pleasures that they have come to look upon as rights.

Career sacrifices are not the only toll experienced by caregivers. A recent study of elders and caregivers found that the adult caregiver was three times more likely than the cared-for elder to report symptoms of depression and four times more likely to report anger. Caregiving children spoke rather poignantly in these studies of the guilt, frustration, and occasional desperation they were experiencing. One respondent wrote: "There is a constant feeling of depression in the inability to bring happiness to the older person whose friends are gone, whose body is worn down, and who knows he is disrupting his child's life."[4]

When these emotional stresses are coupled with the strains of the erosion of the caregiver's own health, the caregiving role can become unbearable.

Guilt: The Gift That Keeps on Giving to the Caregiver

Yet, time after time, caregivers refuse to admit "failure" because of the guilt they internally nurture. "Didn't Mom care for me? Isn't it my turn to care for her?" Many caregivers make the faulty assumption that they must take care of their parents the same way their folks took care of them. They even believe their parents expect or want them to provide around-the-clock care. Although there are many similarities between providing care for aging parents and parenting young children, there are important differences. Most parents look forward with eager anticipation to the birth of their child. By contrast, most lament, rather than delight in, the prospect of having to care for helpless parents. Ironically, their parents, too, dread the day when they will need their children's care.

In most cases, a child's need for assistance in the activities of daily living is only temporary and moves rapidly toward the child's delighted self-discovery of independence. The elderly, however, when afflicted with senile dementia, are moving in the opposite direction on the independence scale and have increasing needs for assistance every day.

The child knows no world outside the one parents provide; aging parents, on the other hand, often bring into our homes a perspective on the world that differs greatly from our own, accompanied by a disapproval of the lifestyles we have chosen.

Although caregivers suffer much self-inflicted guilt, parents themselves can be outstanding inducers of guilt. Gerontologists know that certain personality traits, even the unfavorable ones, can become more pronounced as a senior gets older.

Since childhood, Jon was known to have a problem with selfishness. Not surprisingly, this attribute caused numerous problems with siblings as well as playmates throughout his early years. By necessity, Jon learned to bridle his natural inclination toward selfishness in order to maintain rewarding relationships. Unfortunately, as Jon approached his later senior years, his selfishness became more extreme as he experienced a loss of the social skills he had "learned" throughout his lifetime. Friends stopped calling and loneliness set in, causing him to place greater social demands on his children "who had to tolerate his selfishness." Jon began to become an expert at using guilt to manipulate his daughter to cater to him in even his most frivolous requests.

For many adult children, getting institutional or noninstitutional support in caring for a parent remains a forbidding last resort. They see the need for such assistance as a failure and will only seek help after a forceful recommendation from their physician who is more worried about the caregiver's health than that of the senior.

A number of signals will warn you as a caregiver that you are experiencing role overload and need help. If you notice any of the following symptoms, you might have fallen into the trap of taking on too much to the extent you will eventually need medical and psychological treatment:

- Your relative's condition is worsening despite your best efforts.

- No matter what you do it isn't enough.

- You feel that you are the only one in the world enduring this.

- You no longer have any time or place to be alone for even a brief respite.

- Things you use to do occasionally to help out are now part of your daily routine.

- Family relationships are breaking down because of the caregiving pressures.

- Your caregiving duties are interfering with your work and social life to an unacceptable degree.

- You're continuing in a no-win situation just to avoid admitting failure.

- You realize you're all alone—and doing it all—because you've shut out everyone who has offered help.

- You refuse to think of yourself because "that would be selfish" (even though you're unselfish 99 percent of the time).

- Your coping methods have become destructive: You're overeating/undereating, abusing drugs/alcohol, or taking it out on your relative.

- There are no more happy times; loving and caring have given way to exhaustion and resentment; and you no longer feel good about yourself or take pride in what you are doing.[5]

The Family as a Parent-Care System

"It is well known that one mother can take care of ten children, but ten children cannot take care of one mother."

There is much wisdom in this ancient proverb. It underlines the need for sharing the responsibility of caring for an older parent.

Much of the caregiver burnout so prevalent today could be avoided if the family had the strategic participation of most of the family members on a regular basis.

As already discussed, our role as caregivers is complicated by our own attitudes toward aging and the behavioral quirks of our senior parents. As if the complications of caregiving were not stressful enough, family members can also turn the whole event into a civil war.

Caring for an older relative does not necessarily have to be a time of family division. A shared problem, such as the caregiving needs of a parent, can bring out the best in every family member, drawing everyone closer together as each finds hidden strengths in themselves and each other.

In many families, the senior parents have served as the unifying agent and the family news service. They maintain balance and perpetuate ties between the children and their families. When their physical or mental capacities become severely limited, the family is forced to realign itself to absorb the changes. This time of realignment can be especially painful when unresolved sibling rivalry reemerges after many years. This interfamily relational dissonance can also make the caregiving process unbearable.

Competitiveness, favoritism, and rivalry can all bubble just below the surface resulting in behavior that can be unhealthy for all involved. Over-solicitous behavior toward senior parents may mask the anger a grown child feels for having to take second place, but it also may be a way of saying, "Look how good I am to you. Now, won't you love me best?"[6]

Even with the alternative arrangements available, it is estimated that most elderly people live in a family system, and a fair number live with grown children. As much as your mother never wanted to be a burden to any of her children, there may come a time when she will have no choice but to turn to someone in the family for help. How that someone is chosen can have an explosive impact on the entire family.

Studies have identified five different caregiving styles that offer further understanding about the way families mobilize to meet their parents' needs:

Routine Caregivers: Incorporate regular assistance to the parent into their daily activities, for example, regularly doing a parent's weekly shopping, laundry, or housecleaning. Daughters, oldest children, parental favorites, and "reliable" children are more likely to assume this style. Often more than one sibling in a family is a routine caregiver. The personality that an adult child was assigned within the family impacts the expectations others have in this person's participation in caregiving.

Backup Caregivers: Are reliably available to provide assistance on request, but don't voluntarily initiate involvement.

Circumscribed Caregivers: Provide help within carefully defined limits that other siblings recognize and respect, for example, calling a parent once a week, but not being available for other help.

Sporadic Caregivers: Provide assistance at their own convenience, for example, taking a parent along on an occasional outing.

Dissociated Caregivers: Cannot be reliably counted on to provide assistance of any kind. They may not even be involved in family discussions of the parent's problems.

The studies point out that sons are more likely than daughters to be circumscribed, sporadic, or disassociated caregivers. Daughters are more likely than sons to serve as backup caregivers.

In families with more than two siblings, conflict resulted when one became dissociated from the caregiving system.

Finally, the studies indicated that adult children whose spouses were actively supportive of their caregiving role had more flexibility as to the caregiving style they could adopt.[7]

Another study's findings point to some important differences in the way husbands and wives seem to approach caregiving. This study indicates that men usually have a more "instrumental" focus, concentrating on tasks, goals, and problem-solving. Women, on the other hand, have had a more "person-oriented" focus, concentrating on relationships, feelings, and the effects of their behavior on others. Some experts in caregiving think the male approach may have advantages. Men's tendency to focus on the tasks, rather than the relationship, may allow them to plan and conduct their lives in a way that more easily allows for activities outside the caregiving role.[8]

Clearly, there is no one formula for choosing appropriate caregiving roles. There are reasonable and circumstantial factors such as geographical proximity, giftedness, emotional strength, age, task orientation, and the aged parent's choice or preference. There are also unhealthy reasons that can enter into the selection process as well, resulting in damaging consequences.

Some aged parents place unreasonable demands on their caregivers. Sometimes these caregivers, because of their own complex feelings toward their parents, place unreasonable demands on themselves. In their zeal, they insist on handling the entire responsibility single-handedly and discourage anyone else from sharing in it in any way. Eventually, those who freely offered to help feel shut out after repeated rejections. It is at this point the caregiver/martyr begins to complain bitterly to anyone who will listen about the heavy burdens and the selfishness of her family. Truly the aging parent can become a pawn in family power struggles.

Those families who have most successfully mobilized themselves in the caregiving of a loved one have developed an uncanny, unselfish "sensing system" that safeguards the caregiver as well as the senior parent. They look for opportunities to "spot" one another without being asked. They do not limit the focus of their caring to the parent but include the well-being of all caregivers and their families in their considerateness. They are careful not to play the role of the "critical sniper" taking well-aimed shots on the way care is being delivered by others. And when well-intentioned relatives and onlookers offer unsolicited advice or criticism, they defend each other with encouragement and support.

Such shared caregiving is more of a challenge when family members live in different communities as is common today. If the families are scattered, it is more difficult to maintain a shared decision-making process. Siblings can, however, offer each other support, even from far-flung locations. It's especially important if only one is the primary, on-site caregiver for a parent. A phone call, letter, or delivered bouquet that thanks the caregiver may be just the right therapy for a caregiver who feels worn and neglected. This type of participation offers therapy to the distant family member as well, by stemming feelings of guilt and anxiety.

SUMMARY

Today's Christian families are unprepared for their caregiving roles. The unpredictability of the aging process, the lack of knowledge in general about seniors, gerontophobia, and the lack of prior generation role modeling all play key parts in our being unprepared as caregivers. Yet the likelihood that we will be impacted either directly or indirectly by the caregiving needs of a senior relative is growing.

Most caregivers today are women known as the "sandwiched generation," wedged between the responsibilities of meeting the needs of their children and their parents. These caregivers seem regularly to confront guilt. Sometimes this guilt is self-inflicted and other times it is induced by the manipulative behavior of a parent.

To alleviate caregiver burnout, it is important for the family to participate strategically as a caregiving system. As each family mobilizes to care for a parent the members of the family take on different caregiving styles. Although there is no one best formula for choosing appropriate caregiving roles, it is important that the caregiving system include shared responsibilities which safeguard the primary caregivers as well as the senior parent.

Many Christian caregivers understand that the Scriptures command us to "honor our fathers and mothers." Clearly, those who answer the call of caregiver for their parents are demonstrating obedience to this command and responding to a call that is equally as valid as any Christian calling to child-rearing or other career vocation. It is important to recognize that God's special blessings are bestowed upon those called to care for their parents or loved ones. The next chapter will delineate this calling to care as it was expressed and modeled in Joseph's relationship with Jacob.

2

When Someone in the Family Is Sick
Jeffrey A. Watson

Jeff's Story

The same startling dream was haunting me. In my nighttime theatre, I'd be tip-toeing past the bed of my sleeping grandmother. Just when I thought I was past her, she'd sit up with a frightened look on her face, whisper "Jeff," and lie back down with a sigh. The dream troubled me as a ten-year-old boy, especially when my vivid mental picture changed her bed into a coffin and our bedroom, the funeral parlor. For a quiet introspective kid, it felt as if I were sleeping next to a beloved corpse—one which could suddenly be disturbed back into life.

Over time the dream visited less often and the feelings of fear grew milder. My first brush with death had hurt a lot and filled my

JEFFREY A. WATSON is the Senior Pastor of Grace Bible Church in the Washington, D.C. suburbs. He also serves as Professor of Gerontology at Washington Bible College and as a Bioethicist for PersonaCare Nursing Homes. Previously he served at The Prince George's General Hospital and Medical Center, The Joseph Richey Hospice and The National Association for Families Caring for their Elders. As an active member of The Gerontological Society of America and The Foundation of Thanatology, his writing and broadcast ministry have focused on pastoral care for the aging, dying, and bereaved. Rev. Watson is a graduate of Capital Seminary (Th.M.), Catholic University (M.A.), Dallas Theological Seminary (D.Min.), and The University of Maryland (Doctoral Certificate in Gerontology). He lives with his wife Nancy and their two sons, Ryan and Steven, in Bowie, Maryland.

mind with questions. As was the case with young Timothy in the Bible, my faith in Jesus Christ owed its origin to a godly mother and grandmother—but now our veteran mentor was dead.

PERSONAL EXPERIENCES AS AN ELDERCARE FAMILY

I can still remember the day Grandma moved in with the Watsons, into that attic-turned-bedroom. I was lucky . . . I got to sleep up there too, just yards away from her bed. With both of my parents growing up in broken homes, I was especially delighted to know even one of my grandparents. There must have been a hundred mornings when this little early bird would try to go tip-toeing past Grandma's bed to silently use her bathroom. Just as I would get between her bed and the big rocker where we used to read children's Bible stories, she'd startle into a sitting position. Instantly, her widening eyes would meet mine. "It's only Jeff," she'd remind herself and fall back to the pillow.

On my tenth birthday, cancer took her away from us. In the days that followed, we spent what seemed to be eternally long afternoons and evenings at the funeral home—looking, talking, remembering. My dreams were blending the two powerful pictures into one. My barefoot ballet on the cold linoleum had merged into the deafening stillness of death. Repeatedly talking it out, reminding myself that she was gone, faded the dream into a memory.

Can't My Family Take Care of Me?

When elderly persons can no longer live alone safely, their first choice is almost always to be cared for by family. That's what Grandma wanted, that's what we wanted. We weren't perfect caregivers; but then again, she wasn't a perfect grandmother. But we all did our best as an eldercare family.

I remember the day that Grandma and I were making the downstairs beds and she stepped on that slipper. No one else was home as she went down with a crash on the wooden floor. With her hip shattered, I tried to lift her onto the bed. Unable to budge her, I sped out the door to the nearest neighbor for help. My mother drove in from the grocery store as they loaded her into the ambulance. It was a while before she was back with us, but we were glad when she came home.

For every elderly person who is receiving the much needed care of a hospital, hospice, or nursing home, there are between four and five other older adults being cared for in private homes.[1] Sometimes, the caregiving family moves in with the dependent elder or it may work the other way around. Sometimes, the adult children coordinate a team effort, a wide array of services to be brought to the aged mom or dad. No matter how it happens, the family is America's number one resource for eldercare. More importantly, the family is God's number one resource for eldercare.

The Kin-Keeper

When an older loved one becomes ill, the family usually looks to one of its females, its "kin-keepers," to provide the care. Not only was my mother the primary caregiver with my grandmother, she was also trying to raise three children at the same time. She was the woman "caught in the middle," in the "sandwiched generation" of childcare and eldercare all at once. She lived in a crucible of pressure and was a chief candidate for burnout.

The typical kin-keeper is either a wife caring for her dependent husband and his family, or she is a daughter by blood or marriage to the person needing care.[2] I've seen this noble role carried by women time and again, sometimes to the shame of men who could help.

My own wife was rock-solid the day the court placed my father in my custody when I was in my mid-twenties. In his own demented way as he stood in that courtroom, he pointed at me and told the judge: "You see that man over there? That's my son, Jeff. Whatever he says to do is right. He loves me." Whether his confusion could be traced to his Parkinson's disease, obvious overmedication, the World War II head injury, or his dysfunctional childhood, we will never know. What we did know was that he needed care. From an overnight in jail, to an acute care hospital, to a nursing home, to a VA psychiatric hospital—his needs had outstripped our personal ability to cope. Following an early disability retirement and a prolonged reclusive stay at home, his problems only became manageable with the help of an institutional care team. Our family has learned for more than a decade now to sing caregiving harmony to the primary staff's melody.

When my mother suffered massive hemorrhaging and an emergency surgery, it was my kin-keeper wife Nancy who helped hold things together. Complication followed upon complication until my once-strong mother lay in a coma. She was the victim of post-surgery heart, lung, pancreas, and kidney failure. For a period of time, neither my mother nor father was dead—but neither could make a decision for themselves either. As my mother responded to treatment and began to recover, Nancy became a live-in nurse. For some weeks, she and our toddler took care of his "Grandma."

No Two Cases Are Exactly Alike

In the brief stories of my grandmother, my father, and my mother, there is a cross-section of how families care for their elders. Sometimes the elder moves in with the caregiving family, as my grandmother did; and sometimes the caregiver moves in with the elder, as Nancy did for my mom. Sometimes the care is needed on a permanent basis, such as for my grandmother and dad, while on other occasions it is short-term, like my mom's. And then there are times when a clinical setting becomes the only reasonable option for caring families, a decision we eventually came to with my dad.

One thing is for sure, eldercare is here to stay. With people living longer and having fewer children, no American family should expect to avoid indefinitely the challenge of being caught "in the middle." With a clear sense of biblical priorities, no Christian family will want to avoid the rich opportunity of ministering to and receiving ministry from a beloved elder.

A BIBLICAL MODEL OF AN ELDERCARE FAMILY

In the closing pages of the Bible's first book, we meet an eldercare family. Blending the inspired narratives of Genesis 12–50 with a little bit of realistic imagination, we could invite the kin-keeper in that household to meet us for an interview. Interviews like these that combine the first-hand story of primary caregivers and the interpretation of a caregiving specialist provide the best mix for new learning about eldercare. We'll imagine that we are at a caregiving conference for eldercare families. First, we'll meet Joseph and his kin-keeper wife, Asenath. We'll have them tell their story about being primary caregivers for Joseph's elderly father, Jacob. Then we'll invite a specialist to follow their presentation with some commentary on what they were experiencing and why.

Why Don't You Folks Introduce Yourselves?

"My name is Joseph and I serve as the Secretary of Agriculture in Pharaoh's cabinet down here in Egypt. This is my hard-working wife, Asenath. She's smiling at me that way because she likes me to go by my Egyptian name, Zaphnath-Paneah. That's a mouthful, isn't it? I prefer 'Joseph' because it's the name my parents gave me when I was born. Jacob and Rachel, my parents, sensed that God was going to expand and multiply his people through me and so they chose a name that meant 'increase.'

"You can tell by this whole name thing that I am not an Egyptian by birth. In fact, I never even saw Egypt until I was seventeen years old. I was born up in Canaan to Jacob and Rachel but was sold as a slave destined for the Egyptian market out of hatred by my ten older brothers."

Why Were You Sent to Egypt, Joseph?

"For a while, it was hard to put all the pieces together about what happened, but I think I have a handle on it now. My dad, Jacob, loved my mom very much. When he proposed to marry Rachel, her family tricked him. Jacob was far from home at the time and fleeing from his brother who wanted to kill him. Because Jacob was distantly related to my mother's relatives, I think he expected to find refuge with them and to be treated like family. Instead, he became an indentured servant and had to work for Laban, my maternal grandfather, for twenty years. It was kind of a package deal where he ended up marrying Rachel, her homely older sister Aunt Leah, and two handmaids, Bilhah and Zilpah. Ten sons and a daughter were born to Leah, Bilhah, and Zilpah before my mom had me. I think I was dad's favorite because I was the first child Rachel had.

"My dad was like a ranch-hand for Laban and got jerked around a lot. His wages, for instance, were changed ten times. I think Laban wanted to frustrate him enough so that he would just leave in a huff and then all of the herds could be Laban's. It didn't work like that though. Instead, Jacob took off one day as though he was in a three-day herd drive to find new pasture. Secretly we packed all the household belongings, including some of Laban's stuff, and high-tailed it. We obviously got a three-day head start and that's how Jacob came back to Canaan from Mesopotamia."

My Mother Died When I Was Still a Child

"All that heartache was compounded shortly after we were back in the Promised Land when my mother died. Rachel and Jacob were away on a short trip when time came for my little brother Benjamin to be born. My mom died trying to deliver him and had to be buried on the road, far away from the family tomb. I didn't even get to say 'goodbye' to her. Even as a little kid, I could tell when my dad returned home without her that he was holding onto me even more tightly. I thought he was showing a lot of love to all of us; but now that I look back at it, I think he was holding onto me as a way of holding onto Rachel. Years later, after I was sold as a slave bound for Egypt, he started holding onto Benjamin the same way.

"I learned later that another family tragedy happened at the same time my mother died. It was something I was too young to appreciate then but now I realize it nearly killed my dad. When the messenger arrived to inform us that Rachel had died during Benjamin's childbirth, and that Dad would be delayed as he buried her, Reuben seized the moment. He was the oldest of the twelve sons and fiercely jealous of me. He figured that Jacob would never voluntarily give him control of the clan so he decided to steal it. It was a major power play. What he did was to march in broad daylight into Jacob's tent and rape Bilhah, Rachel's handmaid. His power rape announced to the whole family, 'Whatever used to be Jacob's is mine now. I'm in charge of the clan, the herds, the wealth . . . everything! And when that old man comes back, if he ever makes it, he'll be a tag-along. I'm in charge from now on.'

"Well, I don't know what Dad did when he arrived back, but he dethroned that saboteur, Reuben, in no time. From then on, Reuben hated me even more and Dad held on all the tighter. One of the ways this tension manifested itself was in the shepherding business the family had. Dad made the other boys care for the animals, and he used me as middle management. He gave me a brilliantly colored linen tunic that signaled my role. It was long sleeved and the robe part went all the way to the ground. The only kind of people who wear these tunics are people who are conspicuously wealthy and who aren't supposed to roll up their sleeves and get dirty. You can imagine how that went over."

And Then There Were the Dreams

"I guess what made things worse were my dreams. I had several visions at night that seemed to further reinforce the priority I was destined to have in the family. In one, I saw all the sheaves in a field bowing down to one sheaf—my brothers bowing down to me. My dad didn't mind that one. But when I had another where all the stars, along with the sun and moon, were bowing down to one star, that one upset him. He could accept the boys needing to follow my leadership after his death. But he had a hard time swallowing the idea that the children and the parents would have to be submissive to me while he was still alive. Needless to say, I learned to keep rather quiet about these dreams.

"Eventually, my brothers couldn't stand the sight of me. I had turned in some accurate reports about their mismanagement of the herds to my father, and I guess they really caught it from him. So the next time they went out grazing, they went as far away as they could to try to avoid my supervision. When I eventually found them, they beat me up and nearly killed me. Some of them wanted to murder me on the spot. Instead, they threw me in an old dried out well shaft for a few days to try and figure out what to do. They were a little superstitious about killing me, so they sold me as a slave to some Midianite merchants who were in a camel caravan bound for the Egyptian markets. To throw off Jacob, they ripped up my tunic and put a lot of lamb's blood on it. When they came back from grazing, they told Jacob that they had found it and wondered whose it was. He immediately knew it was mine and his grief set in over my violent and premature death from a lion attack.

"I have to say that God was always with me. He not only prevented me from being killed by my brothers, he helped me in Egypt. At first I was a household servant who became like an administrative assistant to my boss. Then when I was falsely accused of attempting to rape my master's seductive wife, I landed in prison—exactly where God wanted me. In prison, I rose to be the warden's liaison with the inmates. When two of Pharaoh's former cabinet officers began serving time, I helped them understand their dreams. One of them was executed as his dream foretold, but the other was released and returned to service. I had asked for only one favor from the one who was to be reinstituted at the palace—that he would mention me to the Pharaoh for a possible pardon. True to form, he forgot his promise and I remained in prison.

"But I believe that this was also a part of God's timing. You see, some time later Pharaoh began having dreams about an upcoming famine in Egypt—only he couldn't understand the dreams. This triggered the memory of the former inmate whom I had helped and I was released to assist Pharaoh. I was commissioned to prepare Egypt agriculturally for the seven years of famine that were coming. This upcoming famine was the thing that would put me back in touch with my family in Canaan and would fulfill the vision of the sheaves and the stars."

And Will You Also Do Us the Honor, Asenath?

"Well, unlike Joseph, I've lived my whole life in Egypt. I was born in Heliopolis, a city famous for its worship of the sun. Born into a noble class home, my father was a priest for the sun god, Ra.

My mother was an Egyptian princess, a daughter of the last Pharaoh and one of his lesser wives.

"As a child, I grew up believing that the sun god controlled everything. We had sacrifices in the temple just before sunrise to bring Ra back to life. Every time the sun came up over the horizon, we became more convinced that our religion was true. We heard stories of plants, or animals, or even human beings that were kept in permanent darkness—they always died. Those stories completely proved to us that life was in Ra. Scorching droughts were obviously punishments sent by Ra because we were not faithful enough in our service to him. Our hope was that we might please him enough that we could travel with him beyond the horizon where there is no darkness . . . that we would never die."

And How Did You Two Meet?

"I still believed all this about sun worship when I met Joseph. He was a brilliant young man whom the Pharaoh had appointed Secretary of Agriculture. As he told you, the Lord had allowed a lot of adversity in his life to put him in a position where he could direct Egypt's famine relief program and could help his own family back in Canaan. Part of his reward for excellent service to Pharaoh was that he could marry me, the current Pharaoh's niece.

"I have to say that I made out better in the deal than he did. I was a young, spoiled, pagan woman. On the other hand, Joseph was handsome, intelligent, and very self-disciplined. One thing I have always admired about him is his contagious optimism. He can look at the kind of problem that would crush most people and believe that God wants to do something good through it!

"I guess our marriage is an example of his positive outlook. I saw our marriage as something that was going to pull me away from my family and my Egyptian roots. For me, it was a big problem! But he saw it as the opportunity to love somebody who wouldn't let him down and to start his own family. He also was optimistic that he could introduce me to the Lord, the true God of Abraham, Isaac, and Jacob. I fought that until he helped me realize that he worshiped the Creator of the heaven and the earth, the originator of all things . . . including the sun.

"Joseph taught me how the sun was a very important agent of life, but not the *Source* of Life. It was like the water, or air, or food. They all helped sustain life but were ultimately under the control of the Lord God. Whether my family did morning sacrifices or not, the sun was going to come up. It came up all over the world, regardless of morning sacrifices. It really wasn't all that powerful if it died every evening as the sun set. Now that I know the God of Abraham, Isaac, and Jacob, I have a lot less fear and superstition. I'm learning a lot more about trusting and loving people because God is that way toward me."

Tell Us about Your Eldercare Experiences

"Joseph and I actually became an eldercare couple very early in our marriage. Before our boys were born the famine hit. Joseph was working night and day; I rarely saw him. Then one day he came home from work with the most surprised look on his face. 'You're not going to believe who came to buy rations today—my ten brothers!' 'Did they recognize you?' I asked. 'No, they didn't seem to . . . it's been years. With my Egyptian name, hairstyle, and clothes, they didn't have a clue. I could understand everything they said in Hebrew but I spoke back through the interpreter as though I knew only Egyptian.'

"'What are you going to do?' I wondered aloud. 'Well, I'm going to find out if they are any different than they used to be. They say that my elderly father Jacob is alive but starving up in Canaan. My only fear is that they are lying when they say that my little brother Benjamin is up there with him. I have worried all these years that after they got rid of me, they would go finish off Rachel's other son to guarantee control of the clan.'"

God Meant It for Good

"I have to say that my admiration for my husband grew tremendously during those days. I knew how much he had been hurt, but he didn't take revenge on his brothers. He kept his composure when they were negotiating for rations, but he wept in private with me as he relived all of those hurts. He set some tests in motion to figure out whether they were being fully honest about Jacob, about Benjamin, and especially about what they had done to Joseph when he was only seventeen.

"Although it took several months and a couple of trips back and forth between Egypt and Canaan, he concluded that they were changed men. When he revealed to them who he was, they were petrified and fell on their faces. But instead of punishing them, he hugged and kissed them, especially Benjamin. You see, he's a man of justice, yes. But he's also a man of mercy. If people do wrong, they should take responsibility for it. But if they own up to it, they should be forgiven. That's the way he felt toward my sun-worship and that's the way he felt toward them slave-trading him to Egypt. Besides, he could see God's purpose in letting them do what they did. After all, it allowed him to be in a strategic position to keep the whole family alive during the famine. Those dreams about the sheaves and stars bowing down, they have all been fulfilled. He kept repeating one phrase: 'You meant it for evil but God meant it for good!' That's my good husband's spiritual optimism I was telling you about."

Finally, Jacob Arrived

"As soon as the family was reconciled, Joseph sent word that Jacob should move to Egypt where we could care for him. We were convinced that he could no longer live safely on his own. We knew he was a proud and independent man so we tried to honor that but also look out for his best interests.

"The day we received word from a messenger that Jacob's caravan was approaching the border of Egypt, Joseph flew out of the house. He told me later that he never pushed his team of chariot horses so hard. He felt almost like a teenager again, he said. And when he saw his father's wagon on the horizon, he ran out to him and fell in his arms like he had just been lifted out of that dry well shaft! They hugged and kissed and wept before they ever spoke a word. You know, a dignitary like Joseph could easily have waited in town here until Jacob was properly presented to him. But not my Joseph—he's an intensely genuine person, full of public affection for his elderly dad."

Seventeen Years of Love

"When Jacob arrived, he was one hundred and thirty years old. We took care of him for seventeen years before he died last summer. Who would have thought that he would have lasted that long? When he arrived he was gaunt, depressed, and malnourished. But that didn't keep my husband from being as excited as a little kid.

"Shortly after Jacob's arrival here, Joseph got him cleaned up and marched him off to meet the Pharaoh. You have to appreciate what this was like. Egyptians typically hate the nomadic shepherds of Palestine, you know. They are like the lowest of the low, 'scum of the earth,' you might say. Joseph was 'okay' because he was fully Egyptianized. He didn't even speak with an accent since he had lived more of his life in Egypt than back in Canaan. But Jacob wasn't about to change; he was a nomadic ranchhand through and through.

"When Joseph came home and told me how the meeting with Pharaoh went, I was aghast. The normal protocol when people meet a head of state like Pharaoh is to wait until they are spoken to. Not Jacob! As soon as Joseph introduced them, Jacob launched into a big Hebrew blessing. Of course, Joseph had to interpret for him. You know, Joseph could have tucked his father off in some corner so he wouldn't offend anybody. But not my husband; he was so proud of his father and the way God had worked to keep their family alive. Well, fortunately the Pharaoh was very good-natured. I think he was really happy to see how excited Joseph was.

"Apparently, after Jacob was done with his paternal blessing on Pharaoh, the Egyptian ruler's curiosity was aroused. 'How old are you?' he queried my father-in-law. After all, one's length of life is a mark of favor with the gods down here in Egypt. If you make it to one hundred and ten years, you are considered very blest. Jacob's answer was worse than his breach of etiquette: 'My life has been full of trouble, a lot harder than my ancestors had it! And I'm not going to live nearly as long as my own father and grandfather did. I'm a hundred and thirty right now, and I can tell I'm on my last legs.'"

A Chronically Negative Outlook

"I think it was Jacob's negativity that bothered me most in the early days. We had hoped that the whole way God had worked to put Joseph in charge of Egyptian food supplies would not only save lives, but serve as a testimony to Egyptians who didn't know the Lord. While Jacob could confirm the facts of this unusual story, he really didn't share Joseph's optimistic outlook on life. He was so focused on what went wrong that he couldn't see what was going right. Well, Pharaoh didn't seem to mind that much. We think he basically tolerated Jacob and the clan out of his deep respect for Joseph.

"Joseph wasn't as discouraged about his father's depressed outlook as I was. For one thing, Joseph is so positive that he expected that we would eventually rub off on Jacob; we'd help him develop a better perspective on things. I think it also got to me more than it did Joseph because I was more involved in the daily care. I logged more hours with Dad Jacob. I don't mean to imply that Joseph was aloof, but he was very busy in a nationally important job. He certainly took financial responsibility for his father's needs and tended to the spiritual oversight of the family. But I was more in the thick of daily caretaking, especially before the boys were born. We also had hired help in the house that provided some of the care for Jacob."

Getting Started at Caregiving

"Because I was spending more time with Jacob, I found myself dealing with certain hangups. For instance, I had to deal with my own cultural prejudice against nomadic shepherds. At first, I had to try to love Jacob just because he was my husband's father. The Lord had to give me patience and understanding that I had never had opportunity to build over a lifetime together. The man had never nurtured me as a child growing up.

"I tried to pick out something that I could truly admire about him and to milk it for all it was worth. That was an easy choice; I wanted to learn more about his spiritual heritage. I wanted to learn more about the Lord and his covenant relationship to people. This curiosity actually seemed to kill two birds with one stone. Jacob was very interested in reminiscing about the past, and I was very hungry to learn more about the God he had served over the years."

Reminiscing about the Past

"Jacob started off telling me about his grandfather, Abraham. Abraham's courage to leave his pagan roots back in Mesopotamia and to follow the Lord was an encouragement to me. I realized that his decision back then was no less difficult than my decision to leave my family and the sun worship of Ra after I married Joseph. And God truly blessed him with a family, a new homeland, divine protection, large flocks, and numerous offspring who would bless the world.

"When he told me story after story about his father, Isaac, I sensed the same spiritual continuity. Isaac and his beautiful wife Rebekah were richly blessed by God. God answered prayer for them and gave them a family that would grow into a large nation someday. His crops and his herds were multiplied one hundred fold because of the generous wells of water to which the Lord led them."

Regrets about the Past

"But you know, there was a sad theme running through all of this family history. Jacob basically felt like he was a failure. When he rehearsed the deep spiritual experiences of Abraham and Isaac, he pictured himself mostly like an outsider trying to look in. He talked about the time he wrestled with an angel to get his blessing and got injured in the process. He clearly felt like his father and grandfather were far more blessed than he was in resolving family conflicts, something that always seemed to curse him.

"With the mention of 'Egypt,' you could just see him wince. I never thought it was such a bad place to live but I guess if your whole family identity is based on holding your ground in the 'promised land,' it would be. I picked up that he felt like he had let everybody down to move the whole family to Egypt on a semi-permanent basis. 'After all,' he would remind me, 'Abraham and Isaac both went through terrible famines—but they never moved the family to Egypt!'

"The whole subject of family rejection came up often. I didn't realize that Jacob was a twin until he told me how much his dad loved the other twin, Esau. It seems like Esau was a cunning hunter, a very independent macho man. That favoritism seemed to drive Jacob into becoming a momma's boy, a conniver, somebody who learned the art very early of playing favorites and alliances in the family. The bottom line seemed to surface whenever things didn't go his way—maybe God was rejecting him too! 'If God let Abraham live to be one hundred and seventy-five and Isaac a hundred and eighty, why am I ready to kick the bucket at one hundred and thirty?' he'd repeat endlessly. 'Worse yet, Abraham enjoyed his Sarah and Isaac his Rebekah well into their old age. All four of them are buried together in the family tomb at Machpelah. But what about me? My beloved Rachel died far too young and I had to bury her at the roadside in Hebron. I'm ready to die but I'm hundreds of miles away from home.' These conversations were very heavy for me to handle. All I could really do was listen and show him love."

The Last Stages

"I felt like Joseph had a real knack for ministering to Jacob, especially at the end. He helped him get some things back in perspective that were a little bit exaggerated. For instance, since Joseph had forgiven his ten brothers for their near murder and slave sale, he thought Jacob should too. If God had so planned to use the brothers' treachery to preserve the family, at least Jacob should be grateful for God's use of the trial. Just recently we reread the deathbed will of Jacob. There's no mention of the sin of the brothers against Joseph. That's nothing short of a miracle when we consider how bitter Jacob was over that and how readily he reprimands various sons for other sins in his will.

"Near the end, Jacob was blind and bed-ridden. But Joseph continued to visit his father and to bring along our sons. Ephraim and Manasseh were small enough that they could crawl around on the bed or sit on Dad Jacob's lap. Jacob loved being with these boys and responded affectionately to them. I was pretty relieved when I saw how accepting he was of them. After all, they were only half Hebrew and half Egyptian. But he used to say, 'You two are like my own boys!' Then he'd give them a big hug and kiss. Those visits seemed to literally make Jacob come alive and get re-energized. They were good for us too; we had felt pretty cut off from both sets of parents. And Jacob took it seriously too. He tried to predict and suggest the direction our boys should go in the future. He was a prophet and a loving grandfather, so we took his influence as from God.

"Joseph was strong enough spiritually to talk openly with Jacob about death. Jacob wanted him to promise to bury him up in the Cave of Machpelah where Abraham and Isaac were. Of course, we promised that. I am convinced both Jacob and Joseph believed strongly that they would see each other again when they both were 'gathered to their people.' I think using the family burial site was another way of saying, 'It's just a matter of time before God takes us back to Canaan.'"

We Grieved—But Not as Those Who Have No Hope

"I had to admire Joseph when his father eventually died. He struck such a nice balance between Egyptian customs and Hebrew beliefs. He could easily have said, 'It's going to be Egyptian all the way!' and offended his family's tastes. Or on the other extreme he could have thought, 'We're Hebrew and that's that; nothing Egyptian in this funeral!' When Jacob died, Joseph wept, kissed him, and closed his eyes—something we always do. He ordered the forty-day embalming procedure and treated his father like a head of state with a seventy-day mourning period. We understand this period well because it allows people to get the news and travel from a distance to pay last respects. And of course, during this formal mourning time, Joseph didn't speak directly to Pharaoh. Pharaohs are superstitious about things like that.

"For Joseph's family, the embalming sciences allowed them to transport the body for several months through the desert. I was glad when Joseph refused to let the sorcerer-priests do the embalming for Jacob. From my family background I know how occultic that stuff is. The physicians understood body systems just as well so they did an excellent job without any of the magical rituals. The family traveled up in a caravan and spent a week at Machpelah doing the interment before the trip back. That's been several months ago so we are just now getting back to normal. As hard as it was, we've all said how much we miss him and how we had gotten used to having him around as part of our family. I know we'll all look forward to seeing him again some day."

CAREGIVING GUIDELINES FOR THE ELDERCARE FAMILY

As somebody who frequently teaches on family caregiving, I like to picture eldercare as a large rubber band. This eldercare band shows strength and flexibility as it is stretched between and looped over two pegs. These pegs hold the rubber band in place so that it can work. At times these pegs flex farther apart, testing the strength of the rubber band, while at other times they flex closer together, relaxing the stressed band. These two pegs are called "Nurturance" and "Assertiveness."

The "Nurturance" peg represents all the needs of the dependent elderly person. These needs are complex, important, and worthy of our loving attention. The "Assertiveness" peg represents all the needs of the caregiver(s). These needs are no less complex, important, and worthy of our loving attention. Any approach to family eldercare that focuses on one peg at the exclusion of the other is bound for serious trouble.

Picture what would happen if somebody slipped the rubber band off the "Nurturance" peg. The eldercare rubber band would shoot off in the direction of the caregiver's needs and probably overshoot to an extreme. This obsession with "what I need" could result in the passive abuse of the elder, perhaps in the form of neglect or abandonment.

Similarly, if we slipped the rubber band off the "Assertiveness" peg, it would overshoot in the direction of the care recipient's needs. That obsession with "what the loved one needs" could result in caregiver burnout, breakdown, or even active abuse of the loved one.

While an overcommitment to "what I need" could create caregiver irresponsibility, the opposite overcommitment to "what the loved one needs" could result in a caregiver hyperresponsibility. The former experiences no true guilt for failing to meet legitimate needs while the latter suffers from much false guilt for failing to meet unrealistic expectations.

Irresponsibility —	Assertiveness —	Nurturance —	Hyperresponsibility
•no true guilt	•needs of caregiver(s)	•needs of care recipient	•much false guilt
•passive elder abuse			•burnout
			•active elder abuse

If I were to give two caregiving guidelines for the eldercare family, one would represent the "Nurturance" of the elderly person and the other the "Assertiveness" of the caregiver(s). Respectively, the principles would be:

> *Don't Lose Sight of the Big Picture!
> [The Loved One's Needs Are Great]
> *Remember, You're in a Marathon Not a Sprint!
> [Your Needs Are Great Too]

Even though we will discuss these two principles in consecutive order, there is no sense that one is more important than the other, nor that one should be completed before the other is begun. This is not an "either/or" scenario; it must be "both/and."

Don't Lose Sight of the Big Picture!
[The Loved One's Needs Are Great]

The caregivers have lost sight of the big picture when life to them has become nothing more than endlessly parceling out medications or changing colostomy bags. The elderly person is too complex a creature just to serve as a valve between ingestion and elimination.

Life in the Basement

Each human being is like a two-story house with a basement.[3] In the basement are basic physical and security needs. Activities carried out in the basement attend to finding food, drink, sleep, shelter, and protection from danger. Depending on the injuries or diseases that affect a given individual, the basement may also focus on oxygen, hearing aids, wheelchairs, dialysis equipment, and drug prescriptions, etc.

In this basement we would find various things, such as my grandmother's cancer and hip replacement, my father's Parkinson's disease, my mother's emergency colonectomy, and Jacob's malnutrition and blindness. Love that goes beyond "word and tongue" to "deed and truth" must minister on this level. However, if the caregivers and their loved one cannot communicate on matters outside the basement, the relationship is either colored by a severe medical condition or a sterile love.

Life on the First Floor

Upstairs on the first floor are social and emotional needs. It is common up here to overhear questions asked and answered that sound like this: "Am I really loved? Do I belong to anybody? Am I accepted for who I am?" People have various ways of asking these questions and we have verbal and nonverbal ways of sending our messages back to them.

Jacob seemed to struggle a lot on this level. He was plagued by unresolved grief over Rachel's death and Joseph's disappearance. He suffered from a "victim" complex, believing he was frequently exploited by bad luck or the trickery of people like Laban and Reuben. It is very likely that he became temporarily disoriented by being forced to move so late in life, a feeling with which many of our elders can identify.

Fortunately, Jacob was part of a family that was highly skillful in ministering to his social and emotional needs. You can tell in that first embarrassing exchange between Jacob and Pharaoh that Joseph was willing to let his father be an individual. He didn't stereotype "all elderly" in an age-prejudiced way. He seemed to understand that as we age, we become more like ourselves—our individuality becomes enhanced, not diminished.

Over time, I believe, the family helped Jacob resolve some of his unfinished grief. Joseph probably helped him become more realistic in clarifying the facts while Asenath allowed him to share many of the feelings that accompanied those losses. Of course, Ephraim and Manasseh gave him a joyful excuse to reinvest in life.

There's More Upstairs

In the upstairs of this house are the spiritual needs. Up here we ask ourselves, "Am I everything God wants me to be? Am I closing the gap between what I am now and what I ought to be?" Psychologists tell us that the older adult is trying to resolve a developmental crisis. This they label as "Integrity vs. Despair."[4] In weighing his or her life, the elderly person is trying to find a unifying whole that summarizes or integrates all the particulars of the past. Elders need to believe that they have made some meaningful contribution to what they now see as truly important.

In the context of "Integrity vs. Despair," one can understand why so many older adults spend considerable energy thinking about the past. Their life review may fill them with despair if they conclude they spent their life for things that really don't matter—or if they were a failure at achieving the things that did. Elders who hold to family relationships as paramount will be tortured if they look back and see that they ignored the family or that the family is currently alienated from one another. Elders who see serving God as the ultimate value will suffer pain if their reminiscing reveals that they primarily lived for career advancement and money. These feelings will be especially acute if the elder sees his or her own example being reproduced in their children's lives, perhaps in lifestyles that displease God.

Jacob was clearly filled with regrets as he reviewed his life during his move to Egypt. His idealized version of Abraham and Isaac left him feeling that he was a failure. Few of us can imagine what it would be like to be the third generation in a line of famous achievers. If Henry Ford became world famous for the invention of the automobile and Henry Ford, Jr. consolidated the business empire that followed from his dad, who would want to be Henry Ford III? The shoes that needed to be filled would be so large that an average performance would look like a failure.

Furthermore, the family history was told in such an idealized way that Jacob missed all the miserable humanity of his predecessors: Abraham lying to Abimelech, Sarah laughing at an angel, and both of them mistreating Hagar and Ishmael; Isaac lying about Rebekah as she in return deceived her dying husband about the twins' birthright. Even the beloved Rachel stole idols from her father Laban and deceived him when he caught up with her.

The Importance of Family Visits

When Joseph began ministering to Jacob and bringing his grandsons for visits, it further prompted the much needed reminiscing (Genesis 48:1–4). Although such reminiscing may have seemed to be an unnecessary bore to these visitors, it was therapeutic to Jacob. He actually was "strengthened" in the process.

Such an example as Joseph's, of course, reminds us that the average elderly person enjoys many visitors, phone calls, and notes. Families who depend on the primary caregiver, "the strong one," to do all this loving listening, are short-sighted. Similarly, when I receive a phone call asking, "Pastor, will you visit my elderly relative?" I respond: "Sure. When was the last time you visited? How are they doing right now? When are you planning to go the next time? Do you want to go together?"

The Importance of a "Ministry of Maturity"

Joseph also helped his father by encouraging a "ministry of maturity." Jacob had a lot of life experience to draw upon, and he liked to channel it by giving guidance to younger people. This is what he was doing when he "blessed" Pharaoh, his own twelve sons, and his two grandsons.

We are missing the boat when we pity our elders and patronize them as though they have all the problems and we have all the assets. Although their short-term memory may be failing as they forget something you told them twenty minutes ago, their practical wisdom and long-term memory are usually good. They enjoy being asked advice and leaving a godly heritage of influence. Ministry should not just be "to" the elderly, but "with" and "by" them.

The Importance of Body, Work, and Ego Transcendence

Ultimately, the elder in search of spiritual integrity will need to accept three ideas over time:[5]

1. There is more to me than my body.
   [I can't be obsessed with my physical complaints.]
2. There is more to me than my work.
   [I can't be obsessed with my seeming lack of productivity.]
3. There is more to life than just me.
   [I can't be totally self-centered.]

With all the assurance of the Word of God, we can be confident that God is a companion to any elder who sets out on this powerful journey.

Remember, You're in a Marathon Not a Sprint!
[Your Needs Are Great Too]

When Jacob arrived in Egypt, he probably had no idea that he would live another seventeen years under the care of Joseph and Asenath. The eldercare experience for that family was a lot longer than any of them might have imagined. It was more of a marathon than a sprint.

The Eldercare Period

Similar to Jacob's experience, the average eldercare family in America spends five years providing home-based eldercare before their loved one dies or becomes institutionalized. In the Greater Washington, D.C. area, the average for home-based caregiving lengthens to seven years.[6]

It's about time we recognized that the calling to eldercare is just as noble as the calling to childcare. Despite the inattention to the subject, caring for our elderly parents is every bit as biblical as being good parents to our kids (1 Timothy 5:1–20, especially v. 8). Even as we typically spend five or six years taking daily care of our children before they enter first grade and an additional twelve in somewhat less structured caregiving, so it may be with our parents.

Eldercare Planning

Regardless of the particular length of the eldercare period, families must strike a balance in planning. On the one hand, they can't write the script too far in advance. They need to be flexible, taking one day at a time. The health and finances of the elder person change . . . the family's resources change . . . the noninstitutional services available in a given area change.

On the other hand, however, families ought to look ahead realistically. Just as Jacob's sojourn in Egypt was prophetically foreseeable (Genesis 15:13–14, 16), families can learn about possible future scenarios. Many families have found it helpful to update their wills and to discuss nursing homes, artificial life support, and funeral arrangements before a crisis arises. A good question to ask of physicians, nurses, social workers, ministers, and attorneys is: "In your experience, what kinds of things should we be thinking about right now as we look toward the future?"

One of the most commendable traits of Joseph is that he spoke openly with his father about his wishes and his upcoming death. Many loved ones feel that they cannot speak this openly out of a concern "to protect Mom or Dad." They may have brittle or adaptive denial.[7] In the former case, they refuse to admit even to themselves that death is coming; in the latter, they simply refuse to discuss it. However, the fact is that such a "conspiracy of silence" is usually self-protective and only stops communication, not active thinking. Furthermore, most patients know they are dying and want to say a few things while they have the chance. Even if such open dialogue brings some strong emotions to the surface, this preparatory grief can be very cleansing and therapeutic (Luke 22:41–44; cp. Hebrews 5:7–8).

Eldercare Family Dynamics

While family dynamics are always important, they seem to surface boldly during times of acute or chronic stress. Isaac's favoritism for Esau and Joseph's bias toward Manasseh are but a part of Jacob's family fabric. Conflicted relationships like these threaten to prevent the family from making high-quality decisions. Any "ounce of prevention" that can be practiced over the years to build strong family dynamics is deeply appreciated in times of major stress.

Based on surveys taken at the U.S. Naval Home in Philadelphia, we believe that over one-third of institutionalized elderly may be distressed about their family relationships.[8] This distress seems to go beyond the elderly person simply wishing that he or she would receive more visits from relatives. Instead, there seems to be active concern over things like hostility, refusal to communicate, divorce, infidelity, juvenile delinquency, abandonment, lying, selfishness, etc.

Another family dynamic that surfaces in eldercare is "caregiver guilt." When caregivers feel guilty for wrongs they believe they have done in the past, they sometimes try to purge themselves through obsessive caretaking. Or perhaps they feel guilty that they are younger, healthier, and happier than their loved one. Sometimes we feel guilty if we can't "cure" the problem and find "solutions." Instead, we can learn to "care" about the person and find "support" for him or her.

At times, the elder subtly or overtly manipulates the guilt level of the caregiver. While "honoring mother and father" is a lifetime commitment, "obeying your parents in the Lord" only lasts as long as childhood. Our ability to say "no" to our children when it is in their best interest is a skill we may need to draw upon with our parents.

Eldercare Burnout

No matter how the guilt originates, it is an unhealthy and dangerous pattern for the elder and the caregiver alike. A caregiver who sits twelve, fourteen, or sixteen hours a day with the institutionalized elder not only prevents him or her from "fitting in" at that institution, but invites caregiver burnout. A home-bound elder who refuses to take responsibility for himself in reasonable ways or refuses to allow someone else to step in, is inviting the caregiver into a breakdown. The caregiver who is stubbornly determined to become this kind of martyr needs to rethink his/her "selfless-styled" selfishness.

The well-balanced caregiver, like Joseph, doesn't try to provide all of the around-the-clock care alone. Not only did Joseph have a nationally important job which required much of his attention, but the narrative reflects that others provided much of the direct care for Jacob. "And the time drew near that Jacob would die and he called for his son Joseph. . . . [Later] One told Joseph, 'Behold, thy father is sick.' And he took with him his two sons. . . . And one told Jacob, 'Behold, thy son Joseph cometh. . .'" (Genesis 47:29a; 48:1-2). It is very likely that while Joseph provided finances and spiritual oversight for his father's care, others like Asenath and hired servants were often more engaged than Joseph in the direct care.

I believe that Joseph and Asenath were sensitive to their own needs and to the first sign of burnout—resentment toward Jacob. When we become so locked in to "the other person's needs" that we can't break free for a day off, we become chief candidates for burnout. When we become unable to take a badly needed vacation, we are in a position to slip easily into elder abuse. Learning to be resourceful while we still care deeply is an art. For the Good Samaritan, it involved leaving "two pence" with the innkeeper until his return (Luke 10:35). Adult daycare, visiting nurses, or meals-on-wheels are modern ways to "love your neighbor as yourself" (Luke 10:27-28). Fears that using such services will invite the family to abandon their elders have been unfounded. Using these services actually allows families to continue a higher quality of caregiving over a greater period of time.

Eldercare Financing

There is no doubt that God prospered Joseph financially in Egypt. He probably had the equivalent of a triple-digit salary when his starving family arrived in Egypt. In his shoes, many modern-day Christians might have reasoned: "Look, everything I have, I earned the old-fashioned way. When I needed you, where were you? Don't come to me with your hand out!"

Such a self-centered attitude was actually being taught by some religious leaders in Jesus' day. Those spiritual leaders had hopes that the young, upwardly mobile professionals would become the financial backbone to the Temple, even at the exclusion of their elderly parents (Mark 7:9-13). They, of course, were sharply reprimanded by our Lord for ignoring the fifth commandment. Perhaps such a rebuke is also warranted when we so structure our family finances in such a way that we couldn't help with eldercare, even if we wanted to.

The Eldercare Blessing

The way in which the Book of Genesis ends is a powerful affirmation of Joseph. Because of his excellent character, he was given a "double blessing" (Genesis 48:22). Instead of just having descendants who would become the tribe of "Joseph" with their own land area in Canaan, his descendants so multiplied that they became the tribes of "Ephraim and Manasseh." God furthermore underscored Joseph's excellence by allowing him to live to the ideal Egyptian lifespan of one hundred and ten years (Genesis 50:22, 26).

It would be fair to say that Joseph's commitment to excellent eldercare was an expression of his rich life in God and one basis for God's blessing in his life. To use New Testament terminology, Joseph had "true religion" because he helped care for those who no longer had parents or spouses alive to help them (James 1:27). It is likewise predictable that God will richly honor and support those who give compassionate attention to their modern-day elders in need.

A Modern-Day Joseph

I admire the biblical Joseph and any modern "Josephs" I am privileged to know. I met one such modern "Joseph" several years ago as I arrived to pastor my current church in the suburbs of Washington, D.C. Irv and his wife Frances impressed me the first time I saw them. As Irv stood at the front of the church with his snow-white hair and generous share of wrinkles, he explained how he and his time-wisened wife had come to know the Lord "later in life." *Now there's a couple who are willing to keep on learning, and growing, and changing despite their years,* I thought to myself.

As I've come to know Irv and Frances over these years, I see a lot of parallels between them and Joseph. Like Joseph, they experienced more than their share of hardships at a young age. On his own by age seventeen, Irv had to develop a mental toughness to survive family rejection and the premature death of his mother. By God's grace, he chose to have a positive outlook and was led to a fine life partner like Asenath.

This couple models the "ministry of maturity" to which each of us should aspire in the later stages of life. Not only do they prepare the Communion elements for our church and deliver weekly sermon tapes to all the sick and shut-in, they are also avid readers. Books that have ministered to them frequently become gifts to people with special needs. "Harvesters," our ministry to older adults, was co-founded by them to reflect the harvesting principle after years of sowing. Burdened for the homeless and for environmental pollution, they have prompted our church to improved action in these areas. They were heartbroken when their thirteen-year-old granddaughter put a shotgun in her mouth, attempting to end her life. Logging hundreds of hours as her hospital chaplains, they learned sign language so she could speak to them. Ministering steadily, they were delighted when this rebuilding child prayed to receive Christ—a joy they have shared several times in their ministry to family members.

Once when I was doing a Bible study with our Harvesters, I was interested in knowing who in the group still had parents alive. My hunch was that few did. But as I am learning, many "young-old" (those between sixty-five and seventy-five years of age) are still responsible for their "old-old" loved ones.[9] Irv surprised me when he told me that he was responsible for his grandmother. In a nursing home at age one hundred, she also recently prayed with Irv to receive Christ. "There's something," she said, "that I hoped you would talk to me about on this visit."

This modern-day Joseph and his wife do not fit our age-prejudiced stereotypes. They clearly understand the basement, first floor, and upstairs living as they eat wisely, exercise regularly, seek counseling as needed, and exemplify a vital Christian life. They also strike the right balance of nurturance and assertiveness as they reach out to others while taking good care of themselves. While caregiving is a lifestyle, they also know when it's time to take a week with their dog at Myrtle Beach, their place for renewal. They, like Joseph, are due a "double blessing."

SUMMARY

1. Eldercare is a growing priority in America with people living longer and having fewer children. More than 80 percent of dependent elderly are being cared for by their own relatives in private residences with the strict minority of elderly going into nursing homes.

2. The typical eldercare scenario has a female "kin-keeper" caring for the elder, usually a wife, daughter, or daughter-in-law to the dependent elder. This scenario usually lasts for five years before the elder dies or becomes institutionalized.

3. The Bible provides sound examples and principles for family-based eldercare. These caregiving guidelines suggest that under ideal circumstances, the elder should both give and receive care. Furthermore, the caregiver ought to put priority on his or her own needs as well as the needs of the dependent elder. Precaution should be exercised to prevent active and passive elder abuse as well as caregiver burnout.

3

The Age of Loss
Timothy S. Smick

Carol's Mom Tells Her Story

I'll never forget the loneliness and fear I felt when my husband Ray died of a heart attack so many years ago. The funeral had been two weeks earlier and I had been totally consumed with the bustle of activity generated by out-of-town guests and the numerous personal and financial matters that had to be administered shortly after Ray's death. I had been a pillar of strength until that day I sat at my kitchen table and became overwhelmed by the sudden realization of my loss. Ray was my best friend. He was gone, and although I had impressed many of my friends and family with my personal strength and fortitude, the loss of Ray's calming presence in my life had really shaken my personal confidence.

It was only after years and months of depending on the spiritual strength of the Lord's presence that I began to function socially again. I'm sure that some thought I had finally gotten back on my feet again. Most people, however, didn't realize how fragile this appearance of self-sufficient independence was from day to day.

Eventually, I developed new relationships with other widows that gave me considerable support both spiritually and socially.

Although life seemed rather empty and unfulfilling after Ray's death, I began to find a new sense of purpose by volunteering my administrative gifts at our church's child day care center. Not only did the presence of these wonderful children add some spark to my life, but I felt I played a significant part in nurturing these young lives in their understandings of spiritual things. I especially enjoyed the weekly time I spent in leading the "Bible story" session with the children. The camaraderie I enjoyed with other staff members added to my feeling of belonging as we ministered together. I do have to admit, however, that as much as I grew to love those kids, I was glad I wasn't charged with their care in the evenings!

I enjoyed my role as Grandmom with the grandchildren although I only see my grandson on an irregular basis since my son Tod and his wife Mary and their three daughters had moved to the Midwest years ago. My oldest daughter Carol and I were just becoming comfortable in our relationship with each other. Somehow, we just seemed to have the most difficult of relationships during her teen years. I could do nothing right in her eyes, and I'm sure she felt I was just as critical of her. Now we visit regularly for Sunday dinner after church.

I don't quite remember when I became aware that my memory began to fail. Missed dental appointments, burned dinners, and forgotten social engagements started to mount up embarrassingly. One day, I noticed a horrible burn mark on my forearm and had no idea how it had gotten there. Ashamed of my memory lapses, I wore long sleeved dresses and blouses for weeks during the hot summer months to hide the telltale scar.

I dared not tell anyone of this incident for fear that word would get back to my children and they would worry about me. I was very certain that I wanted never to be a burden to my children. It was clear to me during my short visits that they led very full lives. They did not need the disturbance of a needy parent who was a danger to herself.

Secondly, I was a little unsure of my relationship with my daughter Carol. Yes, we had settled into a happy equilibrium as far as our relationship was concerned, but the memories of past parent/child bitterness still lingered in my mind. It's kind of funny that I can remember these unpleasant events and yet cannot recall whether I turned off the stove this morning.

I'll never forget that horrible day I fell and broke my hip last year. I was in such pain that I was immobilized. To this day, I have no idea what caused the fall. I can remember the fear that even transcended the pain as I began to wonder if anyone would ever find me. The hours I waited seemed like days. Finally, Mrs. Serio, my landlady, hearing my muffled sounds, used her master key to enter my apartment and found me contorted in pain lying on the floor.

The trip to the hospital and the surgery preparation was as frightening as it was bewildering. After what seemed like hours, I caught a glimpse of my daughter Carol. As scared as I was, it was at that moment, clutching Carol's hand, that I decided I was going to get through this ordeal and do whatever it took to return home. I was determined not to let this accident get the best of me. Yes, I needed my daughter Carol now as I'd never needed her before, but I was determined not to be a permanent burden either to her or her family.

The weeks that followed were some of the toughest weeks in my life. I looked forward to my physical therapy sessions in spite of the terrible pain the exercises caused me. I knew these exercises were the key to my fight to return to my independent lifestyle.

Once I was discharged from the hospital, Carol insisted I come to their home. As reluctant as I was to be a burden to their family, I accepted this offer since it was certainly preferable to being admitted to a nursing home which was my only logical alternative as I was unable to mobilize myself without the assistance of my therapist or family. I regret not communicating my grateful feelings to Carol for her gracious invitation. I guess it was pride that caused me to act as if it was expected that my family would care for me in their home.

The first week of my stay with Carol and Tom was a pleasant relief from the hospital. Carol and Tom found the novelty of having me as a boarder a pleasant change from regular hospital visits. I enjoyed the opportunity to be part of their everyday family life and contemplated my eventual return to my own apartment in eight to ten weeks.

I was gaining strength as each week passed and diligently kept the schedule of exercises the therapist had designed for me. In fact, my therapist complimented me on my concentration and discipline and decided to alter the program to accelerate my rehabilitation.

Monday was to be the day the extended exercise sessions would begin. Carol knocked on the door with a quick "good morning!" that seemed to hint of a need to hurry because the entire family was behind schedule for the morning. As I stood to grab the cane she held at my bedside, I felt a sudden sharp pain in my hip. No longer able to hold myself up with the cane, I sank to the floor in agonizing pain. I recognized the seriousness of my situation as I saw Carol nervously call for help as she dialed the number for the ambulance. It seemed that in the short time it took the medics to arrive to Carol's home, I lost all my resolve to fight for my own independence. I had instantaneously drawn the conclusion that I would never return to my apartment as I had planned for the last three months. As highly as I valued my privacy and untethered freedom to come and go as I pleased, it seemed that my body was insisting that I relinquish these claims for independence.

Since I had experienced this surgical operation before, the only difference seemed to be my lack of resolve for successful rehabilitation. Instinctively, I knew Carol also understood that I did not have either the physical or emotional stamina to fight my way back again. The fear I had experienced before had given way to hopelessness.

I had now become dependent on Tom and Carol for so much— bathing, toileting, sometimes even feeding me. Accompanying my indifference toward any rehabilitory goals was a lethargic attitude about my dependency for assistance in even my most basic of daily activities.

As much as I love my daughter Carol, who has been absolutely stoical about her role in caring for me, I've come to resent her as I become increasingly reliant on her selfless physical and emotional support. Even our relationship has changed—no longer do we communicate adult to adult. Now it seems as if she talks to me as the "dependent little child" I've become. I rally for the phone calls I receive from my other children primarily because of the brief conversations we have that "restore" me to my parental and adult status.

To be fair, I know I've added greatly to the tension in this household. I can't say as I blame them for any resentment they might direct toward me. After all, this situation is precisely what I had hoped would not happen when I lost my husband, Ray.

* * * * *

It is popular belief today that the above story is representative of all elderly. It is not. Although most younger Americans perceive the population over 65 to be lonely, inactive, sick, poor, and useless, these notions are not true. In fact, most men and women over 65 are healthy and wealthy enough to carry on their normal lives. Only 15 percent are not.[1] Seniors have shown a remarkable ability to adapt to the changes that the aging process brings.

Yet, as Carol's mom's story illustrates, the senior years are truly a time of loss. Loss comes in so many forms. It can come in a single blow, such as the loss of a spouse or a very sudden stroke. Or, the loss can be experienced in many overlapping forms such as the loss of work, combined with the loss of social status, combined with the loss of health, combined with the loss of the ability to perform favorite hobbies or activities. Clearly, unlike any other time in a person's life, the senior years are significantly impacted by various losses. A senior's ability to adapt to these losses is the key to determining whether they experience a satisfying and rewarding old age, or an unhappy and totally dependent one.

If the potential losses of old age were merely physical, they might be easy to deal with. Unfortunately, these problems are almost always interwoven with emotional, financial, and social concerns. To help older family members cope with the changes brought forth by their old age, it is helpful to understand the nature of these losses and how they impact the seniors experiencing them.

Loss of Physical Health

Unconsciously, children seem to presume that they will enjoy good health. In most instances, children and even young adults show little concern for the frailty of the human body, subjecting it to considerable abuse. This abuse can be of the nature found in the bumps and bruises of normal play or of the willful neglect that results from smoking, alcohol, and drug addiction. Usually, it isn't until the later adult years that we become aware of our body's physical vulnerability. Often, we respond to this new awareness with crash diets, life insurance purchases, and an overall increased consciousness of our own mortality.

Cancer in its various ugly forms has taken three of my dear friends in the last few years. All of them were relatively young—in their mid-thirties and forties. Although, as a health care professional, I have seen the ravages of this disease on countless individuals, it wasn't until my attendance at my friends' funerals that I caught a glimpse of the wisdom that Moses pleaded for when he asked his Lord to teach him to number his days.

By the time most adults reach their senior years, they have become well-schooled in the knowledge that advanced age often brings with it a variety of physical problems and diseases. In fact, most caregiving family members charged with the care of an elderly relative have confronted their own mortality a number of times. Now they vicariously wrestle with their relative's loss of physical health as a poignant daily reminder of their own mortality.

Sensory Losses

Clearly the loss of sensory perception is one of the inevitable results of aging. By age 60, most people have lost functional hearing of the higher frequencies, and it becomes harder, if not impossible, to discriminate between similar sounds. Comprehension of speech can be diminished in a noisy room. Unfortunately, many caregivers attempt to be heard by shouting to someone who has experienced a hearing loss. Shouting, however, raises the pitch of the speaker's voice, thus creating sounds that are more difficult to discriminate and embarrassment for the person being addressed. Caregivers would be better advised to be more deliberate in speaking, giving special attention to facial expressions and gestures, since most communication is nonverbal.[2]

The aging process usually brings visual losses as well, such as in the lenses and the ciliary muscles. Most people need lenses for close work and reading. The eyes do not adjust to the dark as easily and cannot discern colors as well.

Gerontologists inform us that even as young as the age of 50, the sense of taste also changes. Because of fewer taste buds and a decline in the sense of smell, it becomes harder to taste all four basic tastes—salt, sour, bitter, and especially sweet. Because of the reduced sense of smell, many seniors install smoke detectors if they have not done so and give themselves visual reminders to turn off the gas.

Even the skin's sensitivity to temperature is decreased with age, making it necessary for many seniors to set their hot water temperature to no higher than 115 degrees F in order to avoid accidental scalding.

Loss of Health

As problematic as these sensory deprivation problems appear to be, they often are the forerunner of even more serious diseases and disorders that signal the loss of some seniors' physical well-being.

Clearly the number one culprit causing dehabilitating damage or even death with seniors is heart disease. Heart disease is a loose description of all kinds of heart ailments. Most heart disease in older people results from hypertension (high blood pressure) or from arteriosclerosis (hardening of the arteries). Ultimately, these diseases can progress to where a senior experiences a heart attack which is simply a disruption in flow of blood to the heart, causing death of the tissue.

Angina pectoris, the suffocating pain in the chest that results when the heart muscle is not getting enough oxygen as a result of the blood supply being impaired, can be controlled by the routine use of nitroglycerin. There is no reason for persons with angina not to live normally, provided they're not having unusually long-lasting symptoms and take reasonable precautions to avoid physical or emotional stress.

It is very important for both seniors and their caregivers to understand the importance of pain as a signal or symptom, of medication, diet, and prescribed routines. One of the toughest problems you will have as a caregiver of a senior with heart disease is getting that person to follow diets or live emotionally with his or her disease. Very often, the sufferer of heart disease is disabled emotionally by the disease and very difficult to treat.

Some seniors plagued with heart disease can take very little or no exercise and therefore become isolated and depressed. Others decide to take their chances and "live a little," mindful of the risks that departing from a restricted lifestyle brings.

Longer life for many cardiac patients has resulted from technological and surgical advances such as open-heart surgery, pacemakers, valve replacement, bypass surgery, and laser surgery. Age really isn't a criteria for determining good candidates for these surgical procedures. Most physicians rely on general medical and mental condition. Quite often, the Type A personality (the most likely personality to suffer heart disease) is also the ideal personality for a cardiac patient because of his or her steadfast determination to "lick this thing."

Hypertension (high blood pressure)—the silent killer—is so prevalent in the aged that many physicians consider it a normal, inevitable aspect of aging which does not require treatment. This is simply not true. Once diagnosed, hypertension is a lifetime disease that must be monitored regularly. Low-salt diets and exercise combined with medication will usually keep high blood pressure in reasonably good control.

The majority of stroke victims are among the male elderly. Stroke is a major cause of long-term disability and nursing home placement. A stroke is a sudden disruption of the flow of blood to an area of the brain. The area of the brain affected, and the extent of damage or death to brain cells, determines the level of disability the senior will experience, usually thwarting his or her ability to regain an independent life. Yet, many stroke patients do benefit from rehabilitation programs that usually begin in the hospital and are later continued in a rehabilitation center, nursing home, or private home. Some recover quickly, others take months or even years.[3]

Cancer is probably one of the most dreaded of diseases afflicting seniors because most have been witness to the devastation it can cause. An enormous variety of cancers are all characterized by uncontrolled, abnormal growth of cells that can invade or destroy healthy tissue.

Acknowledging the fact that there are no sure answers to this disease is one of the first challenges presented to the cancer patient. It is a challenge to overcome the initial fear and dread a diagnosis of cancer provokes. The fact is, real progress continues to be made in improving the survival rate among cancer patients. As the result of the use of modern treatments, many cancer patients die of other diseases before they die of cancer.

One of my friends, who was stricken with this dreaded disease several years ago, alerted me to the social stigma attached to cancer. Although friends admired his brave fight with the disease, they did so only from a distance. Even his wife, his primary caregiver, found herself increasingly isolated at a time when she was in greatest need of support from friends and acquaintances.

Diabetes, pneumonia, hypothermia, heat stroke, prostration, arthritis, osteoporosis, fractures, Parkinson's disease, accidental falling, cataracts, glaucoma, retinal disorders, foot problems, incontinence of bowel and bladder are just some of the significant list of other ailments that rack the bodies of the senior populace today. Each of these medical problems, usually in concert with one or more of the others, plays a part in the seniors' sense of loss of control of their own bodies. Each of these ailments triggers somewhere within the senior the lost sense of physical well-being previously enjoyed with a younger body. And yet, it must not be presumed that all seniors are bound by these physiological disorders. As mentioned earlier, only 15 percent of all seniors experience these debilitating medical problems.

Loss of Intellectual Functioning

As devastating and stressful as the physical ailments mentioned above can be to the senior, they somehow pale in comparison to the penetrating loss of mental or intellectual functioning that can accompany many forms of senile dementia.

Senile dementia is the current terminology for those who, in old age, clearly suffer impairment of intellectual functioning as the result of any of a number of diseases. Many people confuse dementia with psychosis. They are not the same. Psychosis involves loss of contact with reality, but no substantial intellectual impairment or loss. Dementia involves the loss of intellectual function.

Unfortunately, our society suffers a senility phobia that stimulates a great deal of worry and anguish each time a parent's behavior begins to change. Many jump to conclusions that their parent is becoming senile and will soon lose any ability to lead an independent life. It is important for caregivers to understand that such symptoms may result from a number of different causes, some of which are temporary and reversible and others that are more serious signs of deterioration.

In the last decade, Alzheimer's disease has gathered most of the headlines as the most devastating form of dementia and is at the top of most seniors' lists of fears. Interestingly enough, it is not a normal part of the process of aging. Although we do not have precise figures for those suffering Alzheimer's (partially because it is so difficult to diagnose), we know that only between 5–7 percent of those over 65 are severely demented.[4] Obviously the majority of seniors are spared. Most elderly are blessed with many years of independent living with their intellectual faculties intact.

Whether young or old, most humans suffer from forgetfulness from time to time. Yet when forgetfulness occurs in the lives of the elderly it is often more irritating, embarrassing, and most of all, frightening for the senior. Worries about becoming senile are needless since most memory lapses can be overcome by the use of memory aids such as lists, paper and pencil by the phone, calendars, and alarm wrist watches that can signal the wearer when it is time to take a pill or leave for an appointment.

Forgetfulness, however, should not be ignored as a symptom. If forgetfulness is accompanied by other changes and symptoms, a doctor should evaluate its significance. Choose your physician carefully and do not settle for a simplistic diagnosis of "she is just getting old." After all, old age doesn't cause dementia. Disease does.

On the other hand, caregivers should avoid overreacting to a parent's reduced intellectual capacity. Some form of limitation in many seniors is to be expected. If a parent does turn to you for help be sure to adjust the level of assistance to his or her precise needs. It is important that parents continue to function independently wherever and whenever they are capable. Too often, at the first sign of a parent's limitation, children attempt to "take over" in areas where no help has been requested and where help is not really needed. It is important for children to keep in mind that if parents don't use it (their intellectual functioning), they will lose it.

Alice, who had experienced considerable mental confusion as a result of overmedication, gradually became dependent on her children for many activities of daily living. Assistance in eating, bathing, and even toileting had become daily rituals for the entire family. Eventually Alice and her family became distraught over the tensions her increasing need for care was placing on the family. Shunning the family's advice to enter a nursing home, she decided to move into a senior retirement hotel that provided both housekeeping and meal preparation. Within the first week, Alice developed a romantic interest and simultaneously a renewed vigor to live life independently. Dramatically, she became capable of feeding herself, toileting, grooming, bathing, and even tidying up her room. Her family was astonished with her "quick recovery" and learned a valuable lesson about themselves and their approach to caregiving.

Many dementias are reversible and can even be eliminated if they are diagnosed quickly and treatment is promptly instituted. These dementias can range from mild confusion to stupor or active delirium. Among the possible causes for this behavior are malnutrition, vitamin deficiencies, medication, surgical or emotional trauma, social isolation, depression, viral infection, congestive heart failure, transient or small stroke, coma from diabetes, malfunctioning kidneys, alcoholism, dehydration, vomiting, or diuretics.

No treatment, however, will halt the progress of the diseases causing irreversible dementias. Although the symptoms can be intermittently interspersed with normal behavior, they will increase as the disease progresses, and irrational and uncontrolled behavior will eventually predominate.

Alzheimer's accounts for almost half the cases of irreversible dementia. Unlike dementia caused by stroke, this brain damage is not yet visible through noninvasive techniques and at present is only verifiable in the United States by autopsy.

Unlike the sudden destruction caused by a massive stroke, Alzheimer's has a gradual onset. It is progressive and increasingly destructive to the victim's ability to function. Alzheimer's patients can live five to ten years, depending on the age of the patient and the promptness of the diagnosis. The earlier the onset usually is indicative of a more rampant path and earlier death. Seven years is now seen as the average survival time for Alzheimer's patients. This extended involvement with the disease causes the caregiver daily to witness the decline of a loved one. And this is responsible for 50 percent of relatives caring for Alzheimer's patients who eventually suffer from depression.[5]

Paul, whose wife was admitted to one of our nursing homes in her early sixties with the diagnosis of Alzheimer's, was a faithful daily visitor. Some days, his wife would remember events from twenty years before, causing him to wonder if the person he had been wed to for

forty years had been misdiagnosed. Typically, the next day the confusion in his wife would be even worse. It was most devastating to Paul
and his children when his wife could not even recognize them.

Over the months, Paul found himself with a schedule that allowed for little more than daily visits to the nursing home and his job.
He was neglecting himself both physically and emotionally. His doctor,
who also functioned as the facility medical director, told me that Paul
was not atypical of most Alzheimer's family members. As the attending
physician, he found it necessary to treat not only Paul's wife, but the
family as well. He encouraged Paul to reduce his visitation to the nursing home to alternating days with limits of one-hour duration for each
visit. He also advised Paul's involvement in a support group of family
members caring for loved ones stricken with Alzheimer's. After several
weeks of reopening his social life, Paul found the support group to be an
excellent catalyst for him to reveal to himself his real feelings about his
wife and her dreaded disease. It was in these meetings that the grieving
process started. Paul dealt not only with the symptoms of his spouse's
decline but also with the personal loss of demonstrated love, companionship, and intimacy that in some ways was more cruel than death
itself. The physical person of his spouse was indeed present, with ever-
increasing need for care, while her emotional, social, and, indeed, intellectual side seemed to be lost forever.

The inevitable day of his wife's death was not a day of mourning.
Indeed, Paul had spent the last three years grieving over the "loss" of
his Alzheimer's-stricken wife. Instead, the day of her death was a cause
for relief—emotional, physical, and financial.

Social Loss

Retirement can be a wonderful time. Retirees are blessed with
time, and, if backed up with careful financial planning, the money to
pursue the travel and leisure impossible during the career-building
and child-rearing years. One of the often overlooked drawbacks of
retirement is that the patterns of living, of working, of communicating, of socializing, built up over the previous 65 years, often break
down completely or are at least very difficult to maintain. The world
of seniors tends to become a smaller, more confined space, with
missing faces of friends, relatives, and co-workers.

As with physical losses, seniors are impacted by these social
losses in different ways. Some, who are self-sufficient, make new
friends and maintain vigorous social lives. Others find the loss of a
spouse to be so devastating that they shrink into a cocoon, afraid of
the challenge of living life as a widow or widower. Abilities to cope

with these social losses depend on a myriad of factors, not least of which is the level of social skills they have developed during their earlier years.

The inability to cope with change is no small factor contributing to the social isolation many seniors experience today. Reluctant to leave the inner walls of the familiar homes in which they have raised families, they become trapped in unfamiliar, rapidly declining neighborhoods. Their children unsuccessfully beg them to move to safer suburban areas near them, yet their parents often prefer to stay locked "snug" in their familiar homes. They are comfortable with them on the inside, yet so frightened of them on the outside.

Loss of Comfortable Roles

For men, retirement can be such a profound life-changing event that it can result in depression and even suicide. Many men, successful in their roles in the business world, have seen their very personhood and self-respect become intimately entangled in the job roles they have worked so hard to attain. Status, prestige, self-actualization have all been fed by the elixir of their professional success. Often, they have had to forego success in other roles (such as that of father, husband, and church leader) in order to attain their success in the work place. Although they wouldn't dream of coming to an important business meeting without being thoroughly prepared, they are totally unprepared for the sudden and dramatic loss of their job-related roles. Their one-dimensional professional roles do not serve them well in their need to adapt to the role changes that retired life demand. Their part-time "positions" as crossing guards or babysitters offer little to strengthen the fragile sense of self-esteem they have built through the years.

Women who retire from work appear to make significantly better adjustments than men, perhaps because they are already geared to household activities. In fact, the greatest threat to a woman's role may be her compulsive spouse who is always "underfoot" with his interference in the management of the house.

Russ, a recently retired bank executive, was experiencing more marital turmoil with Jane during his first year of retirement than he had during the sum total of all the previous years of their marriage. Unfamiliar with retired life's new roles after his forced retirement, he was daily devoting himself to numerous household chores. He cut out the food coupons, checked the paper for supermarket bargains, baked cakes, did the laundry, and washed the dishes with increasing regularity. At first Jane enjoyed this new-found leisure, but she soon found Russ's new role to be a threatening imposition on her role as the homemaker. Not until Russ found a part-time consulting position with an accounting firm did this role tension subside in their marriage.

Once again, as with many aspects of the aging process, each individual senior copes differently with role changes. The senior's ability to adapt skillfully to new and varied roles without seeing his self-esteem dwindle is largely contingent upon the successful development of his ability to have found fulfillment in a number of roles as a younger adult.

Once you hear a sudden upsurge of stories of past glories that signal how little satisfaction your parent is deriving from his current activity, you should be prepared to offer some counseling support. More importantly, anything you can do in anticipation of your parent's retirement may soften the trauma of transition.

Loss of Financial Well-Being

As with the other losses sometimes experienced by the aged, loss of financial security has a social, emotional, physical and sometimes, medical impact on their lives. Many seniors for the first time in their lives find themselves to be poor. Spiraling inflation severely erodes the savings that at one time were felt by the senior to be considerable. Social Security benefits amount to only a fraction of what was expected by the seniors as they faithfully made contributions throughout most of their working lives. As a result of mandatory retirement, many seniors find their incomes severely reduced overnight.

To complicate matters, pride causes many seniors to be reluctant to talk with their children about their financial dilemmas. Some elderly parents squirrel away assets and plan to surprise their children with a legacy. Others are ashamed of how little they have to show for a lifetime of labor.

Pat had an inkling that his dad had some money "socked away." Yet, he wasn't sure. For some reason his dad had presumed on each of his children for considerable financial support ever since his mom had passed away. Pat knew that his dad had to be receiving his railroad retirement check each month, but Dad never mentioned it and lived his remaining years as a pauper.

Money had always been a private matter within Pat's family, causing him to be very reluctant to satisfy his curiosity about his dad's pension income. Pat and his brothers were only too happy to provide financial support for their dad—financial support that took care of all his personal expenses with the exception of a few minor Christmas gifts for the grandchildren.

Pat's curiosity was satisfied only after his father's death. It was at the reading of his father's last will and testament that Pat discovered how very important it was to his father to be able to "leave something to the kids" so that he would be remembered after his death.

Financial insecurity and money concerns are problems for most lower and middle-income elderly. Even those seniors with debt-free cars and mortgage-free homes (and numerous other valuables collected over a lifetime) are worried about what will happen to them once these assets are depleted.

As always, seniors cope with their financial struggles with varying degrees of success. The poor elderly are obviously impacted the greatest by the inability of their fixed incomes to successfully fight the war of inflation. Sometimes, their economic woes seem incomprehensible to the middle-aged yuppie who is desperately fighting his own battle to "keep up with the Joneses." Yet, the seniors' economic plight does not always correlate with their coping abilities. Relatively affluent seniors can suffer severe emotional trauma related to their considerably reduced incomes, while poorer seniors sometimes seem to function very successfully utilizing the financial skills that a life of frugality brings.

The loss of financial security, whether real or imagined, has significant emotional consequences for the elderly.

SUMMARY

Throughout our turbulent middle-aged years we are often consumed by the hectic activity of raising families, building careers, maintaining friendships, and somehow "getting the kids through college." Somewhere in the deep recesses of our minds we have inadvertently collected romantic images of the golden senior years of retirement. The demands of the moment don't allow these thoughts to be further developed, and we are therefore content to allow these positive images of extended travel, visits from the grandchildren, and warm holiday family gatherings to occupy that section of our minds reserved for the retirement years. And in many ways these years *are* golden. Unfortunately, these golden years are tarnished by the continued reminders that this period inevitably leads to the natural end of the life cycle. Many people, who have lived very successful and enriching lives, find themselves totally unprepared for the consequences of growing old. In fact, to many of them, aging seems to be a fate worse than death.

Probably no word better describes the most dramatic consequence of growing old than the word "loss." Loss may seem like a simple concept. Yet it has a very profound and traumatic impact on the elderly because they have so very much to lose. Loss comes in many forms. It can come in a single blow such as the death of a spouse, or it can be multiple when the loss of work combines with the loss of social status, health, and favorite activities.

The Most Devastating Loss: The Loss of Autonomy

When these losses are combined it can often result in one of the most devastating losses of all—the loss of autonomy. This loss can be the most debilitating because it attacks the senior's self-esteem. It usually comes in bits and pieces. The inability to meet a rent payment prompts the need to "borrow" from the children. Or one has to ask to be driven to an evening appointment because her eyesight isn't quite good enough after dark. These may not seem like major events to their children, but they pack devastating and stunning blows to the senior's self-esteem. Some seniors are forced to change their living arrangements out of necessity. Because "home" is a profound symbol of personal control and independence, making the choice to live somewhere else often means a great sense of loss. The senior's daily battle for maintaining independence is not merely a fight, it is understandably a war.

One's ability to adapt to these losses is the key that determines whether seniors experience retirement as the satisfying and rewarding "golden years," or unhappy, dreary, grim, and tragic years of total dependence.

There comes a time for many seniors when they cannot cope with some of life's simplest activities without the aid of another human being. Often, they look to their children for the support and assistance they need. Although some seniors are fortunate enough to have children nearby who are not only available but also skilled in providing this needed assistance, many do not. Those seniors who do not have children nearby, however, can attain this assistance by utilizing the numerous support services in their community that have been specifically designed with the seniors' needs in mind. The following chapter offers an overview of the numerous services that are available to seniors and their family caregivers.

Clearly, God does not expect any of his children (even those who have lived seventy or more years) to live dreary lives of monotony. With appropriate assistance, today's seniors can have nine disabilities and four impairments and continue to live vital lives that glorify God.

* * * * *

"But the godly shall flourish like palm trees, and grow tall as the cedars of Lebanon. For they are transplanted into the Lord's own garden, and are under his personal care. Even in old age they will still produce fruit and be vital and green. This honors the Lord, and exhibits his faithful care" (Psalm 92:12–15 TLB).

4

Getting Assistance for the Caregiver
Timothy S. Smick

Steve had left work a little later than he had planned and knew his 79-year-old mother would be anxiously awaiting his arrival at her apartment. It was a Wednesday evening, the night that had become the traditional evening for his Mom to join Steve and his family for dinner. This dinner had served as a casual way to keep in touch with his Mom after his Dad had died nearly six years before.

As his Mom opened the door, he couldn't help but notice a very large bruise on her right arm. Seeing the concerned look in his eyes, she volunteered that she'd had a very "nasty" bump while in the department store the day before.

"Don't be worried. Dr. Harris has looked at it and said everything was fine," his mother defensively claimed.

Steve made a mental note to call Dr. Harris as soon as he arrived home.

As the children greeted Grandmom at the front door, Steve headed upstairs to change and give Dr. Harris a call.

"Dr. Harris, I'm sorry to bother you like this, but I couldn't help but notice the large bruise my mother has on her upper arm. She said you examined her and everything was all right," Steve began with an inquisitive tone to his voice.

Dr. Harris was reassuring when he said, "Steve, your Mom is a very fortunate woman. Most women of her age would have certainly suffered a fracture. I x-rayed her arm, however, and it appears she only suffered a very bad contusion." Steve was relieved to hear this until Dr. Harris added, "Steve, I do want to alert you to the fact that your mother's Parkinson's disease is progressing more rapidly than I had hoped. Up to now, we have been able to alleviate some of her tremors with medication. Now it seems as if the effectiveness of the medication has been reduced and will require careful monitoring. I'm not positive, but I think her Parkinson's attributed to her accident in the department store."

Steve thanked Dr. Harris as his mind pondered this new information. He couldn't put his Mom in a nursing home, and yet he knew neither he nor his wife, Maggie, could care for his Mom in their home. Both had jobs and the family had grown dependent on the income that each parent earned. Their home was small and could not accommodate another adult. Even if his home were larger, Steve knew that it would only be a matter of time before Mom and Maggie would declare war on each other. Theirs had been an embattled relationship from the start. Maggie had a taste of what living with Mom was like when Mom joined them for a two-week vacation in the mountains. She could not tolerate Mom's tendency to control. No, Mom living in his home would not work.

Steve went downstairs to dinner, saying nothing about the phone call. He was quiet at dinner as he watched his mother's slight tremors with renewed interest. He was frustrated that he didn't have an answer to this delicate problem.

When an older person begins to lose the ability to manage independently, concerned relatives too often think of only two options: 1) assuming the responsibility of total care themselves, or 2) placing the older person in a nursing home.

In practical terms, the option of assuming the responsibility of total care in your home is not realistic for many families today. Today's housing is built for the nuclear family, not the extended family. With 54 percent of women entering today's work force, the majority of households no longer have a full-time primary caretaker who can provide all the services an elderly parent in failing health might need.[1] In addition, the habits of independent living, formed over so many years, might be very difficult for both the aging parent and their children to break. Although some adult children feel a responsibility to take their aging parents into their own homes, many simply cannot. And many older people would prefer not to be dependent on their children in any case.

Many potential caregivers, who have only a casual passing knowledge of the numerous services available to seniors today, assume that the nursing home is the most practical solution for elderly family members unable to function independently in their own homes. For a number of years, many older people and their families had no alternative to nursing home placement once aging relatives could no longer care for themselves. Fortunately, in recent years, as the elderly have become an increasingly large and vocal part of the American populace, both the public and private sectors of the medical community have been recognizing and responding to the need for other forms of assistance. Today there exists in most metropolitan areas of the United States a wide range of noninstitutional alternatives for seniors who can no longer manage for themselves. The major goal of these programs has been to keep elderly people out of institutions for as long as possible by providing them with a community-based continuum of supportive services. These allow them to remain in their own homes and communities, close to their family and friends.

Comprehensive community programs for the elderly include far more than medical or health care services. They offer, as well, a wide range of supportive services to meet the residential, homemaking, social, emotional, and nutritional needs of older people.

If you are not absolutely certain that your relative requires the round-the-clock care which a skilled nursing home provides, you should investigate the alternatives your community has to offer. Until the necessity arises, most people have no idea of the range and number of supportive programs for the elderly that continue to spring up in their communities. The availability of these services varies greatly from one locality to the next. Large metropolitan areas generally have the widest array of services as well as the best coordination of the services. If you should live in a community where the services are rather fragmented, your biggest job will be to locate and coordinate the required services.

The most efficient way to begin your exploration of the alternative programs in your community is to contact the central social services agency in your area. Nearly every area of the country now has the special information and referral sources they need.

An abundant amount of useful information is provided by your local telephone directories. If you haven't done so already, take a close look at the blue pages in the back of the regular directory. The detailed listings for city, state, and U.S. government offices are preceded by the "Easy Reference List (of) Government Offices" arranged by the functions provided. This list contains the address and phone number of local offices of Medicare and Medicaid, Social Security and SSI, senior citizens services, the Veterans Benefits Administration, and the like. More detailed information can be found in the blue pages headed "State Government Offices," under headings such as "Aging," which lists local Area Agencies on Aging; "Health Services," "Housing," "Home Care," and other state-sponsored programs that might be of assistance to you or your senior relative. The "yellow pages" directory provides current information under headings such as "Home Health Services," "Nurses," "Nursing Homes," "Convalescent Homes," "Rest Homes," "Senior Citizen Service Organizations," and "Social Service Organizations."

To help you begin exploring possible alternatives to nursing home placement for your older relative, the remainder of this chapter will be devoted to describing the various nonresidential types of programs and services designed to prevent or delay the need for institutionalization. The following chapter will concentrate its attention on the wide array of housing products that have been specifically designed for seniors. Although you may not find all these services available in your parent's community, advance knowledge of all the possibilities will help you to focus your search for the most appropriate kind of care for your relative.

Home Health Care

Sons, daughters, and spouses continue to be the most active participants in the care of the ailing elderly (at least five million Americans are caring for a parent on any given day).[2] However, even when family members are willing and able to accept these responsibilities, there are simply no longer as many of these potential caregivers around as there used to be. Some are scattered to other parts of the world, and those who are around are likely to be working all day. As a result of these changes in the modern-day family structure, home care has become a major industry today.

At their best, home health service agencies can provide a continuum of care for the elderly, coordinating the services of registered nurses, home health aides, and housekeepers to meet the particular needs of the individual. These agencies are almost always community-based. They may be public or private, nonprofit or profit-making organizations. The services they offer can be grouped into three broad categories: home health care, personal care, and homemaking assistance.

Home Health Care or Visiting Nurses

Home Health Care and Visiting Nurse programs provide both skilled nursing and restorative care. Depending upon the medical needs of the older person, registered nurses or licensed practical nurses can come into the home on a regular basis to assess the patient's health and to perform the treatments required, such as administering drugs, moving indwelling catheters, or changing dressings. Restorative care services can bring physical therapists, occupational therapists, or speech therapists into the home. Some health service agencies can also offer the aid of a medical social worker who can help the patient and family deal with problems associated with a medical condition and assist them in finding community resources to meet their needs.

All these services can be employed on a permanent or temporary basis. The schedule of home health care visits varies according to the acuity level of the senior. Sometimes the nurses come in every day or several times a week, for a few minutes or longer. They supervise medication, carry out special procedures, provide nutritional counseling, and offer general guidance about household management.

Mary is a Visiting Nurse employed by a nonprofit organization. She describes how the purpose of her regular visits with 85-year-old Mr. Smythe includes much more than the supervision of his medical well-being:

"My relationship with Mr. Smythe began when I was asked to oversee his convalescence from a recent hospital stay. Eventually, the necessity of my involvement for medical reasons was reduced as Mr. Smythe recovered rather nicely from his ailments. As I gradually reduced my visits, it became apparent to me just how much comfort Mr. Smythe found in having a 'medical professional' visit. When I suggested to his family that we discontinue the visits, they set up an appointment to discuss with me the continuance of Mr. Smythe's care."

"We would really like to see you continue to visit Dad, even if you need to reduce the frequency of your visits," said Mr. Smythe's son, Fred, at the start of the conference, a certain pleading tone in his voice. "I guess Dad is not too different than a lot of people his age in that he is preoccupied with his health. It is very soothing for him to know that he can expect a visit from his nurse. You've not only ministered to Dad medically, but socially as well, with your ongoing interest in his personal life. I know the latest baseball standings and reports of minor aches and pains are not central to your care regimen, but they mean an awful lot to Dad. Besides, we have found your advice on how we might restructure our own caregiving responsibilities to be invaluable."

Personal Care Home Health Aide Services

These personal care professionals meet the nonmedical personal needs of older people who require some help with the activities of daily life—eating, bathing, using the toilet, dressing, grooming, and walking. Home health services agencies can arrange for a home health aide to perform these functions, either as a live-in companion if constant care is needed, or on a less intensive schedule. Homemaker/home health aides are trained in household and personal care and usually work under the direction of a nurse, social worker, or other health professional. The amount of care necessary in each individual situation is usually determined jointly by the family and the sponsoring agency; it may be once or twice a week, every day for a few hours, or round-the-clock in special cases for short periods.

Homemaker-Chore Services

Homemaker services provide help in maintaining the household. An older person can arrange for a housekeeper to come regularly to cook, do laundry, shop, run errands, and perform other light housekeeping duties. If more assistance is needed, a home health aide can assist with both personal care and more extensive housekeeping chores.

If you've already taken on the responsibility to set up a short-term home care arrangement, you know it is not a simple matter to implement a plan satisfactory to all concerned. But even though it may be far from perfect and may require much time and effort in terms of changing personnel, sudden crises, and parental complaints, properly organized home care has great advantages over unsuitable institutionalization. Care within the home offers the older person the benefit of feeling safe and secure in familiar surroundings. It also offers seniors at home a sense of independence and control over their treatment. The informal presence of family and friends can often hasten recovery. Even home-cooked meals can mean a great deal to an older person set in his ways. Most importantly, the presence of family allows each family member to make useful contributions to the senior's well-being.

If you are the family member charged with making the home health care arrangements, you will find it advantageous to work with an established home health agency that can coordinate the services of trained personnel to produce a program of care tailored to individual needs. The first question to ask is, "Can I get a complete evaluation and a case management system?" If you're told, "Yes, we have a committee that does a patient evaluation," you'll know you are on the right track. Your parent's needs may change as a condition improves or deteriorates, and case management allows for an appropriate shift in the type of home care provided.

Be prepared to ask a number of questions of any home health care provider. No matter how many references they have, check all of them with the Better Business Bureau, the Area Office on Aging, as well as previous clients. Keep in mind that anyone coming into your home is a stranger so you want to find out if the agency is licensed, if the person is bonded, and what training and responsibilities he or she has had. Just because a nurse is licensed does not mean that the license is in good standing.

The following checklist can also serve as a reminder to you of the preliminary work you can do to assure a smooth working relationship with your home health care employee:

• Check with your state's nursing board to determine that the license has not been suspended, revoked, or limited in some way.

• Find out if the aide is properly trained (in some states certified) for his or her required duties, and who his or her supervisor is.

• Insist on routine contact with the supervisor.

• Have a schedule of tasks for every visit that the aide is expected to follow.

• Provide emergency telephone numbers.

• Agree on costs, expenses, Social Security, or fringe benefits as well as arrangements for payment before the aide begins work.

• Require the aide to furnish receipts on any purchases he or she makes for you.

In some locations neither commercial for-profit nor nonprofit agencies are available. In these cases you might look to nurse registries and employment agencies who will, for a fee, find and place caregiving personnel for you. In this case, you are the employer and you pay the home-care worker directly and are responsible for Social Security and taxes. Many of these agencies take no further responsibility for supervising workers or monitoring quality of work. That is between you and the home-care worker.

Many small towns and rural areas, which may not have formal health care agencies or nurse registries, almost invariably have an informal network of people who perform these services. Often, physicians, social workers, or clergymen can be good sources of access to this informal network of caregivers. You should be aware, however, that government assistance programs will not reimburse you for the cost of these services if they are not provided by a licensed agency.

Unfortunately, not everyone who would benefit from the services of home health care will be able to arrange for this kind of care. Today, there are an estimated 100,000 home maker home health aides to meet an estimated need of 300,000.[3]

Even if these services are available in your community, many people will not be able to afford the amount of care required. The cost of in-home services varies greatly according to the status of the agencies, some of which base their charges on a sliding scale and the kinds and intensity of services the older person requires. Although home health care can be less expensive than institutional care in many cases, it can be far more expensive if intensive, skilled nursing and rehabilitative services are required for an extended period of time.

Who Pays for Home Care?

Depending on the state in which the seniors live, the condition of their finances, and the nature of their needs, home care services may be paid partially or entirely by Medicare, Medicaid, supplementary insurance, a group insurance plan, a health maintenance organization, and/or by community programs subsidized by philanthropic organizations or local efforts. Veterans and their spouses as well as their children may benefit from the Veterans Administration's "improved pension program" when there is a need for "aid and attendance" for a nonservice-associated disability.

Many seniors may have a portion of their home care costs reimbursed by Medicare. Today's current Medicare rules demand that certain eligibility requirements are met by the patient in order for this federal program to pay for home health care. To qualify a patient must:

- Possess a valid Medicare health care insurance card.

- Be under a physician's care.

- Need intermittent skilled nursing care or physical therapy or speech therapy. There must be a recurring medical need for these skilled services. The treatment must be performed by or under the direct supervision of a registered nurse or therapist in accordance with a home health care plan established by the physician.

• Be confined to the home due to injury or illness. Generally, homebound patients require considerable assistance from other persons and/or supportive devices such as a cane or wheelchair in order to leave their residences. Occasional absences from the home, primarily for medical care, are allowed.

• Receive services from a Medicare certified home health agency.

In the event these eligibility requirements are met by the patient, Medicare coverage for skilled nursing care, physical therapy, speech therapy, occupational therapy, medical social services, and the services of a home health aide will be reimbursed. Occupational therapy, home health aide care, and medical social services prescribed in a physician's care plan must be started in conjunction with skilled nursing, physical, or speech therapy, if they are to be paid by Medicare.

A sampling of the specific types of programs and services Medicare will pay for includes:

• Evaluating an unstable heart or lung condition.

• Evaluating the effects of a new medication for a changing unstable condition such as high blood pressure.

• Evaluating the patient for therapy needs.

• Evaluating a respiratory condition such as pneumonia.

• Determining when a significant change in health or function is probable with home health nursing or therapy.

• Teaching a newly diagnosed diabetic the symptoms of the uncontrolled disease, how to give insulin, possible complications, and diet.

• Teaching the family how to care for a bedridden or terminal patient.

• Teaching a stroke patient therapeutic exercises.

• Teaching a chronic lung disease patient energy-saving daily living skills.

• Teaching a patient with a fracture, in-cast care and use of equipment, e.g., crutch or cane walking.

• Teaching a therapeutic diet.

- Teaching and assisting with the care of a new colostomy.

- Providing wound care and evaluating healing.

- Changing, irrigating, and teaching catheter care.

- Filling insulin syringes for a blind diabetic.

- Assisting a weakened patient with bathing, skin care, oral medications, meal preparation, light housekeeping, and range of motion exercises.

- Developing a bowel and bladder program for an incontinent patient.

- Giving monthly B12 injections.

- Continuing a rehabilitation program for a heart attack patient.

- Setting up a medication system for an occasionally confused patient.

- Assisting in obtaining appropriate medical or safety equipment and mobility aids.

For most families of modest or middle income, the problems of payment begin when insurance coverage for maintenance care expires. Most seniors don't realize how a lifetime of savings can be wiped out by living long beyond one's expectations. Even though home health care purchased for a dependent parent is a deductible allowance under the federal tax law, it's still quite costly. If the care goes on indefinitely, there's no reason to expect even the most devoted children to impoverish themselves and their own families in the process.

Although it is clear that it is desirable to keep the elderly out of institutions until it is absolutely necessary, often neither government assistance programs nor private insurance will provide adequate reimbursement for those needing home health care. Both Medicare and private insurance programs may cover part of the cost of skilled nursing care for a limited period of time, but they will not reimburse the cost of custodial or homemaking services alone. Medicaid's (a state and federally funded program designed to pay the health care costs of those who are indigent) coverage of in-home care is as restrictive as that of Medicare, except that in most states custodial care for Medicaid-eligible elderly people is covered under Title XX of the Social Security Act.

These financial considerations play a central role in determining the choice between in-home services and nursing home care. Once limited Medicare benefits are exhausted, the costs of regular visits from a nurse, a home health aide, or a therapist plus regular living expenses can often exceed typical nursing home costs by $1,000 to $1,500 a month.

Making the Decision to Get Help

Many caregivers make use of home health care services after they have attempted to supply all the care for their parent over a prolonged period of time. As a result of mounting family and career pressures and the physical toll demanded by the role, these caregivers reluctantly concede their parents' care to a non-family-member paid professional.

"Either you make the arrangements or I will," Jean's family doctor insisted at the end of her examination. "I don't know what you are trying to prove, but I do know that you will not survive another month of this type of stress. It is physically and emotionally draining for you, and I'm sure, the rest of your family."

Jean knew that Doctor Morgan was right. For five months she had made a gallant effort to care for her mother. Reluctantly, she called the social worker Doctor Morgan had recommended that morning. The social worker made an appointment with the Visiting Nurse Association for the next day. At her husband's urging, she elected to have a home health aide present twelve hours daily.

Jean expected to feel instantly relieved once the aide's schedule had begun. What she felt, instead, was a sense of loss. Indeed, she had lost her role as the caregiver for one of the most important people in her world. For the previous five months Jean had been her mother's primary companion, nurse, comforter, and housekeeper. Now she felt she was without any crucial role in her mother's care.

Participating in Home Care

Children who utilize home health services to care for their parents play a vital part in the administration of loving and attentive care for their parents.

Often seniors are reluctant to question anyone in the medical profession. Remember, today's seniors are a generation that preceded today's "get a second opinion" mindset. Instead, they wrongfully place physicians, nurses, and other medical professionals on a pedestal. Their children can offer their boldness to question, challenge, and, most of all, clearly understand the medical advice they are being given.

It is a good idea to be on the premises from time to time when the visiting nurse or therapist is scheduled to appear so that you can write down special instructions and discuss these with the health aide. If the therapist requires that particular exercises be done on a regular schedule, you can ask the aide to make sure the schedule is followed. In addition, your presence and interest in your parent's progress can contribute immeasurably to his or her morale.

Sometimes you will have to play the role of mediator between the aide and your parent. Obviously, if the aide's performance is conspicuously unsatisfactory, the complaints should be presented to the agency or her supervisor. But it also should be taken into account that your mother is feeling depressed about her diminishing competence and independence. The idea of another person taking over her domain is calculated to make her resentful and irritable.

Whatever the reason, it is not uncommon for the parent to place the caregiver under close and critical scrutiny. Even though she might be competent and agreeable, you may hear complaints about her "gabbiness," "sloppiness," poor cooking, or her "pokiness." And if on one occasion a grocery receipt is misplaced, you may hear muttered suspicions about being "robbed blind."

The best solution to this problem is to hang around in an inconspicuous way, if possible, so you can make your own evaluation. Unless there is a major mismatching of parent and caregiver, it is best to act as intermediary and tactfully iron out most misunderstandings.

Most reputable home health agencies offer their employees instruction on how to do their jobs. Ideally, the agency has a supervisor who visits periodically to make certain the regimen is being implemented. The family member, however, also functions as a supervisor of home care and should make his expectations known. The following performance expectations might prove helpful as a guideline:

- Meal planning, preparation, and cleanup.

- Making beds and changing sheets with the recipient in or out of the bed as required.

- Brushing, combing, and shampooing hair.

- Giving bed baths and/or assisting with tub baths.

- Brushing teeth when the recipient is unable to do so.

- Cleaning and cutting fingernails and toenails (except for diabetic service recipient).

- Shaving with an electric razor.

- Giving assistance in transferring to and from the bed to a wheelchair, walker, or chair.

- Assisting with ordinary self-administered medications (opening bottles, getting water).

- Performing such household services (if related to medical need) as are essential to the service recipient's health and comfort at home (i.e., changing and laundering bed linens, rearranging furniture so that the recipient can move about more safely and easily).

Most agencies that provide in-home services also add these rules as well:

- No use of service recipient's car.

- No consumption of service recipient's food or drink.

- No use of service recipient's telephone for personal calls.

- No acceptance of gifts or tips.

- No bringing of friends or relatives to the service recipient's house.

- No consumption of alcoholic beverages, or use of medicine or drugs for any purpose other than medical, in the service recipient's home or prior to service delivery.

- No smoking in service recipient's home.

- No solicitation of money or goods for personal gain from the recipient.

- No breach of service recipient's privacy/confidentiality of records.

- The personal care workers may eat personal lunch in the service recipient's home with the consent of the service recipient.

- The personal care worker may use the service recipient's bathroom facilities.[4]

Although these "rules" might appear rigid, they offer a helpful baseline from which to structure a relationship that is preferable to beginning with an "anything goes" attitude.

Promote Self-Reliance

Many caregivers and most family members have a tendency to be overly conscientious in their assistance to seniors who are convalescing. You will need to be vigilant in watching that all involved in the care of your parent are looking for opportunities to promote self-reliance. Very few people need to be totally dependent on others for all the activities of daily life. Most seniors take pride in fending for themselves when the tasks are within the range of their capabilities. Sometimes a home health aide needs to be tactfully reminded to foster the patient's independence and not his or her capitulation to helplessness. This will initially require more effort on the caregiver's part. After all, it is much quicker for the aide to button the sweater with her nimble fingers than to wait for Mr. Jackson to awkwardly finish the tedious process of buttoning eight buttons.

Other Noninstitutional Community Resources

Home health care does not stand alone as the only resource available to caregivers and seniors hoping to avoid institutionalization as they cope with the activities of daily life.

Meals on Wheels

There is no question that poverty is a major cause for malnutrition in our society. Another reason for malnutrition among the elderly is their inability to prepare adequate meals for themselves. Low cost or free meals are offered more frequently now to both the poor and disabled. Many major metropolitan areas have voluntary programs to seniors either free of charge or on a sliding scale based on the seniors' ability to pay.

The delivered hot meals not only provide nutrition, but they offer the side benefit of a daily visit from the volunteer delivering the meal. These volunteers might be the only human contact the senior has had all day and they offer vital mealtime "chats" and report back to their organizations on the well-being of the seniors they serve.

Telephone Reassurance Program

Bill and Gail had alternated days on calling "Mom" who lived on the other side of town. Although these calls were social in nature, they served Bill and Gail as a means to relieve them from worry about the well-being of Gail's mother.

Bill's career soon required a transfer to another state. The costs of regular long-distance phone calls became burdensome. Still both Bill and Gail needed the reassurance that all was well with Mom. Gail discovered the existence of a commercial telephone checking service in their former town. For a cost per week that amounted to less than one typical long-distance call to Mom, a service would place a call. Once again, the call served as a vital link with another human. If for any reason Mrs. Glover did not answer the phone, help would be immediately sent to her door. If she did not answer the door, nearby police or fire station personnel were called to determine if anything life-threatening had happened.

Senior Centers

Most metropolitan communities have established senior citizen centers. These centers usually provide a hot lunch and a wide range of engaging activities that are recreationally, socially, and intellectually stimulating. Quite often, these centers provide an excellent source of information concerning other local service for the elderly.

Senior Transportation Programs

Many areas have "senior ride" programs that provide door-to-door transportation service for those older people without a means of transportation and in fear for their own safety when using conventional public transportation. Specially equipped vans for easy accessibility from the curb are often utilized by these transportation programs.

Legal Services for the Elderly

Once again, these types of services are generally found only in the large metropolitan areas. However, where they exist, they can be of tremendous assistance to the senior in circumstances such as eviction, public assistance difficulties, property losses, and various consumer problems.

Adult Day Care Programs

Although not widespread in availability, adult day care centers are an excellent resource for serving the needs of seniors requiring nonintensive medical services. Quite often, these centers are contiguous to functioning long-term care facilities. Adult day care programs usually provide daytime supervision, health monitoring, and physical therapy to seniors who are dependent on wheelchairs and walkers but are not bedridden. In addition to health services aimed at maintaining the senior's physical condition, day care centers provide hot lunches, snacks, recreational activities, and, sometimes, transportation to and from the center and the senior's home. Most often they are used by seniors living with a relative who is away from home during daytime hours. Unfortunately, the cost of such programs is not covered by government assistance programs. Typical costs range from $10 to $25 per day.

Respite Care

It had been five months since Joyce had assumed the caregiving responsibilities of her mother-in-law. Both Joyce's family and her mother-in-law had successfully adapted to this new living arrangement. Unfortunately, Joyce's husband had no siblings with whom to share the caregiving responsibilities and therefore Joyce willingly and lovingly cared for "Mom" in her own home, using the spare bedroom.

Her husband Jeff arrived home from work one evening with the news of a business conference in Hawaii. The real news, however, was that spouses were invited for an extended stay following the conference. Joyce had always dreamed of a Hawaiian vacation and saw this exciting opportunity slipping from her grasp as she considered the caregiving task she had assumed. While sharing her dilemma with a friend over coffee one day, she discovered that the community nursing home had a program designed for families finding themselves in this type of situation.

Upon visiting the nursing home, she gathered more information about their respite care program. This program was specifically designed to give family members some relief from the constant strain of caring for an older relative. The nursing home was prepared to care for her mother-in-law on a temporary basis for a week or even a weekend.

Long after the Hawaiian vacation was over, Joyce found the existence of this program to be a welcome emotional relief. The fact that she had a means of "escape" from the pressures of juggling her caregiving role with the many other roles she assumed made her feel more willing and able to keep her mother-in-law in her home.

Hospice Care

Until 1974, most terminally ill patients and their families did not have much choice about the kind of care that would be available to help dignify the last few months of life. Today, there are over a thousand hospice organizations nationwide providing for the emotional as well as the medical needs of terminally ill patients. They offer a wide range of supportive services not readily available in conventional hospital or nursing home settings. Designed for people for whom no active therapeutic treatment is being pursued because it is no longer deemed appropriate, hospice programs emphasize care and comfort, not rehabilitation. Hospice care is very deliberate in its attempts to embrace both the patient and his or her family, and the services it provides extend through the bereavement period.

Hospice refers to a carefully designed program and not a building (such as a hospital) where this program is administered. In fact, whenever possible, hospice care is administered in the patient's home and not in the hospital.

The underlying philosophy of all hospice programs is that for a person with only a limited time to live, symptoms should be relieved and pain alleviated. Another aspect of the philosophy is that it transfers control of patient care to the patient and the family.

When hospice care is operating at its best, it views the patient not just as a physical being, but as a social, spiritual, and psychological being, with needs in all those areas. The program attempts to treat the patient and the family as a unit. In so doing, it helps to ease the pain of the loss for the family as well as the physical pain of the patient.

For Christians, hospice care is most beneficial for all involved when the eternal, spiritual perspective is intertwined with the anticipated temporal loss of the patient. Clergy, skilled in pastoral counseling, can be an essential part of the hospice team as they minister to the patient and the family during these trying times of pain and bereavement. Clearly, the Christian message of hope and the assurance of eternal life with our Father in heaven removes much of death's sting and imparts a lasting meaning to the end of earthly life.

Making the Arrangements

Sometimes the most valuable role you can play for your dependent parents is that of administering a combination of community-based services. It is certain that the effort in arranging these services is more time consuming and complex than simply entering a nursing home where these services are provided under one roof. Some seniors prefer the worry-free simplicity and security of nursing home care. However, most feel the emotional rewards of more independent living are worth the time and effort it takes to establish and monitor a program of care.

Considerable help in finding various resources is available from the professionals who staff many community-based services for the elderly. In the event no one single program can meet all your parent's needs, health care professionals may be able to direct you to other community services that provide the necessary supplementary assistance.

If your parent is hospitalized, the hospital's discharge planner usually is an excellent resource and assistant in selecting the right combination of services for your relative.

Unfortunately, the development of these community-based resources is uneven across the country. In many rural areas, a nursing home will be the logical choice for your parent merely because no other alternative forms of care exist. In a suburban area, however, the array of choices available to the senior will require days of investigation to select the combination of services best suited to your parent.

SUMMARY

The option of assuming the responsibility for the total care of an elderly parent is not realistic for many of the readers of this book. Fortunately, there exists today, in most metropolitan areas of the United States, a wide range of noninstitutional alternatives for seniors who can no longer manage for themselves. These community-based programs include far more than medical or health care services. They offer, as well, a wide range of supportive services to meet the residential, homemaking, social, emotional, and nutritional needs of older people.

The efforts involved in setting up and administering a customized set of services that meet the in-house needs of a parent can be quite taxing. Many seniors and their children still find the extra effort to be worthwhile in that it postpones the parent's need for institutionalized services.

Although many seniors find it highly desirable to remain in the familiar surroundings in which they raised their families, others find the burden of maintaining their homes to be rather laborious. Therefore, these seniors are not only in the market for supportive services but a move to a worry-free and labor-free residence as well. Just as there are numerous choices of support services available to seniors today, there is an amazing array of residential products specifically designed for the needs of today's seniors. The next chapter will be devoted to offering the reader a survey of these residential products and their particular features.

5

Housing and Health Care
Alternatives for the Elderly
Timothy S. Smick

"Pop" was as active at 87 as he had been in his sixties. A widower for
the past two years, he still maintained a mental sharpness and wit
that was truly impressive. His sense of humor and ability to produce
the "perfect" pun made him a favorite with people of all ages.

Although he had retired from his medical practice twenty-five years
earlier, he continued to be well known among his previous patients and
physician colleagues. The huge Victorian home in which I had been
raised had almost become a historical landmark in my hometown. The
ornately detailed home was commonly referred to as "Ol' Doc Wilson's
place." As proud as Pop was of that fine old house, it pained him not to
be able to take care of it as he once had. The maintenance required by
the home consumed most of his available time and yet he still was losing
ground to the forces of Mother Nature.

Moreover, Pop's body was also "losing ground." For many years
he had been dependent on Mom to do the cooking. Now without her,
he had not been eating regularly. Instead, he skipped eating a day at a
time, not because he forgot, but because he didn't want to take the
time to cook and clean up.

If the neighborhood boy was not faithful in promptly mowing the
lawn, Pop was out pushing the mower till he felt exhausted. When it

snowed, he would stay indoors for days feeling trapped by the snow-covered walks.

One day I suggested to him that the home might be getting to be too much for him to handle. After all, a 5,000-square-foot home was an awful lot for even a younger man to maintain. Pop's response to my suggestion was adamant when he said, "There's no way you are going to put me in one of those nursing homes."

We dropped the subject until about six weeks later when I was shocked to find him hallucinating during one of my regular visits to the house. Our doctor had me bring him to the hospital where he was admitted and an I.V. was started immediately. He was dehydrated, slightly malnourished, and exhausted. Within a few days he was back to his old self again, but the time had come for us to have a serious talk about his future.

I had met with the hospital social worker who also functioned as a discharge planner. She was well acquainted with all the housing options available to seniors in the area. Armed with brochures and an abundant amount of information, I headed toward Pop's hospital room for a heart-to-heart talk.

During our discussion I made an important discovery. At the time Pop retired from medicine, there were not many options for seniors in his situation. In fact, nursing homes and some "run-down" boarding homes were the only alternatives available to seniors. When I showed him the array of options available to him today, his resistance to selling the house melted away.

The next week I took a couple of days off work to visit some of the facilities brought to our attention the previous week. Pop and I were amazed at the options available to him. We narrowed our selection to two excellent senior housing choices.

At first, Pop was leaning toward a high-rise retirement facility comprised of about 150 apartments. The facility provided one hot meal a day and the residents used their small apartment kitchens to provide their own supplementary meals. It was clear that there would be little maintenance or apartment upkeep concerns for anyone living in this congregate care facility.

Pop, however, chose the new continuing care retirement community that had just recently opened on the outskirts of town. I found a great deal of comfort in the fact that this community was prepared to accommodate Pop's needs even if he eventually needed the medical attention a nursing home could provide. Although Pop showed some interest in this feature, he was most persuaded by the fact that some of his friends had already moved into the independent living portion of this mid-rise facility.

Shortly after making this decision, Pop put his house on the market and began packing those items he intended to bring to his new home.

Most people today are not aware of the many housing options available to seniors. Unless you are actively in the marketplace for senior housing, you have no real need to consider the current senior housing choices. Instead, you most likely rely on the general belief that the senior's only options are either to live with children or in a depressing nursing home.

Indeed, twenty-five years ago there were not many choices for seniors. Yet, as a result of today's exploding senior population, the marketplace has responded with numerous products to meet the very specific housing desires of this population. No longer are seniors perceived as one large demographic group. Instead, they are perceived as a highly segmented audience with dissimilar needs and desires. Within the 75+-year-old cohort are seniors with dissimilar financial positions, lifestyles, physical fitness, tastes, marital situations, and overall medical health.

One thing most seniors do have in common with each other is a general reluctance to live with their children as a solution to a health or financial problem. They have an even stronger reluctance to enter a nursing home.

Perhaps you, too, are not aware of the many residential options available to seniors. Even if you have been thinking about possible alternative arrangements, you may have discovered that getting reliable information on which to base your planning is not easy. Chances are, the facts available have come to you in somewhat random fashion. Perhaps you have seen newspaper or TV ads for retirement communities—one commodity heavily marketed to older people these days. Quite possibly, you have wondered if there are other, less publicized alternatives you might prefer. If so, what are these alternatives and how do you compare them? In the remainder of this chapter we will attempt to examine the entire continuum of senior housing in order to enable you to select the accommodations most appropriate for you or the senior you are assisting.

Determining Decision-Making Criteria

Once seniors have determined for themselves that a move from their current residence will bring about a significantly improved living situation, it is important to establish priorities to be considered in the selection process. *Consumer Reports* includes the following items for a senior's consideration when reviewing various nonmedical housing options:

- Climate
- Neighborhood safety
- Visual appearance of the neighborhood
- House or apartment security
- Visual appearance and state of repair of the exterior
- Visual appearance and state of repair of the interior
- Structural features (elevators, ramps, handrails)
- Cost (rent or mortgage payment)
- Access to public transportation
- Proximity to medical care
- Proximity to shopping
- Proximity to church
- Proximity to recreational center
- Daily presence of another person in the home or very close by
- Assistance with heavy cleaning and housekeeping
- Assistance with light housekeeping
- Assistance with personal chores (bathing, laundry, shopping, cooking)
- Privacy
- Proximity to family (close enough to visit weekly)
- Proximity to friends (close enough to visit weekly)
- Neighborliness[1]

After completing the prioritization of these items it is also important for seniors to take stock of their financial position. Many seniors look to their children to assist in this confusing process. Others may insist on the utmost privacy in these matters and prefer to determine for themselves what they can afford. Whether seniors elect to solicit your help or the assistance of an accountant, it will be very important for them to determine their monthly income, assets, and total net worth.

About 75 percent of those looking at senior housing alternatives are women. There are times when some women are not particularly aware of their financial well-being because they had relied on
their spouse to manage their financial affairs. Now widows, they believe their net worth to be depleted because they have little understanding of the asset values of their homes, antiques, art, stocks, and
bonds. They are amazed to discover the "hidden" wealth that can be
converted to cash to fund their housing and living needs.

Remaining in Your Own Home

Sometimes, the best option for a senior is to remain in the house
in which he or she presently resides. As seniors weigh the trade-offs
of a move (financial and emotional costs, distancing themselves from
familiar friends, loss of personal furnishings or possessions), relocation
sometimes doesn't make sense. Given their druthers, 85 percent of
seniors would not move from the home where they probably have
lived for as long as thirty years.[2]

For those seniors desiring to remain in their present home
there can be financial obstacles to address as well. Although most
seniors own their own homes and no longer have mortgage payments, they sometimes feel overwhelmed with the inflationary increases of fuel, taxes, and home maintenance. Recognizing this
dilemma, some financial institutions offer home equity conversion
plans that allow seniors to tap into their home equity. Reverse mortgages pay the homeowner a set monthly income which is considered
to be a loan against the equity in the house. The loan does not
have to be repaid (along with the accrued interest) until the home is
sold to satisfy the debt fully. In the event the senior outlives the
term of the loan, payments can be deferred, with the lender and
the homeowner sharing in the home's future appreciation.

The catch is that these plans are not widely available. Legal
restrictions in some states discourage local banks and savings and
loans. Also, lenders are wary of making fixed-rate loans based on
mortality risks, fearing that some older persons will outlive their
home equity and that some heirs will contest the sale of the home to
pay off the loan. The federal Department of Housing and Urban
Development agency initiated a pilot program in 1989 that insures
2,500 mortgages to elderly people. With this type of federal backup,
it is felt that banks will become increasingly more willing to enter
the reverse-equity market.

Seniors sometimes share their homes with other seniors to
help defray the cost of upkeep. Assuming success in finding a com-
patible housemate (not always an easy task for those set in their

ways), they receive rent and companionship that makes independent living both affordable and socially pleasurable. In many metropolitan areas there are shared housing resources that can assist in locating match-ups of seniors who desire to stay in familiar homelike settings and yet need to defray housing costs.

Congregate Housing or Senior Apartment Complexes

Group living arrangements in which most if not all the residents are older people come in many shapes and forms. High-rise, mid-rise, opulent and expensive, modest and affordable, government-subsidized, accommodations for a dozen or 300, most of this type of housing takes the form of apartment-style living. Most offer companionship, security, and a modest amount of assistance with tasks such as cooking and cleaning.

Subsidized Senior Apartments

Subsidized senior apartments are probably the most widely known form of low-cost congregate senior housing. Many are built with the aid of federal and state funds. They often range in size from 100 to 300 units. Typically, each apartment is a self-contained unit with its own dining area and kitchen. Most of these housing projects include a central dining area as well as recreational space, small libraries, emergency call buttons and security systems, grab bars, handrails, ramps, and smoke detectors.

Many are sponsored by private nonprofit agencies: Area Agencies on Aging, church groups, fraternal orders, neighborhood and civic groups, and local housing authorities or planning departments.

The housing is specifically designed for low-income seniors and is often partially subsidized by HUD (the U.S. Department of Housing and Urban Development) under its Section 8 program. Rentals for HUD-subsidized housing are calculated according to complex formulas. They are based primarily on annually updated "fair market rents" for each community and each type of dwelling unit.

Luxury Senior Apartments

The segment of seniors most willing to move from their own homes are those with college degrees, annual household incomes over $32,000, men and women under 70 who live alone, and people with serious health limitations.[3] Quite possibly, one of the reasons affluent seniors are so willing to relocate is the wide array of acceptable choices made available to them in most metropolitan areas. The majority of seniors today do not move to the Sunbelt retirement communities surrounding golf courses and resort beaches. Instead, most independent seniors who sell their homes for one reason or another, elect to remain within a fifteen- to twenty-minute drive from their network of friends and relatives.

Once again, these seniors are unpredictable and have demands that are not exclusive to their generation. Some retirees cherish the community spirit found in many retirement communities and senior apartments. They appreciate the fact that there is plenty to do, and they make good use of the recreational facilities. They feel secure with readily available but not intrusive medical and maintenance assistance. They enjoy not having noisy skateboarding children cluttering up their lives.

Others don't like being surrounded by so many elderly people talking about sickness and death. They feel somewhat cramped by community or senior apartment regulations and by too many planned activities. They relish having younger people around and feel cheated by segregated living arrangements.

One thing these affluent seniors do have in common is that they have an appreciation for the catered lifestyle. Most likely, they have enjoyed the ability for the last couple of decades to employ others to perform life's more mundane tasks. In order to enjoy a weekend of golf or sailing they paid someone else to mow the lawn, trim the shrubs, wash the car, paint the house, and clean the bathrooms. But this catered lifestyle was not always employed by these seniors for the mere pursuit of pleasure. Many seniors find that serving others within and outside the church to be a tremendous source of fulfillment and life satisfaction. Civic groups, hospital volunteer organizations, symphony and art museum drives, and church ministries of all types occupy a significant portion of their busy and satisfying schedules. By not being "tied to home maintenance," they are free to pursue these more fulfilling aspects of their retired years.

Luxury senior apartments have been developed in most metropolitan areas to provide seniors with the accommodations and services necessary to meet these very specific needs. Available on an "a la carte" basis (for purposes of billing for services) are limousine service, full course dining services, dry cleaning service, on-premise beauty and barber services, housekeeping, home health and homemaker services, pharmacy delivery, valet services, concierge and banking services. Added to these, of course, are the standard services of a fully maintained apartment complex with twenty-four-hour security and architectural features designed with the seniors' particular needs and desires in mind. In-house recreational accommodations are also provided. These often include pools, spas, exercise rooms, billiard tables, woodshops, libraries, ceramic kilns, numerous lounges, craft areas, movie theaters, and abundant common areas.

Generally, these apartments are leased by the year and on occasion, some senior apartments are leased on a monthly basis.

Continuing Care Retirement Communities and Life-Care Plans

During the 1960s, "life-care" communities were the new experiment in housing for the elderly. At that time, only a few of these multilevel retirement communities existed and were usually owned and operated by church or denominational organizations.

Continuing Care Retirement Communities (CCRC's), also known as life-care communities, combine a wide range of living accommodations and supportive services, from independent apartments or cottages to skilled nursing facilities, within the same campus or complex that is identified as the retirement community. Most of these communities are loaded with full services and the luxurious appointments that are highly valued by its residents.

The distinguishing feature that is probably most important to the purchaser of this kind of retirement housing, however, is the community's guarantee of lifetime care. Residents usually enter these communities while they are still healthy and vigorous enough to live independently in their own apartments or cottages and take advantage of the numerous recreational and social opportunities that make these communities so appealing. Yet, if it were not for the guarantee of lifetime care and the accommodations to back up that guarantee, these communities would have little or no additional appeal to retirees than the luxury senior apartments previously described.

The ability to "age-in-place" is the major attraction of the CCRC form of retirement housing. In the event of a crisis of failing health, either temporary or permanent in nature, these facilities provide their tenants with a full range of supportive services. These services can include everything from housekeeping and personal assistance to the intensive nursing care found in the best of nursing homes.

Since the lifetime care provision is a key element distinguishing these communities from other forms of senior housing, they require long-term contracts and substantial entrance fees. In some parts of the country these entrance fees can be as low as $25,000 and in other more upscale communities, the entrance fees can exceed $400,000. The representative entrance fee in most metropolitan communities is in excess of $100,000 for a typical one-bedroom apartment. In the

1960s and 1970s these entrance fees were often forfeited if a resident chose to leave the community or died. In some communities the life-care plans required residents to turn over their assets in full. Fortunately, this arrangement has fallen into disuse largely because it was too risky for the resident and certainly not a fair exchange of value. Today, it is very unusual for a community *not* to refund all or a major portion of the required entrance fee if the senior leaves the community for any reason. Those communities that do not refund the majority of the entrance fee usually amortize the entrance fees over a defined period of time.

In addition to the initial entrance fee, residents also pay a monthly charge to cover maintenance, meals, and other basic expenses. These monthly fees can be as low as several hundred dollars and as high as fifteen hundred dollars. They can also be expected to rise as the cost-of-living index increases. In those communities where the entrance fee is used to make periodic payments to a sinking fund (amortization), the monthly service fees are generally lower than those where the funds are fully refundable. Most homes that charge a high entrance fee have included future health care costs in that figure, while those with a relatively low entrance fee generally assess a substantial additional monthly charge for nursing care. Quite often, this additional monthly charge is used to pay the premium of a long-term care insurance policy the community has purchased for its resident. Beware of plans that guarantee no monthly increases; this will almost certainly result in curtailment of promised services, diminished quality, or even bankruptcy.

As expected, the CCRC or life-care community does not meet the needs of many seniors because of their inability to meet the community's eligibility requirements. Since there are no federal, state, or private insurance programs that fund these independent living arrangements, the most obvious eligibility requirement is the senior's ability to meet the financial cost. The cost range is wide and varies according to location, type, and size of housing, as well as services included. Generally, some proof of income continuity must be provided, even if the purchaser is paying the entrance fee in cash. What the management wants to determine is that the buyer will have enough disposable income and insurance to pay for future maintenance, health care, and other costs of living. Experts in the retirement field advise that you should count on costs exceeding what the retirement community predicts by 5 to 10 percent.

Not only must the potential resident's financial health be sound, his physical, medical, and mental well-being must be intact. Most communities demand a medical examination requiring complete disclosure of the applicant's medical history. It is important that the applicant doesn't attempt to conceal important information. If any discrepancy is discovered, the contract for life-care services could be invalidated. Don't assume, however, that if you have ever been ill or hospitalized, you will automatically be disqualified. Decisions are made on an actuarial basis and every community will take some calculated risks. At the very least, most communities require the applicant to be ambulatory at the time of entrance. Each facility defines "ambulatory" in its own way. Some insist on the applicant's ability to mobilize without the use of any aid such as a walker or cane. Others, especially those communities that have been operating for a while, accept seniors who mobilize themselves with the assistance of all types of aids, including electric motorized carts.

Clearly, these communities appeal to many seniors. Community spirit and a sense of belonging as well as the built-in social life provide many opportunities in which to meet people. Certainly there are advantages to on-site recreational and athletic facilities, easy access to services, cleanliness, security from crime and fear of potential criminal activity.

"Shoveling snow, raking the lawn, and mowing the grass just got to be too much for Connie and me," said Al, a retired plumber from Baltimore, Maryland. "We were insistent on not wanting to be a burden on our kids or anyone else, but we wanted to live someplace where we wouldn't have to make another move later in life." So they sold their home in Perry Hall and paid the entrance fee on the Edenwald Retirement facility while it was under construction. It was fortunate that they had the foresight to reserve their apartment because by the time the facility was completed, it had an extensive waiting list of seniors willing to pay the considerable entrance fee as well as the monthly maintenance fee of $1,500. Connie and Al receive three meals a day in a beautiful dining room, housekeeping, full apartment maintenance and repairs as well as an extensive program of trips, crafts, hobbies, and social affairs. They know if they can no longer function independently, they can move into the adjacent nursing home, where, for no additional cost, they can receive nursing care. "We certainly don't like to be reminded of the possibility that we might need nursing care, but when you are our age you have the feeling that something could happen at any time. It sure gives us peace of mind to know that we will be cared for immediately," said Al. He found out how quickly that help could come when he began to suffer chest pains several months ago. A nurse from the nursing center arrived within a matter of minutes after he pushed a call button in his apartment.

"Who knows how long I would have waited for help if I had been living in a regular apartment?" he wonders.

As pleased as some seniors are with their new homes in a life-care community, other seniors do not find the retirement community life to their liking. Middle-income people often find that the rising cost of entrance fees and monthly maintenance fees price them out of the market. Others do not like the community's similarity in age (which typically averages 78 years old), religion, ethnic background, and general attitudes among residents. Some feel uncomfortable with a daily life that might seem too organized and regulated. Certain seniors find the community's privacy to be inadequate and feel there is an unfair distribution of costs for services they are not likely to use, such as golf and swimming.

A choice of this or any other lifestyle comes down to a trade-off of benefits and their costs. Assisting a parent in sorting out the many advantages and disadvantages can be a tremendous service.

Jim was assisting his mother-in-law and her husband with setting up their retirement housing plans. "I told them to begin right now to put their $1,000 refundable deposits down in order to reserve an apartment in one of the two CCRC's now under construction in their area. It seems that the only communities without significant waiting lists after opening are those that may be in considerable trouble. They need to reserve the apartment now so it can even be a consideration for their planning in the next several months."

In most communities, the availability of quality life-care accommodations is in short supply. Jim's advice is good counsel especially for those seniors who say, "I'm not quite ready for that."

In deciding upon a life-care community, the selection of a qualified consultant is very important. The purchase of life-care is every bit as complex as the purchase of a house, and it is worth taking the extra time to find a lawyer, accountant, or financial consultant who is thoroughly knowledgeable in the field. Since these facilities require such a large initial investment, a thorough investigation of the financial stability of the organization should be conducted before your parents commit their financial security to its care. Although most are financially sound, some problems have arisen from "newcomers" to long-term care who have been forced into bankruptcy, leaving their residents in a financially vulnerable position. In addition, all the extensive community rules and regulations as well as the contract should be reviewed by your lawyer and accountant.

Most of the purchase decision in life-care communities revolves around the senior's finding a good "fit" with his or her lifestyle and the services and amenities of the independent living portion of the facility. Yet, responsible planning must include the possibility that your parent may require the medical attention of the nursing home or personal care facility in the future. The tips for shopping for a nursing home offered in the following chapter should be utilized by the person "shopping" for life-care or Continuing Care Retirement Communities.

Assisted Living, Personal Care, and Residential Care Facilities

With the growing number of seniors in the 1980s has come the development of other alternatives to nursing home care. During the 1960s, seniors in need of assistance in the activities of daily living, but with no real medical needs requiring the round-the-clock attention of a licensed nurse, had no options other than nursing homes. Experts in long-term care had determined that even as late as the 1970s, nursing homes housed individuals who really didn't need the intensive medical and therapeutic care they provided.

The latter half of the 1980s has seen an explosion of new facilities that provide the supportive and protective environment needed by a frail segment of the senior population who can no longer live independently in the community. Known as assisted living, personal care, residential care, catered living, domiciliary care facilities, and board and care homes, these facilities are targeted to provide the senior with a need for assistance in everyday living with a noninstitutional, nonclinical alternative to nursing homes.

Today's nursing homes are admitting far sicker patients than they did a decade ago, largely as a result of hospitals' cost-saving motivations to discharge patients to the community much sooner than they traditionally did in the past. Therefore, the "light care" patient feels even more out of place than in the past in the midst of the increasing medical sophistication of the modern nursing home.

Kathy was desperate: "Mom needed help and she knew it, but she was not ready to admit it to anyone else. Her fear was that she would have to live 'in one of those nursing homes.' It was easy to have empathy for her. Through a church volunteer program, I had become a regular visitor in the Oak Manor Nursing Home in our neighborhood. It was clear to me that Mom was in much better mental and physical health than most of those elderly residents. Yet Mom needed help in bathing, dressing, meal preparation, and climbing stairs. The episodes of mini-catastrophes she had experienced of late reinforced the fact that she could no longer continue living in her own apartment without some help.

"We tried getting her admitted to the new retirement community on the other side of town. Unfortunately, Mom's inability to function independently made her ineligible for this type of facility. Just as I was ready to pull my hair out, I heard of the Courtland Gardens Residence. This facility 'billed' itself as a retirement residence that offered a protective environment for elderly people no longer able to live independently in the community.

"My initial reaction upon entering the facility's beautifully appointed living room entrance was that Mom would appreciate the homelike environment. My favorable impression was reinforced during the tour when I observed the private rooms and apartments, the elegant dining room where three meals a day were served restaurant style, and numerous architectural features designed with seniors' needs in mind. Even the handrail was disguised as a decorative chair railing. Although just about every nontherapeutic and nonmedical need had been addressed in the facility's physical layout and service package, the facility seemed to reinforce its residents' desire for autonomy and independence.

"Mom, who was reluctant even to visit the facility, exclaimed, 'This isn't bad,' when she finally toured the facility. The director explained to us that the average age of the residents in the facility was 83. Although each of the residents preferred having meals prepared for them, they still enjoyed 'dabbling' for themselves in the stocked kitchen near each room and apartment.

"The Courtland Gardens Residence proved to be the perfect mix of independence and support for Mom. She has made new friends and even regained some abilities that she had lost while living by herself."

Most of these facilities are unregulated and are becoming available in many different forms. Some nursing homes have built assisted living facilities contiguous to their nursing homes in an attempt to provide a continuum of care for seniors if their medical needs should change. Many other personal care facilities are free standing and located on the same campus as a related nursing home. Life-care communities and CCRC's have begun to provide assisted living accommodations for residents who have initially entered the community in the independent living portions and found their need for supportive services to have increased. Numerous congregate care facilities, which have seen their populations "age-in-place," have segregated portions of their facilities for the provision of assisted living.

Monthly, annual, or even daily rents are the norm for financing this type of care. Presently, no insurance program provides coverage for this kind of living. Elderly people with low incomes who qualify for Supplemental Security Income (SSI), however, can receive substantial cash assistance for this type of housing.

The cost of this type of care varies. Modest facilities may rent for as low as $500–600 per month. Elaborate and elegant projects can cost much more. Most of these facilities have prices that range between two-thirds to 100 percent of the cost of semiprivate accommodations in a community nursing home.

NURSING HOMES

The process of selecting a nursing home for yourself, a friend, or a relative is not the sort of thing anyone anticipates. In fact, the "nursing home" label conjures up all sorts of ugly images in our minds. Newspaper headlines about corrupt nursing home operators warehousing old people in rundown, substandard complexes have been probably observed at one time or another by every reader of this book. In actuality, there are probably still some nursing home horror stories to be told. Media attention focused on these problem facilities has appropriately drawn attention to the need for more stringent regulations to safeguard our nation's elderly. Unfortunately, this same media attention has helped foster a negative image for those nursing home professionals who are dedicated to providing exemplary and compassionate care for the elderly. Fortunately, competent and quality nursing homes are the prevailing rule today, although their professionalism is not what captures today's newspaper headlines.

The term "nursing home" is actually a very general name for several different types of medical care facilities. Although it continues to have the connotation of a "last stop" for the elderly, it actually can be a place for people of all ages to convalesce following an accident or serious illness. Today's modern nursing home is increasingly being used by major insurers as a cost-efficient alternative to hospital care for accident victims needing nursing care and physical therapy. As mentioned in a previous chapter, nursing homes are used quite often as a respite for people needing temporary placement while a family takes a break from caregiving responsibilities or tries to arrange alternative modes of care.

Sometimes the best way to define a complex subject is to tell the reader what it is not. A nursing home is not a prison where the elderly are segregated from society. It is not a drawn-out hospice program where people are waiting for inevitable deterioration and death. Instead, it is a home for people who are in need of rehabilitation and assistance in caring for themselves. It is a place where nursing and medical care, such as injections of medication, catheterizations, wound dressings, physical therapy, speech therapy, occupational therapy, and other forms of rehabilitative services are provided. Personal care is also provided in the form of assistance in eating, dressing, bathing, hair and nail grooming, getting in and out of bed, placing telephone calls, and letter writing. Of course, nursing homes provide numerous residential services such as a clean room, appetizing and nutritious food, a pleasant atmosphere, and an appropriate variety of all types of social activities.

Quite often, nursing homes are judged by the level of care they provide. The care offered by nursing homes is categorized in one of three ways: skilled, intermediate, and custodial. Most nursing homes provide both skilled and intermediate care, while some offer all three levels. With the rise in medical neediness in today's nursing home populations, it seems as if the distinction between skilled and intermediate care is becoming very fuzzy, even to medical professionals working in the nursing homes.

Yet a skilled nursing facility is able to provide a more intense level of nursing care than an intermediate care facility. Typically, the skilled nursing home patients are bedridden and unable to help themselves. These patients usually require one or more therapeutic treatments that have been prescribed by their attending physicians.

On the other hand, an intermediate care facility provides less intensive care than a skilled facility and therefore generally costs less. Usually the patient has a greater degree of mobility and is not confined to bed. Intermediate care facilities also stress rehabilitative therapy programs that enable the patient to regain or retain as many functions of daily living as possible. Once again, the care is supervised by registered nurses and licensed practical nurses.

Custodial care is nonmedical in that residents do not require regular attention from nurses and aides. Although these personnel may be present when needed, the medical condition of the resident does not require continuous care on a regular daily basis. The custodial care regimen is often indistinguishable from the supervision needed by the residents of assisted living or personal care facilities.

Quite often, the shopper for such services wonders what bearing the nursing home ownership has on the quality of care. I'm often asked, "Who provides the best care, nonprofit, for profit, or government-owned facilities?" The answer is not as straightforward as one might believe and depends on a number of factors. For instance, if money is no problem to you and your family, you will find the most luxurious and pampered settings to be in the finer for-profit nursing homes. Hoping to distinguish themselves from the competition in order to be more profitable, they offer higher staffing patterns, more luxury appointments, and outstanding dining to the customer willing to pay the higher price. Medium-priced nursing home facilities tend to offer even quality in service whether or not they are for-profit or nonprofit facilities. On the lower end of the price scale are the facilities which have nursing home populations primarily comprised of welfare patients.

Clearly, the nonprofit facilities serving welfare populations have the best quality of care largely due to their ability to subsidize their operations from contributions from their parent organization (a church or fraternal order). Sometimes, local or state governments operate nursing homes. Often these facilities are classified as public nonprofit institutions because they are funded by tax dollars and municipal bonds. Most of the time these facilities offer, at best, an average quality of care due to the tenuous nature of their funds. The quality of nursing homes is so variable, however, and there are so many exceptions to every generalization I have just given, that nothing can substitute for your personal observation and judgment.

The predominant room type in a nursing home is a semi-private room where a bathroom is shared by an adjoining semi-private room. Most facilities have only a very small number of private rooms and charge a premium for these highly desirable rooms. Some of the nursing homes serving large "welfare" populations often have three and four beds per room that promote economy of scale at the sacrifice of patient privacy.

Nursing homes are the most costly form of senior housing. The reason—close to 70 percent of nursing home costs are attributed to labor. Remember, nursing homes are much more than senior housing. Although a clean room is part of what one buys when making a nursing home purchase decision, it is only one factor to be considered among the many complex and sophisticated services offered in today's modern facility. If a senior does not need the medical and therapeutic services offered by a nursing home, it is foolish to pay for them. The senior is better served by selecting one of the other housing products previously mentioned that cost considerably less than a nursing home. Therefore, it is important that you and your parent assess his or her physical/medical needs and then attempt to match available resources within the home and the community to those needs. This factor, coupled with determining one's financial status, are foundational to helping you decide if nursing home care is the proper option. Unfortunately, in certain rural areas of the country, nursing homes are the only senior housing alternative to caring for a parent at home.

To arrive at a thorough assessment of a person's condition there are two general areas to consider: a person's general health status and the type of health services needed.

The Department of Health and Human Services recommends the following health status checklist that asks the question: Does this person have difficulty with:

- Bathing—requires assistance?

- Continence—difficulty in controlling either bladder or bowel?

- Dressing—requires assistance or does not dress at all?

- Eating—requires assistance, either from a person or via tube or intravenously?

- Mobility—requires assistance to walk or is confined to chair/ bed?

- Using toilet—requires assistance or does not use at all?

- Speech—completely lost or so severely impaired that can be understood only with difficulty (cannot carry on a normal conversation)?

- Hearing—completely lost or so impaired that only a few words or loud noises can be heard?

- Vision—blindness or so severely impaired that television set cannot be seen from eight to twelve feet away (features of a familiar person only recognized within two to three feet)?

- Mental Status—cannot understand (or remember) simple instructions, requires constant supervision or restraints for his/her safety?

The following checklist is offered to determine the health services required by the seniors' physical condition. For intensive nursing care that requires special training and has some inherent risk you need to determine if the senior requires:

- Bowel/retraining (needed when the patient is chronically incontinent)

- Catheterization (needed when the senior cannot empty bowel/bladder unassisted)

- Full bed bath (needed when the senior is entirely bed bound)

- Intravenous injections (usually requires a tube connected to a vein for an extended period of time)

- Oxygen therapy (for patients who cannot breathe with ease unassisted)

- Tube or intravenous feeding (for seniors who cannot eat even with assistance)

For other forms of nursing care that require training, but generally not as much as intensive nursing care and posing less risk to the senior, you need to determine if the senior requires:

- Application of sterile dressing or bandages

- Vital sign monitoring (blood pressure, temperature, pulse, respiration)

- Enema

- Hypodermic injections

- Irrigation (wash wounds or body cavities)

For personal care that requires even less training and risk but is quite labor-intensive and time consuming you need to determine if the senior requires:

- Administration of medications

- Help with bathing, dressing, or eating

- Rub or massage

- Special diet

For therapeutic services performed by licensed, trained therapists you need to determine if the senior requires:

- Physical therapy

- Occupational therapy

- Speech therapy

- Psychological therapy

Nursing home care is very expensive. A quick review of the facilities in your community will demonstrate that some homes are more expensive than others. Therefore, it will be important for you and your family member to determine what you are capable of paying and willing to invest.

Some nursing homes are relative bargains, providing excellent care at a lower cost than their competition. Others are grossly overpriced and provide only average care in return. Generally speaking, however, the more you pay, the more you get.

How much you can afford to pay may put limits upon your ultimate choice, so it will be necessary to once again assess the financial resources available to help support the cost of care in the nursing home.

As referenced in the beginning of this chapter, the development of a monthly income statement is the first step in assessing your financial status. All income from Social Security benefits, retirement plans, interest from bank accounts, stocks, bonds, real estate investments, and other assets should be considered. Nonliquid, nonincome-producing assets such as homes, land, antiques, and other valuables should be appraised for their market value. The analysis should assume the appraised value of these nonliquid assets to be principal placed in an interest-producing account with the corresponding income generated, added to the monthly income statement. If family members are willing to contribute to the cost of their relative's nursing home care, then these supplemental funds should be added to the monthly income.

Many seniors, upon the completion of this monthly income analysis, realize that they are far short of the necessary funds required to pay the costs of nursing home care. With present day nursing home costs averaging $75 to $80 per day in most parts of the country, they soon realize that it will be necessary to utilize the principal that is now presently earning interest to fund their health care. The fact that net worth built up over a lifetime can be eroded in a few short years of life in a nursing home is a painful realization for both seniors and their heirs. Most families come to terms with this financial fact when they weigh the consequences of the emotional and physical stress encountered in caring for loved ones needing constant, round-the-clock attention in their own homes.

There are two other sources used by some qualified seniors to pay for a portion of or all their nursing home care. These programs are:

Medicare

Medicare is a federal health insurance program for persons over 65 that covers hospital, skilled nursing, physician services, home health service, and outpatient care. The program is administered by Social Security through the Health Care Financing Administration. Medicare will pay for skilled nursing care *only* if the following conditions are met:

• It must be a skilled nursing facility and certified to participate in the Medicare program.

• The person must have been in the hospital for at least three (3) days and be admitted to the skilled nursing facility within thi..y (30) days following their discharge from the hospital.

• A physician must certify that the person requires skilled care on a daily basis.

• There must be ongoing utilization review to determine if the person requires skilled nursing care.

• If a determination is made that skilled care is no longer required, Medicare coverage ceases.

Most American seniors believe that their long-term care needs will be paid by Medicare. This is an erroneous assumption. Medicare is responsible for less than 7 percent of the cost of nursing home care in comparison to the 51 percent of costs that are paid out-of-pocket.[4] Medicare is not a long-term solution to paying for nursing home care, since it does not cover intermediate or custodial care. Medicare coverage for 1990 is as follows:

Time Frame in Days	Medicare Pays	You Pay
1–20	100% of costs	Nothing
21–100	All but $74/day	$74/day
101+	Nothing	All costs

Medicaid

Medicaid (sometimes referred to as Medical Assistance) is an assistance program that is administered by the individual states through local welfare departments. The program is funded by both the federal and state governments and is intended for primarily low-income individuals requiring health care services. Medicaid covers a wide range of health services, including both skilled and intermediate nursing home care, provided the person is admitted to a nursing home that is Medicaid certified.

Even if your parent enters a nursing home as a self-pay patient, you should familiarize yourself with this program. Over half of the individuals who enter a nursing home as self-pay patients become Medicaid-supported patients. Today 42 percent of all nursing home care is paid by Medicaid.[5]

Because Medicaid is state administered you will need to check the exact eligibility requirements of your state. Benefits are usually based upon the following: income, savings, property, and other assets. Full disclosure of all financial transactions for the past two to three years will be required, as will full disclosure of any assets owned. Any attempts to conceal or transfer assets is considered to be a fraudulent act against both the state and federal government with criminal consequences.

Once a nursing home accepts a Medicaid patient, it agrees to the Medicaid payment and will not attempt to collect the difference from the patient or the family. Medicaid rates are usually below prevailing market rates and are established by the state. These rates are then agreed to by the nursing homes that participate in the program. Reimbursement will vary from state to state, and it may even vary within a state. The actual costs of operating a quality nursing home are not reimbursed in full by the Medicaid program. Indeed, most nursing homes are not inclined to admit Medicaid patients who have not initially been self-pay patients for extended periods of time. Most states do not attempt to force nursing homes to accept Medicaid patients.

Applications for a determination of Medicaid eligibility are submitted to the local welfare or public assistance office. The office will then determine the applicant's eligibility and notify the applicant accordingly. In some cases, the local offices will assist in finding facilities that accept Medicaid patients. It is not at all unusual for Medicare patients to apply for Medicaid coverage once their skilled-nursing benefits have been exhausted.

Long-Term Care Insurance

Presently, 1.1 million Americans hold long-term care policies purchased in anticipation of their potential need for nursing home care. The president of the Health Insurance Association maintains that "long-term care insurance is the hottest product to come along in thirty years." Although this insurance may be an excellent manner in which to protect the senior's estate from being exhausted by the high cost of long-term care, many experts do not feel the insurance is worth the expense to seniors who don't have large estates to protect. Since there are numerous policies with even more numerous variations of coverage, the best advice that can be given in this book is buyer beware and don't buy a policy that doesn't have a thirty-day "free look" period, allowing you ample time to change your mind. For further information about long-term care insurance, write the United States Health Cooperative, 1334 G St. NW, Washington, D.C. 20055. Your local Area on Aging can also assist you in determining the extensiveness of a specific policy's coverage.

Nursing Homes Can Often Be the Best Choice

Less than 5 percent of seniors will ever need to use nursing home care. Yet, 100 percent of seniors hope their health will remain strong enough that they will never be the recipient of nursing home care.

Admission to the very best nursing homes in our country is still an event that can provoke a great deal of guilt in the family member who feels defeated as a full-time caregiver at home. "I hope you love me enough that you will never put me in one of those places," is an emotionally guilt-ridden statement communicated daily by many seniors to their family caregivers. And yet, when the same person is admitted to a hospital, the caregiver is usually never smitten with guilt. In fact, rushing a loved one to the hospital is considered to be a very practical and responsible expression of love and concern for a family member hurt in an accident or stricken with disease.

Most families involved in admitting a family member to a nursing home are not selfishly shirking their responsibility as loving and obedient children. Instead, they recognize their parent's need for a level of long-term care that cannot be effectively delivered by themselves in their own homes.

Granted, a few generations ago the long-term care of those elderly who even survived their sixties was delivered in the home. Since there were no better long-term health care alternatives available to those tightly clustered nuclear families, caring for the senior great-grandparent in the home with the participation of all the nearby extended family was the typical course of action. Indeed, child-bearing, dentistry, and minor surgery were also medical events that took place in the home.

Unlike those days of yesteryear, our modern health care system has extended its medical care for the elderly, from the acute-care setting of the hospital to the long-term care of the nursing home. The nursing home today is not the dumping ground for unwanted elderly. Instead, it is a highly sophisticated medical environment that attempts also to offer a homelike setting for seniors suffering a myriad of medical and psychological problems.

* * * * *

Summary

Today's senior population is a highly segmented group with distinct needs and desires. Differing financial positions, lifestyles, physical fitness, tastes, marital situations, and overall medical health demand a variety of housing options that "fit" the specific requirements of each individual senior.

An entire continuum of senior housing options has been developing in the last decade in response to the multifaceted housing demands of the elderly.

The first step for seniors who are evaluating these various housing options is to determine if a move from their current residence will actually bring about a significantly improved living situation. Many seniors find the best option is to remain in the house in which they presently reside. Some are making use of reverse mortgages to derive a monthly income from the equity they have built in their homes. Others are sharing their homes with other seniors to defray the cost of upkeeping their homes.

More and more seniors are discovering that some form of group living arrangement is best suited to meet their housing needs. Congregate housing and senior apartment complexes are designed specifically for the elderly and take the form of modest subsidized complexes as well as elaborate and opulent buildings equipped with every service and feature imaginable. Continuing Care Retirement Communities and life-care communities combine a wide range of living accommodations and supportive services that allow residents to "age-in-place."

Assisted Living and Personal Care facilities provide the supportive and protective environment needed by the frail segment of the senior population that can no longer live independently in the community.

Nursing homes are the most costly form of senior housing primarily because so much more than housing is offered. In fact, 70 percent of nursing home costs are attributed to labor. It is designed for only a small segment of the senior population that needs the medical and therapeutic services offered by skilled and intermediate care nursing facilities.

Less than five percent of seniors will ever need to use nursing home care. When medical circumstances require that twenty-four-hour-per-day nursing care is needed for an older parent the family member charged with making the arrangements for admission can feel guilty and defeated. Yet today's caregivers can continue to express their love for their parents by carefully selecting the appropriate nursing home for their relative with the same care they would select a physician to perform life-saving surgery. The next chapter will attempt to aid family members in assisting their parents in the selection of an appropriate nursing home.

6

Selecting a Nursing Home
Timothy S. Smick

Kathy enjoyed a special relationship with her mother. Relationally very close since childhood, their bonding seemed to continue even throughout adulthood. Regular daily phone conversations were always ended with warm expressions of love.

In the past few years, her mother had developed Alzheimer's disease. The resulting dementia had progressed to the point that it was impossible to maintain continuity in even the simplest of conversations.

The onset of additional medical problems and the twenty-four-hour-per-day stress of managing her mother's care at home had caused Dr. Wilkens to insist that Kathy place her mother in a skilled nursing home.

Although the idea took some getting used to, Kathy realized, after some counsel from her husband, that Dr. Wilken's strong recommendation was wisely offered out of concern for both her mother's as well as her own well-being.

The next day, Kathy set out to find the very best nursing home for her mother. She felt that her diligence and thoroughness in selecting the appropriate nursing home would be her means of expressing her love for her mother.

Her mother's strong financial position gave Kathy a real advantage in the selection process. From the local Area Agency on Aging she *found out that the largest number of nursing home options were available to those seniors fortunate enough to be able to finance their care from their own funds. From the agency she received a list of the entire metropolitan area's licensed nursing homes.*

She called Dr. Wilkens to determine just what services her mother would require from a nursing home. Dr. Wilkens assured her that the regimen of medical care needed by her mother was within the capability of most skilled nursing homes. He did offer a helpful tip when he suggested that Kathy give special attention to how a nursing home manages the senile dementia resulting from her mother's Alzheimer's disease.

Kathy had a firsthand understanding of the specific care her mother needed. After all, she had been the one providing that care the past two years. She also knew that her mother could afford the rates listed in the nursing home directory given to her by the agency. Yet she was still not certain of her strategy for determining the best nursing home "fit" for her mother.

* * * * *

Many caregivers have found themselves in Kathy's position. Certain that a family member needs the services of a nursing home, they are unsure about how to find the right one. Unless they have had significant exposure to a medical setting as a result of employment or a prolonged illness, they feel uncomfortable in an environment of medications, therapies, patients, doctors, and nurses.

It is the intent of this chapter to offer the reader an orientation to nursing homes as well as a strategy for determining the quality of service offered in each of the facilities the reader might be considering.

The reader should be aware that there exists in bookstores and libraries a substantial collection of material on the criteria to be considered when selecting a nursing home. I've reviewed much of the material and found it to be very helpful in its overview of nursing homes. These references are included in this book's selected bibliography. Clearly, the criteria offered by these books would enable the reader to differentiate a sub-standard facility from one that consistently offers a high level of care. Unfortunately, much of the literature does not offer the reader the strategy needed to distinguish the outstanding facility from an average one. It is my desire to offer the reader insights derived from seventeen years of nursing home operational experience and on-site exposure to well over 1,300 nursing home facilities that will enable him or her to discern the more subtle clues which distinguish premier long-term care providers from the ordinary nursing home.

Keep in mind that you can be made privy to an in-depth review of any nursing home's compliance with state and federal regulations. Health department surveys are available today, thanks to legislation that makes most governmental files available to the average citizen. Individuals can make appointments with licensing and certification officials in their states to see copies of these reports or they can be made available to you for your review at your local Social Security Administration office.

It is important to remember that each state is charged with the licensing and certification of its own nursing homes. Although the federal government performs audits of each state's surveillance methods, there continues to be considerable disparity from state to state in the accuracy and depth of these licensure reviews. In some states, the slightest error in paper compliance is noted. In other jurisdictions, only much more significant errors are recorded. Regulators of nursing homes have continued to improve in their scrutiny of patient care in the last few years by strategically focusing more of their attention on the patient's well-being instead of the facility's compliance in keeping up with a myriad of required paper work.

In any case, you may need further assistance from the regulators to answer any questions you might have about the severity of any deficiencies cited at a facility in which you are interested. Pick up the phone and give them a call. They will usually not endorse one facility over another, but they will offer clarification about the severity of any deficiency they have cited. Don't rule out a nursing home with deficiencies. Most, if not all hospitals and nursing homes in your area, will be out of compliance in some of the thousands of regulations governing health care facilities. Be alert, however, to a facility that has not been responsive to correcting these deficiencies and stay far away from those facilities that have been cited for life-threatening conditions.

Accessibility to Friends and Family Is Critically Important

The first criteria to use in screening the extensive list of available nursing homes is the location of the facility. Decide realistically where the nursing home can be located. The person residing in the nursing home will need, and is entitled to, frequent visits from family members and friends. If the home is too inconveniently located, these visits will become more and more infrequent and the nursing home patient will suffer as a result. It may be necessary later to expand the geographic region you will consider if a suitable facility is not found close to home. Try for convenience initially, because a senior's constant contact with the family is a very important element of quality long-term care.

Martha had a family reputation for being practical. So it was a surprise to no one in the family when she began her search for a nursing home for her mother at the kitchen table. Armed with a map of the town, the "yellow pages" telephone directory, and a collection of highlighter pens, she plotted each of the nursing homes in her vicinity on the map. She then marked other locations she regularly visited each week. The grocery store, the mall, her church, her daughter's community college, and her husband's office were all circled on the map in bright yellow. Martha knew the bridge crossing the West River was heavy with traffic most of the time, so she eliminated from her consideration the two nursing homes on the east side of town. She also felt unsafe every time she traveled to the southwest side of town and therefore eliminated the Oakdale Nursing Home from her list of "possibilities." It was clear to Martha that there remained six facilities conveniently located in the midst of her family's weekly destinations. Martha was now ready for the next step in the screening process.

Determination of Needed Services

The next step in the screening process is to determine what services your parent currently needs or is likely to need in the near future. By utilizing the series of questions provided in the previous chapter you should be able to summarize the exact health care services for which you will be shopping. Armed with this information, you are ready to call those nursing homes conveniently accessible to you and your family.

When calling these facilities, you will want to obtain the following information:

The level of care offered. Obviously, if your parent has need of skilled nursing services and the home you called does not provide it, you should politely terminate the call.

Special restrictions on the type of patients admitted. Some skilled facilities are reluctant to accept patients who require a great deal of supervision. It is far better to ascertain this information now than at a point much further along in the evaluatory process.

Extensiveness of the waiting list. In those states that are underbedded the very best nursing homes have waiting lists. Unfortunately, most patients in need of nursing home services do not have the luxury of waiting for an available bed. In any case, this information is important in evaluating the home's suitability in meeting your needs.

Medicare or Medicaid certification. If your physician feels that your relative's medical condition might be eligible for Medicare coverage, you will most certainly want to find a facility certified by the Medicare program. Not to do so might mean many thousands of dollars will have been unnecessarily spent.

If your relative qualifies (or will soon qualify) both financially and medically for Medicaid coverage, you will want to make certain that not only is the nursing home certified by the Medicaid program but that it will accept Medicaid payment as full coverage. In many areas of the country, the best "equipped" nursing homes will *not* accept Medicaid patients because of the program's insufficient reimbursement.

Daily room charges and ancillary charges. The room charges will differ based on the accommodations. Private rooms usually cost more than semi-private rooms, and skilled beds rent for more than intermediate care and custodial care beds.

Most facilities have additional charges for personal laundry and/or dry cleaning, TV rentals, hair dresser appointments, wheelchair rentals, pharmacy and medical supplies, and physician visits.[1]

Once you have effectively reduced the number of nursing homes to be considered by screening out those that are inconveniently located, not properly certified or licensed, too expensive, or inappropriate in other ways, you are ready for the most challenging part of the selection process—your own personal inspection of the nursing homes still under consideration.

Your Personal Inspection of the Nursing Home

If you are like most people, you have probably never ventured inside a nursing home before. Please be warned that you are in for an initial shock. Although I have worked in nursing homes for seventeen years, I can still remember my first day on the job when I had the unsettling experience of encountering such a high concentration of infirm elderly people. If you don't sufficiently prepare yourself for the fact that this is what you will encounter in any nursing home, you may be blinded from objectively observing anything else. If your first visit to a nursing home still catches you "offguard," it might be necessary to make several trips to acquire a balanced perspective.

Usually, the first order of business is the arrangement of an appointment to visit the nursing home. Most facilities will have you speak to an individual who customarily meets families to answer questions, gives tours, and solicits appropriate information about the potential nursing home resident. Typically, either the nursing home administrator, the director of nursing, the administrative secretary, facility social worker, or admissions coordinator is charged with being the family's first facility contact. Your initial encounter with this person can speak volumes concerning the type of care offered by the facility and the manner in which that care is delivered. If upon meeting this person you find his or her overriding concern is to solicit medical and financial information, be wary. Or if you are treated as an intrusion or interruption to his or her hectic schedule, you may very well be in the wrong facility for your parent. However, if the person with whom you are meeting displays a compassionate empathy for both you and your parent in the course of the interview and communicates a patient understanding of your desire to be diligent in finding the right nursing home, you have most likely encountered a facility worth further investigation.

As you mentally prepare yourself for the initial tour of the facility, make certain that you are consciously using all your senses during the visit. Envision your parent in the nursing home under consideration. Do not discount your emotional reaction to the facility and its personnel. If you have been effective in overcoming the initial cultural shock of nursing home life, these emotional impressions can be important evaluational tools.

Your interview and tour of the facility should be strategically timed. I prefer to tour nursing homes on or around 11 A.M. Usually, the morning is the most active patient-care time of the day. Thus, it provides the best opportunity to observe staff and patient interaction. If your tour begins at this time, it will generally overlap the lunch hour and offer you the chance to inspect the meal service as well.

The person conducting the tour should not make you feel rushed and should allow you to pursue any path of inquiry you feel is important to your parent. You should, however, be certain that your investigation of the facility under consideration considers the following:

The Building and Grounds

Attractive surroundings can certainly boost your perception of a facility and are an indicator of a well-run nursing home. But it is important to keep in mind that you are buying much more than real estate when you make a nursing home purchase decision. Many family members allow their impressions to be so influenced by curb appeal or impeccable interior decoration that they overlook more important criteria central to their evaluation.

However, the maintenance of the building and grounds can be an excellent indicator of the facility's commitment to quality care. Neat and well-maintained landscaping, litter-free parking areas, well-illuminated walkways, sidewalks that are in good repair, handicap accessible ramps and outside seating areas are indicators that promise good things about the service within the facility. A run-down, poorly maintained physical plant says a great deal about the administration's concern for its residents—and perhaps even more about the institution's financial solvency. Even with this in mind, however, remember that a facility's ability to match your aesthetic tastes is far less important than its safety and comfortable livability.

The health department's licensure survey teams focus much attention on the facility's provision of a safe environment. If you have read the facility's survey reports, as was recommended previously, you will observe areas of concern they have had in the past. You should make certain that your tour allows you to observe these areas of concern to satisfy yourself that the safety concern has been corrected. Sometimes, especially in older nursing homes, certain Life Safety Code requirements are waived by the health department because they were not required at the time the facility was constructed and would prove to be a financial hardship to install or retrofit. The fact that the facility is technically out of compliance does not always imply that the facility should not be considered for your parent. For instance, some facilities constructed in the early sixties do not have the now required eight-foot width in all hallways to allow for the evacuation of hospital beds in the event of fire. Instead of insisting that the interior of the building be demolished and reconstructed to meet this code requirement, the health department and fire department have often waived the required clearance and have had the facility, instead, provide additional fire sprinkler equipment.

A facility with an atmosphere of livability is also an important plus to your parent. Adequately sized and well furnished lounges, dining rooms, activity rooms, lobbies, corridors, and especially patient rooms are very important. Once again, you will want to be certain that the comfort these areas provide, the atmosphere they permit, and their safety features meet your parent's requirements.

The Personnel

Some of the most modern nursing home facilities have beautiful grounds, spacious rooms and furnishings, and interior appointments that rival those of the finest hotels. Yet some of these facilities are little more than elaborate warehouses of the elderly because they lack qualified, dedicated, and well-supervised staffs.

Your evaluation of the staff's availability, competency, and overall demeanor to the patients will be the most important consideration in your facility evaluation. Unfortunately, this is the most difficult attribute to judge because it requires a keen and somewhat intuitive observance of staff interaction.

Once again, I'm not going to elaborate in detail on the types of employees who should be present in a nursing home. The law requires that nursing homes employ licensed nursing home administrators, RN's, LPN's, physical therapists, occupational therapists, speech pathologists, dieticians, and nursing assistants. If your parent's regimen of care requires the specific services of any of the therapists, you will want to inquire further concerning their abilities. It is usually a good idea to request that you be introduced to a particular therapist during the tour. However, just because a therapist is licensed doesn't mean he/she will be well suited to your parent. Ask for references from other families in the facilities who have used the therapist in order to solicit a more candid evaluation of their capabilities.

The demeanor that the staff projects toward residents is one of the most important criteria you will be attempting to evaluate during your visit. It is an evaluation often overlooked by health department survey teams because it doesn't fall into the matrix of regulational compliance they are evaluating. Yet the interaction of patients and staff can speak volumes about the kind of patient care administered in the nursing home you are visiting. You will know you are in the wrong facility when you discern a staff member who thinks of the residents in terms of "dealing with them," or "tolerating them," or "handling," or "putting up with them."

Instead, you should be looking for signs of staff members who understand the sanctity of life, who through their special training, sensitivity, and ability help make the lives of the elderly meaningful. You should be looking for a health care team whose reverence for human life calls for health care services in the context of physical, psychosocial, and spiritual dimensions—a team that knows that each aspect of these patient care services enhances the other. You will be looking for staff members who work well with each other and you as a team. You will be looking for a staff sensitive to the unspoken needs of the patients. In reality, you are looking for staff members who feel called to the challenge and joy of caring for your parent.

Evaluating a staff that will not only care *for* your parent, but also care *about* your parent, is a difficult task. It cannot be done on a rushed tour of the facility and will most likely require further visits. Yet your tour can provide loads of observations that will enable you to form impressions about the demeanor the staff has toward the patients.

While walking through the hallways of the nursing home, study the way the staff members interact with one another. Is there good eye contact? Do they refer to each other by name? As they go about their responsibilities, is there good cooperation between each of them as they lift patients, serve meals, etc.? Are they deliberate in the manner in which they approach their jobs, or do they seem to be wandering aimlessly? Do they offer you a cheerful hello as you pass them in the hall? Is there any indication of staff/supervisory tension?

If you observe considerable tension in the facial expressions of the staff, and they are not responsive to your salutations, you might have stumbled across a facility that is suffering labor relations problems. Squabbles between management and staff usually "cost" everyone involved, including the patients. If you detect a certain uneasiness in the interpersonal relationships of the staff, it is time to terminate the tour as quickly as possible.

Study the way the staff interacts with patients. If they talk condescendingly and disrespectfully to the patients, do not address them by name, and seem to deliver care in a hurried or rough fashion, you can be sure you and your parent will be unsatisfied customers should you select this facility. On the other hand, if you see staff members stooping to make eye contact with residents, holding their hands while they address them by name, explaining exactly how they will be helping them, you have found a staff that is indeed "called" to the challenge and joy of caring for your parent. Look for evidence that the staff respects the patient's right to privacy and dignity. Are cubicle curtains drawn when patients are receiving treatment while not fully clothed? Are patients dressed? Do they show signs of good hygiene and grooming?

Interestingly enough, I have found that facilities where residents are treated with dignity and respect almost uniformly have little or no regulatory problems with health department licensing agencies. These facilities might not have the most ornate of physical plants, but the quality is delivered in bundles to the patients and their families by the staff's responsive, compassionate, and caring service.

The Nursing Care

Quality nursing and medical care is also an important issue to most people selecting a nursing home. After all, the demand for this medical attention is what has made the need for a nursing home mandatory. Once again, the regulatory agencies are a helpful indicator of the competency of a facility's medical and nursing staff. It is doubtful that most readers of this book have the medical training to determine if a sophisticated treatment or regimen is being administered correctly. You most certainly won't have access to medical charts (for reasons of legally mandated confidentiality) that would enable you to determine the staff's medical observation capabilities. Therefore, you will need to rely on health department surveyors for appropriate feedback on the facility's capabilities in the more sophisticated and technical aspects of medical care.

Most of the nursing care received in any nursing home is routine and nontechnical in nature—bathing patients, changing soiled sheets, and so forth. Never think for a moment that the quality of this type of care isn't just as important as the most sophisticated medical procedures.

If anything, it is even more important as far as the resident's dignity, self-esteem, and comfort are concerned. Furthermore, poor physical care and hygiene can lead to life-threatening situations, such as infections and all types of illnesses. These nontechnical aspects of nursing are quite easily observed and should be noted by you during your tour. Some things to look and smell for are:

Halls and rooms free of unpleasant odors. In most nursing homes a substantial number of patients are incontinent of bowel and bladder. Therefore, the existence of an occasional temporary odor is to be expected. However, if the odor is routinely observed through numerous portions of the facility, and exists in the same area where it was previously observed, you can be sure that you have a facility where incontinent patients are not routinely changed and housekeeping is inadequately staffed.

Each resident has a call button within easy reach of his or her chair or bed. Sometimes, the call button is placed out of the reach of an immobile patient's reach. If this happens in more than an isolated case, it is indicative of poor, nonresponsive nursing. Also, be alert to how long it takes a staff member to respond to a call light. The response should be prompt and attentive. Occasionally, patients will be so demanding that the only way to promptly please their every request would be for them to have their own private-duty nurse. Where this is not financially possible, the patient will have to be politely informed by the nursing personnel that his or her nonemergency needs will be met after other residents with more pressing needs are satisfied.

Each resident should have a clean water container and glass in his or her own room.

Patients' fingernails should be trimmed and, in the case of males, their faces cleanly shaven.

Good oral hygiene should be evident.

Patients confined to wheelchairs and gerichairs should not be leaning to one side. Their feet should be supported by footrests and never left dangling.

Look for demonstrations that patients who tend to be immobile are encouraged and assisted to walk.

Look for a nursing station that appears neat, tidy, and organized.

Recreational and Social Calendars

Use your ears during the tour. Sometimes, when touring a nursing home, I've wondered where the patients were. The halls were strangely abandoned and quiet. Were the patients discouraged from coming out of their rooms? This should not be the case. It is important that the nursing home resident feel that he or she is permitted to live in and move around in a homelike, pleasant atmosphere.

A well-run recreational program can add significantly to the patient's quality of life as well as his or her physical well-being. Therefore inspect the activities calendar to see if there are abundant activities that might interest your parent. Make certain that there is a good blend of both active and passive activities to appeal to many different levels of mental and physical abilities. Look for calendars that are rich with diverse events for every day. Typically, poorly staffed and poorly conceived programs have gaping holes in the evening and weekend portions of their calendars. They also have an abundance of bingo games and church services and very little else to stimulate the bodies and minds of their residents.

Food Service

One of the most important events in the lives of the elderly are meal times. Perhaps because meals break up the routine or perhaps because there are few other sensory experiences they can enjoy, meals become a crucial event in nursing homes. Make absolutely sure that your initial tour or subsequent follow-up tour includes your observation of the service of a meal.

You will need to assess the food's aesthetic appeal and its nutritional value. By watching a meal service, you will readily be able to observe the patient's receptivity to the food's taste. Watch to see how much food is left on the plate when the patients leave the table. You might want to order a meal for yourself to sample the food's taste, texture, and temperature. Pay special attention to the appearance of the plates served. To determine whether attention to food presentation has been given, note the use of garnishes and foods of various colors.

To judge the nutritional standards, ask the tour guide for a chance to review a menu cycle. Then try to determine if the cycle is sufficiently varied. Check to see if the meal served matches the one on the menu. See how often fresh fruits and vegetables are served in season. Find out what choices are available to residents who might not like what is on the menu for a given meal. Ask if soups and other parts of the meals are cooked from scratch or are frozen or prepackaged.

After you (and, if possible, your parent) have conducted your on-site investigation and evaluation of the most suitable nursing home in a selected area, you will be ready to make an informed choice. Most likely, no nursing home will strike you as ideal in every way, so you must decide which facility best meets the particular needs of your parent.

Discuss Your Findings with Your Senior Relative

It is obvious that no nursing home can fully replace the compassionate care you gave in your own home or the familiar and memory-filled surroundings of your parent's own home. Yet now is the time for you and your parent to thoroughly discuss the merits of the nursing home of your choice with a clear understanding of the compromises inherent in that choice. It is absolutely imperative to discuss this important event with your parent even if you are certain that what you say will not be understood. Try to explain the situation truthfully. I have rarely seen an admission to a nursing home work successfully when the patient had been told "white lies" to coerce them to enter. Instead, these lies increased the patient's anxiety and adversely affected the person's already tenuous orientation.

Sue had just returned home from taking her mother to the Shady Oak Convalescent Center. She felt awful. Yes, she had been diligent in selecting the best nursing home in the area. She was certain of that. In fact, the facility enjoyed an impeccable reputation. Yet the forlorn look in her mother's eyes as she said good-bye haunted her for the rest of the evening. And now, in her living room, she was reliving the very painful parting as she sobbed with her face buried in her husband's chest. "What have we done? How could we bring ourselves to do such a thing to Mom?"

The next morning Mrs. Bingham, the facility's social worker, called to inform Sue that her mother had rested peacefully the night before and enjoyed a hearty breakfast that morning. Sue started to feel a little better until her guilty feelings had begun to refuel as she thought of the events of the day before. Then Mike called from work to see how she was doing: "Honey, you are a loving daughter. You are forgetting how close the two of you are. Nothing has changed. Your mom is still very much a part of the family, that is, if you will let her be."

Mike was right. Sue needed to devise a workable plan for the future that would assure that her mother remained a part of the family. After shedding the guilt, she could put that pent-up energy to good use by latching on to the simple formula offered by Nancy Fox in her book, *You, Your Parent, and the Nursing Home:*

> visiting
> vigilance
> vocalizing.[2]

Don't treat your parent as if he or she has been excommunicated from the family. Regular visits of both short and extended duration are especially important to anyone living in a nursing home. These visits help sustain the relationships that are key to our healthy emotions. Your parents should be included, and not sheltered, from disappointments, trials, and hard decisions as well as the joy you encounter in everyday life.

There have been occasions, however, when family members have developed unhealthy visitation patterns largely motivated by guilt. Sometimes, children who are unsure of their role in the health care delivery process feel obligated to spend six to ten hours a day in the nursing home. If you or another family member find nursing home visitation significantly hindering you from leading a normal, healthy life at home, then you are most likely a hindrance and not a help to the health care being provided to your parent.

You also play an important role as the patient's "vigilant committee." Be full-orbed in your watchfulness. Some family members, who have no trouble voicing a complaint to the home's administrative staff about their concerns, are as quiet as a church mouse when it comes to questioning their parent's doctor.

Sometimes it is necessary to intercede for your parents. Don't hesitate to speak up if they are unable to do so for themselves. However, if they can speak for themselves, foster their independence by encouraging them to vocalize their concerns themselves. If you observe they are unable to get results, intercede, remembering that "honey attracts more flies than vinegar."

Typically the appropriate channels to most effectively voice a complaint are as follows:

> Charge Nurse
> Director of Nursing
> Nursing Home Administrator

In the event that the administration has been unresponsive to your voiced concern about the care for your parent, the following are external sources that should be considered:

- The Local Health Department

- The State Health Department's Division of Licensing and Certification

- The Office of Aging

- The Nursing Home Ombudsman Office

Your efforts and diligence in determining the best "fit" for your parent will pay satisfying dividends of comfort when you know you have placed your parent in the responsible and loving hands of a dedicated and committed health care team. Clearly, it is advantageous to conduct your nursing home investigation when you are not faced with a parent's immediate discharge from the hospital. Unfortunately, life's events do not always work that smoothly. Still, even if the hospital discharge planner seems urgent to find a place for your parent, do not feel rushed into making an inappropriate placement of your parent in any nursing home.

SUMMARY

Many caregivers are unsure about how to find the right nursing home and feel uncomfortably at odds with an environment of medications, therapies, patients, doctors, and nurses.

Those family members equipped with a general orientation to the services offered by most nursing homes and a strategy for determining the quality of these services are most likely to achieve success in discovering the facility best suited for their relative.

A good strategy will attempt to screen from consideration those facilities not conveniently accessible to family and friends of the patient.

By reviewing health department surveys made available to the public by licensure and certification officials in their state, family members can receive an in-depth review of an extensive and recent professional investigation of a facility's compliance with state and federal laws governing the operations of nursing homes. Those facilities with significant problems should also be screened from the list of potential nursing homes under consideration.

A determination of the type of services your parent will need or is likely to need in the near future is the next step in the screening process.

A strategically timed personal inspection of the remaining nursing home possibilities is critically important. It is imperative that all your senses be utilized during this inspection as you visualize your parent in the nursing home under consideration. This inspection should include the building and grounds, nursing care, recreational calendars, food service, and most importantly, the personnel. Your evaluation of the staff's availability, competency, and overall demeanor to the patients will be the most important consideration in your facility evaluation.

Once a selection is made, it is imperative that you discuss your findings with your senior relative.

After a relative is admitted to a nursing home, your responsibilities as a caregiver are not finished. Instead, your responsibilities have changed from being the "hands-on" deliverer of daily care to that of a watchful visitor who is willing and able to intercede for parents when they are unable to do so for themselves.

As important as your visits are to your relatives, the visits they receive from friends from church are also highly valued by the institutionalized senior. Too often, institutionalized people feel cut off from the Body of Christ as if they were dispensable, unwanted waste paper. The following chapter depicts how the "senior sensitive" church can play a vital role in delaying the need for institutionalization as well as ministering to the caregiver. Admission to a nursing home does not necessarily mean excommunication from the church.

7

The Eldercare Connection
Jeffrey A. Watson

"How can we help these people?" the team leader asked. "There are too many folks landing in nursing homes who really wouldn't have to go there if *we* could work together!"

An Ounce of Prevention Is Worth . . .

A small committee of church volunteers had begun to search for practical solutions to premature nursing home admissions. One member defined their role: "I know there are a lot of senior citizens living alone around Kansas City. If we could help them to take better care of themselves, to eat decent meals, to get to the store and the doctor's, to keep their houses and apartments repaired and safe, and to stay positive, we could keep them from having some of the health crises that put them in the hospital. You know, by the time they are hospitalized, they are pretty sick. And then they often don't have family at home to help them during their recovery. And that puts them right in the nursing home. Sure, the nursing home tries to rehabilitate them and return them to their homes in the community. But too often, it never happens. They never really turn the corner and go back to living at home alone. If we could prevent or delay the crisis that brings on the hospital stay, we could help a lot of good people."

Creative ideas incubated for several weeks. Some dreamed of building a more ideal retirement home through their church. Others countered such an idea: "Look, only one in twenty older adults needs to be in a sheltered setting at any given time. Let the nursing homes do their job and we'll reach out to the 95 percent who want to continue living in their own homes as long as possible! . . . What we ought to do is help the older adults in our community answer two questions:

• How can I get help when I need it in order to remain independent as long as possible?

• What can I do in the later years to find meaning and purpose for my life?

The team agreed and the vision was born.

A Monumental Task

"But who's going to help us do this? We are talking about an enormous task." The answer became obvious in time: retirees would be the main source of manpower. After all, who already *owned the vision* for this kind of ministry? With the average retirement age getting continually younger and with people living longer and longer, there already was a large pool of motivated, competent volunteers. Most of these potential recruits had retired "from" something but needed the challenge of moving on "to" something. Now that they were retired and their "nest" was empty, many had anywhere from ten to twenty years available either to give or receive ministry. Self-esteem could be built by giving the volunteer retirees a sense of feeling needed, bringing joy to another person, and developing new skills.

The name was chosen, "The Shepherd's Center."[1] Reminiscent of Psalm 23, the name held as good a chance as any to create positive impressions, even for those disillusioned by the formal church.

"But who are we actually going to target? If we shoot for doing everything for everybody, we'll fail and lose our credibility! No one will get help that way," one team member warned. The team agreed to target all the adults over sixty-five who were living in a specific geographic area. The Shepherd's Center was not going to be a building. It was going to be a service to people. The committee members imagined a covenant between the Center and those within their geographic perimeter. On the one hand, the Center would make every effort to assist these people in achieving the goals of independent and purposeful living for their later years. On the other hand, these people would need to provide the majority of leadership and volunteer work force for the Center.

Home Services

The first tangible service offered by the Center was "Meals on Wheels." Five men became committed to bringing hot meals as needed to thirty-five different people. Each volunteer was responsible for seven older adults who lived alone and had indicated that they needed one hot meal per day. This service grew rapidly until nearly fifty volunteers were serving two hundred adults an average of twenty thousand meals per year! These meal drivers also became the alert system that set off emergency procedures when a person did not respond to the door. For those who did respond, however, there often were other needs to be attended to. Small errands were usually done by the driver while additional concerns required others to follow-up.

As common needs were noticed, new services began. The "Shoppers Service" attracted younger women to serve as volunteers who would either shop for the senior or take the person shopping once a week. The "Handyman Program" provided minor repairs so that an expensive craftsman or technician would not have to be called in. The "Night Team" took after-hours phone calls and decided whether to call an emergency professional or just to give reassurance. The "Care XX Program" helped low-income adults secure Title XX (Social Security) benefits from public agencies. The "Friendly Visitors Program" organized volunteers from a businesswomen's organization to make regular visits to isolated individuals. The "Companion Aides" provided nonnursing, nonhousekeeping help such as children might do for their parents. The "Security and Protection" coordinator gave regular sessions on personal and home safety techniques. And the "Hospice Team" assisted terminally ill patients who were living at home.

Center Services

While the home services were directed at helping elders survive on their own, Center services developed to answer the question, "Why survive?" The purpose of Center services, offered at area churches, was to help enrich and reconstruct life for these aging seniors. "Adventures in Learning" became a one-day-per-week adult education program. Courses were taught by volunteers on subjects like Bible, budgeting, cooking for one, exercise, travel, books, languages, etc. This program usually lasted from ten to twelve weeks and soon had as many as forty elective subjects and 800 registrants from all the various locations.

The "Life Enrichment" program offered a group counseling experience in a three-hour session once per week. This program was led by a clinical psychologist with basic and advanced groups. The "Health Enrichment Center" offered health lectures, nutrition sessions, exercise classes, screening services, seasonal inoculations, and nursing assistance. The "Gadabout Tours" were low-cost local bus trips to places of interest and historical significance. "Defensive Driving" courses were offered periodically by trained volunteers, as were "Pre-Retirement Seminars" and "Senior Adult Employment Services."

Keeping the Vision Growing

What had begun as a small brainstorming session in a local church had become a blessed reality. In time, twenty-five churches had joined the partnership to offer nineteen different services to the local older adult. In the geographic target area, there were a total of 53,000 people of whom 12,000 were age sixty-five or older. The Center has grown to the place that 350 volunteers offer help to more than 4,000 seniors—one in three in the target area.

The Shepherd's Center has a small salaried staff and is now incorporated. It is officially accountable to a Board of Directors composed primarily of older community leaders. Each program or service has a Chief Coordinator who donates twenty or more hours per week, recruits his own volunteers, and directs their program. Motivation remains high because those serving as volunteers receive appreciation directly from the people they are serving. A Coordinator's Council, comprised of each of the nineteen Chief Coordinators, supervises the Center and reviews suggestions for new services.

Anyone in the geographic region can qualify for a home service simply by indicating that he or she is over sixty-five and cannot provide the service for himself or herself. All services are free, except for a nominal charge on the "Handyman" and "Gadabout" programs. Center services are available to anyone who comes to the service site, regardless of the geographic boundaries.

The Impact of the Shepherd's Center

This creative approach to volunteer networking and eldercare has been overwhelmingly beneficial. Numerous older adults have found new meaning in life. A conservative estimate suggests that more than 100 seniors continue to live independently who would otherwise have been institutionalized. Sponsoring churches have gained new credibility, blending faith and works in a practical marriage.

Ultimately the whole American society may benefit from such model programs. As pressures increase on each tax dollar, tangible services provided by older adults may be sought out at little or no cost: neighborhood-oriented child care, handyman services, security watches, etc. There is certainly little hope that all the services needed by senior Americans can be tax subsidized. Instead, as older people themselves accept some responsibility for the creation, management, and funding of these services, there is a bright prospect of cost effectiveness and the personal touch.

Realists: Apply Within

If you are in an eldercare family today, you don't need to be a "Lone Ranger." There are volunteers and churches who are willing to help you as a part of their ministry. If you aren't in an eldercare family, you can have a ministry by volunteering to help others.

As realists, we understand that older adults fall into a number of categories:

• Many *live alone* quite effectively. These seniors become excellent candidates to volunteer with organizations like The Shepherd's Center.

• Many *live with family or friends* to care for them. These seniors may want to take advantage of the life enrichment opportunities provided by an organization like The Shepherd's Center. Caregiving spouses and adult children may also want to fall back on some of the life maintenance services for their loved one during times of illness or vacation for the caregiver.

• Many *struggle to survive alone*. These seniors either have no family or their family is unavailable to provide care. For these people, life maintenance services are crucial. The services may be needed chronically or just temporarily during rehabilitation from a fall or a surgery. In either case, they are a lifeline to help and friendship.

• Many *live in clinical institutions*. These seniors have at least one acute medical condition requiring skilled care for a time. As an inpatient, they can engage in various life-maintaining and life-enhancing resources, as their health permits. If a particular setting is barren of such opportunities, the elder and his or her advocates can become a constructive agent of change.

Without stereotyping all older people, it is fair to say that every elder could be therapeutically "connected" to the caregiving network. Whether they become care providers, care recipients, or a dynamic combination of both, they are a part of God's creation which he called "good." Through his church, which is founded on the good news, getting old needn't be "bad news."

THE ELDERCARE CONNECTION: FIRST CENTURY A.D.

For any who read the Bible with an eye to geriatric concerns, it is obvious that the early church had its share of eldercare burdens. It is in this context that the brilliant deacon, Stephen, shone as an angel to God's people. After harvesting from Stephen the eldercare experiences of the early church (Acts 6:1-7:60; cp. Leviticus 19:32; Ecclesiastes 12; Matthew 5:16, 18:10; 1 Timothy 5:8; James 1:27), we will be ready to assess the status of eldercare in the twentieth century church.

A Testimony from Stephen

"Almost everyday we see new believers coming to the Savior all around Jerusalem. Some of them are very sophisticated priests, the same ones who crucified our Lord a few months ago. But others are little old grandmothers who wept for Jesus when he was marched up to Calvary. What an amazing combination! Thoroughbred Jews, plain Greeks of every age, all types.

"I think the Lord has used two things to really grab people's attention. The first is the unique love the believers have for each other. They share their food and belongings. And what's more, they don't let their differences ruin their fellowship. The second is the sudden death of Ananias and Sapphira. When they lied to the Holy Spirit in front of the apostles and the whole church, God took them home on the spot. Word really got out: God wants a holy church! Those two things have left people longing to be a part of the deep love in the church but at the same time realizing that it is serious business to be a disciple of Jesus Christ."

Critical Pressures

"Just yesterday the Twelve called a congregational meeting. We had to meet outdoors beyond the Damascus Gate because the crowd was so large. Peter informed us that we had some important needs in the church that were not getting met. For a moment I thought he would be asking for more people to donate goods for some individual. Instead, he spoke about a whole group of needy people: Greek widows.

"Apparently, everyone was still sharing their food in love as before. But the Twelve just didn't have enough hours in the day to deliver the food to all the widows and still spend good time praying for the church and preaching the Word. The worst part of it, according to Peter, was that it appeared the Twelve were prejudiced. The Greek widows had gotten the impression that the Jewish widows came first or were loved more than they. I could tell Peter was close to tears because of his tender heart for feeding the sheep, physically and spiritually.

"Peter continued, 'We know that the Lord doesn't want us to do less praying and preaching. But we'd have to cut back if we went to every widow's home each day with food. And the problem is only going to grow as the Lord adds people to the church.'"

Creative People

"Maybe Peter sensed that some in the group were willing to sacrifice the food ministry to widows to protect the apostles' priorities. But he disagreed. 'Moses commands us to *stand in respect when in the presence of the elderly*—how can we walk past them in disrespect and ignore their hunger? Our Lord emphasized that *we cannot overlook the neediest among us, like widows and orphans*—their angels in heaven will monitor how we treat them. Solomon teaches that *the elderly have special physical and social needs*—we'd have to deny the Word to deny their needs. In fact, Jesus taught that *our good deeds for one another will create a credibility for the gospel*—ultimately helping to win unbelievers to saving faith. The food ministry to widows is actually a part of our praying for conversions and Bible preaching.'

"By now, everybody was curious about Peter's strategy. 'We've prayed and the Lord has led us to create a new team of leaders. We want you to select the seven best men you can find. They will have to have three qualifications:

• '*Honest* (to manage large amounts of donated goods and money without privateering any of it)

• '*Spirit-filled* (to be able to love these widows as Christ loves them)

• '*Wise* (to be able to discern who is truly needy and who ought to be encouraged to be more self-reliant)'

"Everyone sensed this was a plan that had come from God. I was chosen along with six other men. After the congregation was satisfied that the new team was complete, they presented us to the Twelve. Peter and the apostles ordained us for the work and prayed over us in a great celebration service."

Christ's Approval

"Almost immediately we sensed the Lord's pleasure with the new team approach. The Bible-preaching ministry increased because the apostles could concentrate more directly on it. This brought in many new converts, most notably priests. And this wasn't just a movement of the young. Our love for each other and for the needy reinforced the message of Christ.

"Sometimes when we would be visiting an elderly shut-in, we'd have opportunity to minister to his or her neighbors or friends. After seeing us come day after day with food, they didn't have such a hard time believing that Christ had changed us. They could see that Christ had made us a people of love. Sometimes when we'd be asked to pray for the sick in these homes, God would reach down and heal them on the spot. Those kinds of miracles proved to many people that Jehovah was at the source of our movement and had authored our good news message."

Stephen: A Fallen Hero

The testimony of Stephen is rich toward God and man. As a brilliant Hellenistic Jew, he was able to debate with the most progressive thinkers in his day and to defend the claims of Christ. It is marvelous to imagine that a man of his spiritual competence was "washing the disciples' feet" through the food ministry to Greek widows. The power in his public ministry might well have come from the grateful, daily prayer of these dependent saints.

Stephen's holy boldness eventually led him down the same path of suffering as our Lord. Jealous of his popularity, the Sanhedrin produced false witnesses accusing him of blasphemy. Dragged before an enraged Supreme Court, Stephen displayed supernatural calm as if in the eye of a hurricane. Those in attendance later described his face "like that of an angel," a strengthened kind of peace that the world couldn't give.

When asked to respond to the charges, he launched a stinging review of Israel's history. Citing events and phrases from over sixty biblical passages, Stephen illustrated Israel's fickle loyalty. Again and again as God would reveal his truth, Israel would rebel against it. He confronted their unbelief, their disobedience, and their murder of Christ. The trial scene became an uproar. Infuriated justices bared their teeth like growling dogs and rushed Stephen outside the city limits. As the murderous mob gathered stones to crush him, he looked skyward with a sense of familiarity. "Heaven has just opened like the front door to my own home. A brilliant glory is shining out from the throne and Jesus is standing beside the throne, his arms out welcoming me."

With this prayer on his lips, Stephen was quickly bloodied by the brutal rocks. Before he lost consciousness, he collapsed into a kneeling position. As his death quickly followed, a widespread persecution of the church broke out. Believers, strengthened by the courageous example of Stephen, scattered in every direction from Jerusalem carrying the good news of Christ and his love for people.

THE ELDERCARE CONNECTION: TWENTIETH CENTURY A.D.

As one who admires the example of Stephen, I wonder where he would fit into our twentieth-century churches. Would he be shocked at our entertainment-style ministries? Would he discover prejudice that love should have conquered long ago? Would he find lazy pastors and church members who have no time for the elderly? Would he be willing to be pulled off the front lines of the "Greek Widows Food Ministry" so that he could do *more important things* like writing books and presenting seminars? Against the backdrop of Stephen's ministry to the elderly, we can ask two questions:

- How could the church be improved?

- Where should the church be applauded?

How Could the Church Be Improved?

A story may help us see some ways the church could be improved. As I sat in seminary chapel one day, an honored guest was introduced to be our speaker for the day. He was promoting his international youth organization. As he spoke eloquently, he pointed toward the window where we could all see Magnolia Gardens Nursing Home. "Did you know that eighty percent of the people who are Christians today made their decision for Christ before the age of eighteen? So don't waste time over there, holding Uncle Joe's hand and rubbing Aunt Susie's back! Youth are the future of the church."

I was angry and my mind began to quietly debate: "Maybe we put eighty percent of our energy into reaching the young! Maybe we are afraid of witnessing to adults. Maybe the way we cram the gospel into a fifteen-minute presentation and immediately demand an eternal decision fits youthful logic better than mature logic. After all, children and youth often use multiple choice and random guessing as their form of logic. They reason: 'Try this answer; it might be right!' Older adults think more slowly and more accurately.[2] They make fewer mistakes because they reason: 'I want to make the right decision because I intend to stick with it.' Maybe if we surveyed unbelievers, eighty percent of them would also say they made a profession of faith before age eighteen but don't believe it any more."

My mind went to the story of the Good Samaritan (Luke 10:30–37). Some obvious parallels stood out to me:

• The *man who had been wounded*, robbed, and left half dead seemed to personify anybody in acute need, including many elderly.

• The first pedestrian who crossed to the other side of the road happened to be a *priest*. This first potential helper was in the nearest position to care but he couldn't be inconvenienced. He seemed to be a picture of apathetic clergy, like our chapel speaker.

• The second pedestrian who crossed to the other side of the road was a *Levite*, one who helped in the spiritual worship of Israel. To me, he seemed like distracted lay leaders who had "better ministries" to engage in than reaching the elderly.

• Finally, a *Samaritan* came along, one who would have been despised by the priest and Levite. This common half-breed Samaritan had "compassion when he saw him." Instead of apathy or laziness, he looked directly at the need and was moved. He cleaned the wounds, sacrificed the convenience of his own donkey, and brought him to an inn. The Samaritan didn't meet all the wounded man's needs himself. Instead, he included others like the innkeeper to join the team of caregivers.

It seemed obvious to me that if we were going to improve the church by helping the wounded elderly, we would have to:

• Motivate the Priests and Levites, and

• Mobilize the Samaritans

Improved Leadership: The Clergy Connection

Since a river can never run higher than its source, it is strategic to convince church leaders to build "senior sensitive" church and parachurch ministries. Such persuasion must begin in our colleges, seminaries, and ministerial associations. Successful programs like The Shepherd's Center must be showcased to create a healthy jealousy.

Clergy must be taught a "realistic theology" that incorporates the subjects of aging, grief, suicide, terminal illness, the role of healing, the destiny of deceased children, and the nature of life with chronic impairments.

Their training must also include proper "ministry priority." Too often, church leaders accept the age-prejudice in our society: unless we are young, strong, energetic, quick thinking, and beautiful, we are not valuable people. This influences not only what we preach and teach but whom we allow to run our churches. With such age prejudice, we will inevitably create an imbalanced commitment to church programs for those who are young enough and healthy enough to attend regularly, to be enthusiastic, to work hard, and to give financially. Those who can't do this become nonpersons in the community of love.

Finally, Christ's shepherds must be discipled in "caregiving skills." Clinical Pastoral Care must go beyond simply performing funerals. These leaders must be helped to understand the psychosocial tasks of older adulthood, the culture of clinical institutions, the art of conversation with a dying person, the difference between healthy and pathological grief, and the repertoire of coping styles used by sufferers. Perhaps most of all, these caregivers will have to give up the cliché-ridden facades of the pastoral role.

As these Jericho Road "priests" are nurtured in realistic theology, ministry priority, and caregiving skills, they will need in turn to train their "Levites" (the elders, deacons, and directors in their ministries). We cannot teach what we do not know; we cannot lead where we will not go.

Improved Ownership: The Volunteer Connection

In every group of people there are good-hearted "Samaritans" and "Innkeepers." We don't need to give them oil, wine, a donkey, or an inn—they already have these. The most important thing we can give them is permission to minister. Setting them free to use what they already have for ministry is the key to success.

Rather than balking at the thought of new time pressures being placed upon an already frantic church schedule, we need to mobilize our volunteers more effectively. The less people personally invest in their churches, the less it seems "theirs." Churches must conscientiously mobilize the inactive volunteers in the pew to tap the rich resource of their unused talent. After all, church leaders are to "equip" the people so that they can do the work of the ministry along with the leaders (Ephesians 4:11–13).

Since thirty million Americans do volunteer work, the church would be foolish to invite or reward a complacency among its members. Instead, we ought to follow known principles for recruiting and maintaining volunteers:

• *Identify a true need.* Most people are sensitive to the needs of the sick or elderly because of loved ones and friends whom they have known. They also say, "That will be me someday!"

• *Clearly define what you want the volunteers to do.* Include the amount of time needed, to whom they will report, and what resources are available to help them do the job.

• *Allow the volunteers to influence the planning process.* During the training time, let the volunteers know they have support from others on the team and that they can influence the direction of the ministry. Allow them the opportunity to change their assignment from time to time when appropriate.

• *Be ready to join in and help when needed.* You grant the most powerful stamp of approval when you join in from time to time. It also gives you credibility and accuracy in your recruiting and trouble-shooting.

• *Express your appreciation.* People want to feel needed and would like to have their progress evaluated. They don't need cheap backslapping. Allow the volunteers to tell their own success stories and to hear other volunteers do the same. Such feedback sessions can also help pinpoint problem areas.

Perhaps the greatest untapped resource for volunteers in ministry are retirees. Their maturity makes them less inclined to impulsive blunders and they take commitments seriously. One bit of advice, however, is in order. Retirees go through a "honeymoon" phase during the first months of their retirement. During this time, they are reveling in the absence of wearying commitments. They might be open to your planting an idea but don't expect a new heavy-duty commitment. However, the "restless" phase follows when they realize that life cannot be defined as the absence of something. Volunteers who are recruited during this period often carry the commitment into the "project" phase, a long, stable period of redirected commitments. The Shepherd's Center has proven that success can be born of a marriage between true needs and committed retirees.

WHERE SHOULD THE CHURCH BE APPLAUDED?

Anyone who gives even "a cup of cold water" in the name of Jesus is to be commended (Matthew 10:42; 25:40). When such "cups" are rejected or spilled, our Lord receives it even then as if it were given in love to him. When an individual, a family, a team of volunteers, or a whole church program propose to give such "cups" to the elderly, our Lord applauds his people. By defining which "cups" are most needed, we can identify ministries that are having the greatest impact on the elderly and their caregivers.

"A Cup of Cold Water" for the Elder Living at Home

According to the most recent survey of eldercare families,[3] dependent seniors have some unique needs not typically targeted for ministry. In addition to the traditional spiritual nurture of a church, many older adults need:

- Indirect Care
    - 82 percent grocery shopping
    - 79 percent transportation
    - 75 percent housework
    - 68 percent meal preparation
    - 65 percent managing finances
    - 45 percent administering medicine
- Direct Care
    - 46 percent assisting with walker/wheelchair
    - 41 percent dressing
    - 38 percent bathing
    - 29 percent toileting
    - 28 percent feeding

According to common standards, the eldercare relationship exists when a person fifty years of age or older depends upon an unpaid person to provide at least one aspect of direct care *or* two aspects of indirect care. Such a relationship, of course, can be temporary or chronic. With due respect to the privacy of the older adult, there are times when a brother or sister in Christ can offer some of these "cups of cold water" in his name.

University Church

University Church was a congregation typically dedicated to reaching college students in their university town. The founders had located the church just south of the main campus to make it convenient for students who had to walk to church. As University Church matured over the years, it became the spiritual home for children, for middle-aged adults, and eventually older adults too.

One particular need emerged for middle-aged women. Many of the ladies in the church had never attended college. It seemed the common reason was that they had worked to put their husbands through school or had stopped their education to have children years before. Now that their "nests" were emptying and their husbands' careers were stable, their interest in returning to school was renewed. For some of the women, their husbands had died or divorced them, making the return to the workplace imperative. For others, a career change was long overdue.

One challenge seemed to stand in the path of many women returning to school: eldercare. These kin-keepers were expected to look out for *everybody else's* needs:

- the husband
- the adult children
- daughters-in-law/sons-in-law
- grandchildren
- *aging parents*

Whether the aging parent was the kin-keeper's own parent or the spouse's mom or dad, it was *her responsibility*. Among other things, eldercare responsibilities prevented these re-entering women from getting to class. Who would watch mom or dad? Who knew enough to care for their unique direct or indirect needs?

In response to these families, University Church created "The Fellowship Club." Housed at the church, this fellowship of older adults gave dependent seniors a mixture of health maintenance and life enrichment activities. Administered by a Clinical Social Worker, this adult daycare option allowed some families to know their loved one was in good hands for a few hours during class. For others, it allowed them to continue the jobs by which they were paying the bills when the elder became dependent. In some cases, The Fellowship Club provided a place of respite while the primary caregiver fulfilled doctor's appointments and accomplished other errands.

As University Church adapted its facility and expanded its program, The Fellowship Club found young college students their most excited staff members. Many young people found that the joy of learning from adoptive grandparents easily matched the satisfaction they derived from practicing new skills. Through listening to the needs of the congregation and using resources already available, this campus church has become a community landmark for intergenerational ministry.

"A Cup of Cold Water" for the Elder Living in an Institution

A seminary student living in the Philadelphia area became convinced that churches ought to make a priority of ministering to elders who live in long-term care facilities. His burden led him into a major study of the spiritual needs of residents at the United States Naval Home. His doctoral dissertation published the seven highest ranking "spiritual needs" as defined by the residents themselves.[4] They were:

- *60 percent: Anxiety or concerns about dying.* Residents worried about questions like: Is there life after death? Is there heaven and hell? Am I prepared to die? When will I die? Of what will I die? Will I die alone? Will there be pain? How will I be remembered?

- *38 percent: Distress in family relationships.* Residents were concerned about questions like: Why do some of my loved ones not visit, call, or write? Why was I put in this place? How is my spouse doing? my children? my brothers and sisters? my grandchildren? my nieces and nephews? Are these loved ones getting along with each other? Why are they experiencing divorces, alcoholism, juvenile delinquency, conflicted relationships, etc.?

- *27 percent: Alcohol consumption.* Residents were concerned about increasing dependence on alcohol and its effects on their health.

- *24 percent: Procedures for maintaining support.* Residents were concerned about whether they were doing all of the correct paperwork and following the bureaucratic procedures to keep Social Security, insurance, and/or retirement benefits coming.

• *22 percent: Financial problems.* Residents were concerned about whether the money would run out and the impact this would have on their own care as well as their dependents outside of the facility.

• *21 percent: Sexual needs.* Residents were lonely for intimate companionship. Conjugal visits from spouses were difficult due to lack of privacy. These needs were sometimes expressed through inappropriate talking or touching of the staff.

• *17 percent: Meaninglessness of life.* Residents felt life was meaningless, boring, and without sufficient purpose for living.

First Church

First Church was over 100 years old. It certainly should have had its share of elderly saints and an historic commitment to ministering to them. But it hadn't worked quite that way. Having spent its first eighty years in downtown Washington, D.C., First Church's move to the Maryland suburbs had cut off a link to many of its elders. Urban sprawl after World War II had sent the mobile middle class into an exodus from the city. This "white flight" left many of the poor elderly to fend for themselves in the concrete jungle.

Once in the suburbs the church grew again rapidly. With a young staff, most of the new membership came from young and middle-aged adults. As "baby boomers" joined the church in droves, programs were created for children, youth, and young families.

Fortunately the voice of the "sandwiched generation" was eventually heard. Many women were "caught in the middle," sandwiched in between eldercare and childcare responsibilities. Some elders were still living in the downtown area like prisoners in their own homes. Their fear of crime and exaggerated racial tensions had made them live like soldiers behind enemy lines, waiting for supplies to be air-lifted in. Other families had aging moms and dads who had made the move to the suburbs too. These aging families helped First Church to mature in its intergenerational ministry.

First Church began offering a number of learning experiences that helped sensitize the congregation to the needs of those touched by aging, grief, and death. Over the course of a year twelve sermons were preached in a loosely connected series called "So Teach Us to Number Our Days." These messages were so timely that they became a morning radio series.

Lay Caregiving Seminars and adult Sunday school electives were taught to equip individuals and families in eldercare ministries. Some took the training and applied it to their professions in nursing, physiotherapy, and pharmacology. Others took their vision into volunteer capacities with hospice, hospital, and nursing home care.

The congregation was divided into mini-flocks, each with its own Elder/Deaconess team. With this kind of lay pastoral care in place, visits could be made to the elder's private or institutional home. Sermon tapes could be delivered, meals offered, and handyman repairs made if needed. To extend this kind of ministry, a dynamic couple was hired as they retired from the mission field. With their leadership, "The Senior Adult Ministry" was born. Three senior adult Sunday school classes, a mid-weekly fellowship meal, local trips, and ministry outreaches were orchestrated.

This "senior sensitive" church became a key to survival when Willamina developed Alzheimer's disease. In the beginning, the main focus was on supporting the primary caregiver at home. Phone calls, home visits, and encouragement went a long way toward helping the caregiving daughter-in-law. The pleasant distraction of local trips, fellowship meals, and the steady nurture of the Sunday school class helped ease the burdens. Sometimes a surrogate family would invite Willamina for the day while her family attended to other important business.

As the disease progressed, there were several hospitalizations and an eventual nursing home admission. The caregiving team continued to minister through difficult months. At times, Willamina was physically aggressive or verbally cruel to her visitors. Eventually, she lapsed into a coma.

As silent weeks passed, her coma deepened and her family was due a long-awaited vacation. Members of the church who were volunteers through the chaplain's office promised to visit regularly during the vacation. In a farewell conversation, Willamina's son explained to his comatose mother that they would be in the Adirondack Mountains for a week. Still assuming that nothing registered, he promised that the church team would be visiting as he stood to leave the room. From deep in the coma, Willamina said: "Thanks. Thanks a lot. Thanks for everything!" Pleasantly puzzled, the son left the room. Upon his return, the team met him at his house to break the news that Willamina had died peacefully. Grieving with the family, they were able to share the healing thought that the final conversation was one of grateful closure. Willamina had spoken no more words after that final farewell.

"A Cup of Cold Water" for the Elder's Caregiver

In World War I, there were nineteen soldiers behind the lines supporting every one that was at the battle front. Recruiters, trainers, cooks, medics, factory engineers, transporters, intelligence, top brass, etc. all had a role in keeping the front line soldier functioning. Likewise, the support system we provide for front-line caregivers will determine the difference between victory and defeat in the war against elder abuse and caregiver burnout.

We must remember that the majority of caregivers accepted their enlistment in this battle because they were "the only ones who lived close enough" to help the elder. In many cases, there was "no one else to care," regardless of geography. In a lesser number of cases, the caregiver role was assumed because someone had "the closer relationship."

The typical caregiver works a full-time job in addition to carrying the role of primary caregiver.[5] This average caregiver also depends on at least one service to be provided from outside the immediate family. Unfortunately, the majority of these caregivers have found that religious organizations and employers do not provide any of the support services they need.

Based on nationwide caregiver research, we know that many caregivers have had to make changes in their lifestyle to fulfill their eldercare commitment:

- *spending less time with their own immediate family*

- *paying less attention to their own health*

- *taking fewer vacations*

In addition to these lifestyle changes, the eldercare family pays an average of $117 per month of additional expenses. These usually occur in travel, telephone, and special diets or medications. When home nursing or hospital costs are involved, the caregiving family pays out an average of $238–275 per month of its own money.

Caregivers were asked: "What kinds of assistance do you believe you need the most?" They answered:

42 percent—Information about developments in medicine and health care

39 percent—Help in obtaining services from bureaucracies

38 percent—Updates on federal and state legislation that affects us

32 percent—Someone to talk to when we are overburdened

31 percent—Some free time for a vacation

30 percent—Someone with whom to share coping strategies

If we as individuals, families, and churches cannot find anything on this list of "cold water" needs, we are willfully blind.

Grace Church

Grace Church had all the traditional older adult ministries one would expect in suburbia: Bible studies, visitation, pastoral care, fellowship outings, and ministry outreach. But one vital link was missing—how to help the caregiver. In a period of no more than a year, there seemed to be an epidemic of geriatric crises: strokes, heart attacks, broken bones, auto accidents, Alzheimer's, Parkinson's, diabetes, MS, layoffs, divorces, and other personal setbacks. The missing link was figuring out how to help the middle-aged caregivers whose "empty nest" had become "newly full."

Many of the caregivers initially went about their family responsibilities in silence. The job needed to be done and so they set out to do it. In time, the stress from their jobs *and* their family caregiving became enormous. Many had to withdraw from their formal church ministries; some cut back on attendance. It was easy to imagine that everything was "ok" with these beloved caregivers because they weren't the complaining type. But they were like wounded soldiers on the front line of battle without any backup troops in sight.

A church survey exposed this hurting pocket of the congregation. Three questions drew rich responses:

- "Do you have any friends or loved ones over sixty-five years of age who have significant physical, emotional, or spiritual needs?"

- "What can this church do better to help you as you care for these loved ones?"

- "What can this church do better to help the elderly in general?"

Shortly after this survey was taken, "The Eldercare Connection" was created. A network of former and current caregivers began to work together as an informal team. Now that they were identified as part of a common group with a "ministry," they could begin pooling resources. One of the church staff members began to devour everything he could learn about gerontology. The veteran caregivers began to give advice. Telephone calls, cards, and brainstorming sessions brought a fragrance of life into numerous families. The caregivers were ministering to each other.

Alzheimer's disease was to blame for Roger's mom wandering away from the house. It was scary for him to wake up at two o'clock in the morning and find his mom's bed empty. After the time she was found two miles away, the family began talking about a nursing home. An uncle had "a better idea." He installed locks on the doors that would allow him to come over and lock everyone inside at night. Fortunately, somebody in the "The Eldercare Connection" knew a better solution. "You can't lock people in—it's a fire trap that way! Put in a chirper on your front and back doors," he suggested. The friend explained how he had seen these little battery-operated boxes attached to entrance and exit doors at nursing homes. Once the door was opened ajar, a "chirp" sound began. It would become louder and more frequent as long as the door was held open: "chirp . . . Chirp . . . CHIRP . . . CHIRP . . . CHIRP!" Anyone, awake or asleep, would be quickly notified that a resident was coming or going. A quick look would safely locate the unattended wanderer.

When James' father needed care in Alabama, there was only one daughter nearby to help. But that daughter had emotional disturbances that prevented her from assuming any caregiving responsibility. She didn't work; she hardly functioned. If anything, James' dad was still economically and emotionally responsible for the adult daughter. It became obvious that James would have to receive *both* his father and his sister into his home in Virginia. If James were going to care for either, he would have to care for both. The new arrangement was financially exhausting. James' father didn't want to spend his savings "on those shrinks," but the daughter needed help. It was somebody in "The Eldercare Connection" who suggested that they apply for State Medical Assistance. "I guess I always assumed," James said, "that you couldn't get state government help unless you had worked and paid taxes in the state." He was pleasantly surprised and financially relieved.

When Jeff's dad was diagnosed with Parkinson's disease, Jeff found helpful information in the public library. He read everything he could on the disease and was ready when other caregivers had Parkinson related questions:

- "How do you keep them from feeling frustrated when they can no longer button their own shirts or tie their own shoelaces?" *Answer:* Use Velcro® patches instead.

• "How do you keep them from shuffling their feet and losing their balance when they try to turn around?" *Answer:* Deliberately lift one foot at a time and concentrate on forcing the heel to strike first. When turning around, walk in a big circle.

• "How can they get themselves out of a chair?" *Answer:* Choose firm chairs with arms and backs when possible. When rising, slide to the front edge of the seat. Put your heels well under the chair and bend far at the waist before standing. An elevated padded toilet seat can be purchased.

• "How can you help them feed themselves without spilling?" *Answer:* Use two-handled cups and edged plates.

• "How can they get themselves into bed alone?" *Answer:* Sit down on the side of the bed so that your head will end up in the pillow area. Bend the arms and legs into a fetal position. Roll.

When both of Evelyn's parents had massive strokes within several months of each other, the family was devastated. Evelyn's brother refused to consider the rehabilitation hospital or the nursing home. "My parents are never going into a place like that!" he shouted at Evelyn. Against the advice of everyone, he insisted that *he* would care for both of them *at home.* Evelyn paid for visiting nurses to do weekend duty so her brother could at least sleep. In time, he fired them. Months dragged on until Evelyn began to get a sick feeling that her parents were not being cared for appropriately. The brother was burning out. Someone in the eldercare network at church showed Evelyn a brochure on the different kinds of elder abuse:[6]
1) *Passive Neglect*—The caregiver fails to provide food or other health necessities due to his or her own illness, laziness, or ignorance. It is unintentional.
2) *Psychological Abuse*—The caregiver inflicts mental anguish through name calling, insulting, frightening, isolating, threatening, etc.
3) *Financial Abuse*—The caregiver uses the money, property, or other assets of the older person in unethical ways.
4) *Active Neglect*—The caregiver fails to provide food or other health necessities by choice, deliberately denying the older person dentures, eyeglasses, medications, etc. Willful infliction of physical or emotional distress also may occur.
5) *Physical Abuse*—The caregiver inflicts physical pain or injury through involuntary confinement, slapping, bruising, cutting, burning, pushing/shoving, sexually molesting, etc.

With the help of the brochure and the support of the eldercare group, Evelyn was able to identify and confront the passive, psychological, and financial abuses happening to her bedridden parents. "The Eldercare Connection" had become an enabling network for its caregiving members.

"I Have No Hands but Your Hands . . ."

In wartime France, a Christian church was nearly leveled by repeated enemy bombing raids. By morning light after a devastating bombardment, the priest returned to his church. He began locating the pieces of a life-sized Savior that had been fragmented in the church yard. Gradually he repaired the figure until the Christ stood tall again, missing only his hands. The fingers and hands were splintered and could not be found in pieces large enough for reconstruction. Undaunted by the incompleteness, the priest hung a sign around the neck of Jesus: "I Have No Hands But Your Hands. . . ." So it is today that Christ reaches down from heaven through his followers to do his will: caring for one another in the family, in the church, and in the world.

One of the beauties of being "the hands of Christ" is found in the diversity of his body. No two fingers on his hands were exactly alike, nor are we, nor are our churches. Whether we serve Greek widows like Stephen in ancient Jerusalem or whether we serve with The Shepherd's Center in downtown Kansas City, we serve one Christ. Whether we are clergy in search of improved leadership or volunteers in search of improved ownership, we strive for the same excellence: "that ye love one another as I have loved you." Whether the "cup of cold water" we offer the beloved elder is primarily in a home, an institution, or even to the elder's own caregiver, it is done as "unto me."

Many churches have begun to discover the beauty of his diversity in us—the freedom not to be clones of each other or of each other's church. One such church with which I am familiar has developed four intensive people-helping ministries called:

- The Timothy Ministry

- The Abraham Ministry

- The Barnabas Ministry

- The Andrew Ministry

For those who want to learn how to be a disciple of Christ, a "Timothy Minister" is available to them. They work together with a planned program of personal study to master the basic building blocks of Christian thought and lifestyle.

For those who want to minister in the privacy of intercession, an "Abraham Minister" guides them into a lifestyle of prayer for others.

For those who want to help the hurting, a "Barnabas Minister" trains them for four months and then publicly commissions them to serve for the next twelve. Some "Barnabas Ministers" may join the *exhortation team,* offering long-term support and counseling to those in pain. Others may join the *helps team,* providing meals, rides, or housework for those who cannot do so for themselves. The *mercy team* enlists those who will reach out to the shut-ins.

A final group for those who want to share their faith is the "Andrew Ministry."

Two stories illustrate how these ministries mutually support one another in the building of *one* body. A woman in her seventies was escorting her husband to the Walter Reed Army Medical Center. Literally on the doorstep of the hospital, her beloved husband's life was snatched away by a blood clot. Through the Barnabas Ministers she was nurtured in her healing process. With a renewed purpose for ministry, she has become an outstanding Abraham Minister interceding on behalf of others.

When another retired woman felt helpless to minister to her dying neighbor, she called on the church to send a Barnabas Minister. Through the sensitive skill of the minister, this terminally ill unbeliever accepted Jesus Christ as her Savior. For the next thirty days, the timid neighbor friend read Scripture to her new sister in the Lord. On the one-month anniversary of the neighbor's new faith, this new child of God went to glory. With new confidence in God's power to save, the hesitant witness has gone on to become a vital leader in the Andrew Team. To each of us as individuals, as families, and as churches the Lord still says: "I have no hands but your hands. . . ."

SUMMARY

1. There are various models of healthy eldercare ministry:
   - Stephen with the Greek Widows Food Ministry in Jerusalem
   - The Good Samaritan on the Jericho Road

- The Shepherd's Center in Kansas City
- The Fellowship Club of the University Church
- The Lay Caregiving Seminars and Teams of First Church
- The Eldercare Connection of Grace Church
- The Timothy/Abraham/Barnabas/Andrew Ministries of the Brethren

2. Eldercare ministries will improve through:
  - Better clergy training and performance
  - Volunteer ownership of the ministries

3. Eldercare ministries are to be commended if they:
  - Address any of the direct or indirect care needs of elders still living at home
  - Address any of the spiritual care needs of elders living in clinical institutions
  - Offer appropriate information, support, and respite for the elder's caregiver

4. There are five kinds of elder abuse: passive, psychological, financial, active neglect, and physical abuse.

8

When the Going Gets Tough
Jeffrey A. Watson

"If the kitchen is the only room heated during the night, then that's where Mother's bed must be!" The grief-wearied teenager began moving the cupboard out of their simple kitchen so he could slide his own couch and his beloved mother's deathbed near the token warmth. Lying next to her, he could attend her every need.

Throughout their last long night together, Klara's son sat in bed with her, propping her into the least painful position her cancer-filled chest could bear. Staring at the dingy lights of their twisted little Christmas tree, Klara's eighteen-year-old caregiver began to think back quietly and painfully. "When father died I was only fourteen. . . . *Surely, God will let mother live a long time,* I kept telling myself. I needed her too much to lose her. . . . She's too young to die now at forty-seven. . . . What am I going to do? All three of my brothers are dead and so is my sister Ida—none of them made it past their sixth birthday. Why was I cursed to live this long? To bear all of this pain? . . . Then there's Paula, my little sister, an orphan at eleven! . . . I can't raise her!" In his silent torture, he drifted off to sleep without saying goodbye.

Painful Christmases

In the years that followed Klara's death, this melancholy boy would never adjust. He hated Christmases because of their haunting

memories. His confused mind would swim with thoughts of suicide.
That fatal choice would eventually write his obituary.

Still anguishing sixteen years after his mother's death, he
would compose the poem entitled, "Think of It!"

When your mother has grown older.
And you have grown older,
When what was formerly easy and effortless
Now becomes a burden,
When her dear loyal eyes
Do not look out into life as before,
When her legs have grown tired
And do not want to carry her any more—
Then give her your arm for support,
Accompany her with gladness and joy.
The hour will come when, weeping, you
Will accompany her on her last journey!
And if she asks you, answer her.
And if she asks again, speak also.
And if she asks another time, speak to her
Not stormily, but in gentle peace!
And if she cannot understand you well,
Explain everything joyfully;
The hour will come, the bitter hour
When her mouth will ask no more![1]

A Greater Tragedy

Klara Hitler would be spared a tragedy greater than her own
death. Her Adolf would go mad with grief. He would become obsessed with the obvious failure of Dr. Bloch, Klara's surgeon. Locally
known as the "poor people's doctor," this Jewish physician would
personify Adolf's domestic enemy. The unsuccessful treatment for
Klara's cancer would prove Hitler's racist theory of Jewish incompetence sold at exorbitant prices to the harm of the common person.

Though there would be many sources for Adolf Hitler's
demonic hatred of all non-Aryans, one cannot ignore his disturbed
childhood. Overwhelmed by the death of her other four children,
Klara smothered her "sickly Adolf," breastfeeding him until he was
five with hopes that he would survive past childhood. Enmeshed
like siamese twins, Adolf "lived only for his mother." Bitter from
more losses than one young person should have to bear and twisted
by a pathological mourning, he would never recover from her death.

Young Hitler's room became a lonely refuge and prison, his
public life a reserved corner in a secluded cafe. That sick hatred kept

incubating within his dormant mind until he saw "Jews pushing their way into government posts." To him, they not only held a professional monopoly on Germany, comprising 80 percent of the lawyers and doctors, they had killed his "dear, loyal" mother.

The Jewish Cancer

Reaching back in history to find a social excuse for excising the Jewish cancer from his fatherland, he seized upon religion. "Hadn't the Church of Rome tried to rid our society of this poison?" he remembered. "Didn't that great German, Martin Luther, argue that Jews deserved unique judgment for crucifying Christ?" If the Holy Roman Empire had failed in its medieval purge, and the Weimar Republic likewise left the task undone, it would be up to "The Third Reich" to let Christ rule where now the Jews held a stranglehold.

Satan seized upon a vulnerable mind with an infected grief wound. Evil blame was cast upon the people of Abraham, a scapegoat nation for the same hellish hatred that had sent their Messiah to Calvary.

Spiritual Bankruptcy

At his core, Adolf Hitler was spiritually bankrupt. He failed in all three goals of spiritual life:

1) To Have Hope in God;
2) To Feel Loved by Others;
3) To Grow through Suffering.

Rather than hope in God, he resorted to his own paranoid genius. Rather than receive love from wholesome others, he thrived on the sick loyalty of the Nazi brownshirts. Rather than grow better through his sufferings, he turned murderously bitter.

No matter how badly things go, each of us desperately needs to have biblical hope in Someone beyond us—Someone who relieves us of being the center of our universe. No matter how badly things go, each of us must be lovingly engaged with people around us—people whose love is medicine for the soul. No matter how badly things go, we must grow through our suffering—lest in our despair we dry up spiritually like a hollow corpse.[2]

No matter our age or our degree of wellness, whether a Hitler or a Roosevelt, we have the same three acute spiritual needs. These needs not only call us to action on behalf of others; but they remind us of priorities for taking care of ourselves. To help us explore these three key spiritual needs, we will invite several folks to share about "when the going gets tough." Some are biblical characters, like Nicodemus, James, and Job's wife. Others are twentieth-century believers like Velma, Smitty, and Rowena.

To Have Hope in God

Nicodemus asked a profound question of our Lord: "Can a person be spiritually born again when they are old?" Because his question is still with us today and our Lord's answer timeless, let's have Nicodemus take us back to their conversation (John 3:1-21; 19:38-42).

The Nicodemus Question

"My name is Nicodemus and I'm nearly sixty-five years old. My life has been lived pretty much in Jerusalem and in the surrounding countryside. I gave my early adulthood to studying rabbinic law under the brilliant Gamaliel here in our capital. After I turned forty and got a name for myself, I was appointed to become a Sanhedrin lawyer, one of seventy judges in the Jewish Supreme Court.

"I soon learned there was a lot of pressure with my job. It wasn't just a matter of studying the Old Testament and giving legal interpretations. We had to try to enforce the religious laws of Moses and run the Temple. That wasn't very easy to do. A lot of our people didn't care very much about obeying Moses. The young people spent more time at the stadiums the Greeks built than they did at the Temple. They said they liked the athletic contests . . . but I think it was the immodest clothes everyone was allowed to wear there.

"And then there was the Roman occupation army. They were so godless and they were everywhere. No matter where you looked, they had idols—carved images of some warrior or god. From their coins to their shields, they carried pagan images. They even believed that their Emperor was indwelt by God. Such blasphemy!"

A Frustrated Supreme Court Justice

"A few years ago when our King Herod Archelaus died, those blasted Romans put their own governor in charge of Jerusalem. 'Pontius Pilate,' they call him. We weren't even allowed to have a Jewish king anymore. Then they tied our hands and said our Supreme Court couldn't try capital offenses. We couldn't convict someone of a crime worthy of capital punishment. Basically, the death penalty was taken away, except when the Romans wanted to murder somebody in the name of 'justice.' My job became terribly political, especially when we judges couldn't agree among ourselves. And when we were divided, we still had the Romans to deal with!

"Part of my job was to be out among the common people, teaching them the laws of Moses. Sometimes, I'd come across a rabbi teaching a group so I'd stop and listen. Technically, I was supposed to interrupt and reprimand these teachers if they were in error. Usually that was no big deal since I had a lot of clout and their mistakes were generally simple to correct."

Chaos in the Temple

"The biggest doctrinal debate I ever got myself into was three years ago. The rabbi was Jesus of Nazareth. I had never even heard of him until some rumors of him doing miracles in Cana and Capernaum surfaced. I couldn't really figure out who he was since he didn't go to any of the law schools I was familiar with.

"The first time I laid eyes on him was during Passover week that year. This thirty-year-old radical came charging into the outer court area where the various animals were sold to worshippers for sacrifice. With his small whip he began opening the animal pens and driving out a small stampede of oxen and sheep. He opened the cages for the doves, and the birds took off flying. By the time we realized what was happening, he had flipped the cashiers' tables over and coins went rolling in every direction. When he was done, his eyes were blazing and he was out of breath. He shouted with an authority I'd never heard before: 'This is my father's house! . . . It is supposed to be used for prayer. . . . It is not supposed to be used to steal money from poor people.'

"We were stunned by the whole display; but we were also aware that hundreds of people were standing around completely agreeing with him. A group of us approached him, not knowing if he was going to use the whip on us or not. We asked, 'What right did you have to do this to the Temple?' Without hesitating, he pointed his finger at his own chest and said: 'Tear down this temple and I'll rebuild it in three days.' That seemed so weird to us at the time. After all, Herod's Temple took forty-six years to build. The only way he could pull off that claim would be to have God's power in his own hands. We just dropped it at that point, but we never forgot his words. We didn't really want to give him any more of an audience than he already had."

How Can a Man Be Born Again When He Is Old?

"Throughout the rest of the week, he kept teaching and doing miracles. The crowd following him kept getting larger and larger. That's when I felt I needed to go head to head with him. I chose to seek him out at night when most of the crowds had gone home. I knew I needed an angle with which to approach him before I went public to debate him. His popularity was immense and I didn't want to be embarrassed on my own turf. I was over sixty and I had no intention of getting out-debated by a self-trained, thirty-year-old rabbi.

"I told him I had some concerns about his teaching. But I also told him that his miracle-working power made me think that God was with him somehow. Well, he went right to the bottom line. He crystallized his teaching and the whole point of his confirming miracles in one sentence: 'Unless a man is born again, he will never experience the kingdom of God.' Well, that threw me. I figured I was a leader in the kingdom of God. As soon as we could get rid of the Romans and get more Jews obeying Moses, we'd have the perfect kingdom of God starting right here in Jerusalem. I figured I was born into the kingdom of God when my godly Jewish mother and father gave birth to me. On day one, I was a citizen of God's kingdom, Holy Israel. But he shook his head, 'no.'

"So then I asked: 'How can a person as old as I be born again? Even if my mother were still alive, how could she give birth to me again?' I guess he had heard that one before. He was ready with an answer: 'When you were born before, you were born in a biological sense . . . delivered through a watery sac . . . and people could actually watch the process with their eyes. But people who are born a second time are born in an invisible, spiritual sense. No one else can see it happen. It's between the person and God.'"

Don't Tell Me Moses Taught This Too?

"'How could these things be?' I asked him. That's when he chided me, as though everything he was saying should have been obvious to me from my study of the Old Testament. He reminded me of the time when Moses' people had to look up and 'believe' in order to be saved from a poisonous snake bite. Then he said: 'For God so loved the world that he gave his only Son that whoever would believe on the Son wouldn't perish but have everlasting life.' He assured me that he was the Son and that he hadn't come into the world to condemn everybody. Instead, he had come to bring healing from our poisonous snake bite, to bring us life, to dispel darkness with his light.

"That was the end of our private conversations; but I kept thinking about his words. His miracles gave me the hunch that he was connected to God but his words were strange to me."

A Lynch Mob

"A couple of years later, almost to the day, we met again. I was awakened around 2:00 a.m. on Passover Friday morning. *What could this be? Are the Romans burning down Jerusalem?* I wondered. *Who would be banging on my door at this time of the morning?* It turned out to be a temple servant who was sent out to round up the Sanhedrin judges. 'Some kind of emergency,' he said before running on.

"Well, the emergency was Jesus. The high priest had arrested him earlier in the night. He was quickly convening the court so that we could pass down a guilty verdict and have him executed. *It's illegal to hold a nighttime trial! . . . Why now? . . . Only the Romans can try capital offenses!* These questions burned in my mind.

"Others had the same questions as I but the high priest had answers: 'We'll examine him tonight to save time, but we can reconvene at dawn to slam down the gavel. That will make it officially daytime. It has to be done now because Jesus is becoming too popular. With his popularity, he might disrupt the whole Temple ceremony tomorrow on Passover like he did several years ago. If he does and we do nothing again, it'll be like giving him the Temple. We might as well let him run the religion of Israel then. Our relationship to the Romans is too fragile. If we fight him tomorrow, they'll call it a riot and send in their troops. They've already said if we have one more religious riot, Rome will level this city. We can't let that happen. We have to be willing to let one man die to save the rest of us . . . otherwise, one man lives and the rest of us die.'

"I didn't like the idea of executing Jesus, but I was in a bind. The court had to have consensus on something like this. I figured if Jesus was the Son of God, he could stop us. If he wasn't, he should die for the sake of peace.

"We quickly produced witnesses who had heard him say, 'Destroy this temple and I will rebuild it in three days.' I could even have served as witness to these words but the justices had to be neutral during the giving of evidence. We all agreed: those words were blasphemy, claiming God's power. 'Guilty as charged!' the high priest shouted.

Justice, Prophecy, and the Son of God

"At dawn we reconvened and did the paperwork. It was all legal now. The tricky part came when we sent him to the Romans to see if they would write a Roman execution order for us. From what I was told later, he went to Pilate, then to Herod Antipas, and back to Pilate. They wouldn't convict him of blasphemy since that was not a crime in Rome. Every one of their Emperors regularly blasphemed when they claimed God indwelt them. But we did convince them to bring the charge of treason, since he claimed to be 'King of the Jews.' Certainly, that was as much an affront to their worldwide Emperor as his blasphemy was to our God. They saw it that way too. They beat him mercilessly and almost killed him. Then by 9:00 in the morning they sent him out to Golgotha to be crucified.

"By now I was back home and my head was swimming. I kept remembering the miracles and how lovingly he talked to me about being born again. I had found some places in the Old Testament that he might have been referring to in our conversation. Our prophet Ezekiel had said that 'I will put my spirit within you. I will remove your heart of stone and give you a heart of flesh!' Maybe that's what he meant by 'being born again,' invisibly, by the Spirit. Then I remembered how Isaiah described the Messiah as a 'lamb led to the slaughter . . . silent before his shearers, he opened not his mouth . . . all we like sheep have gone astray; and the Lord has laid on him the iniquity of as all . . . he was taken from prison and cut off from the land of the living . . . he made his grave with the wicked . . . he had done no violence; neither was any deceit in his mouth . . . it pleased the Lord to bruise him because he bore the sins of many people and made intercession for the transgressors. . . .'

"I couldn't stand it any longer. The words of our prophets were talking about him. If he was the Messiah, he wasn't guilty of anything—he *could* rebuild the Temple in three days and he deserved to be King of the Jews. He never fought back against us or the Romans, like a sheep doesn't fight its slaughterers. We've taken him from prison and sent him out there to be crucified with common thieves. My logic had been all wrong. If he is the Messiah, he won't stop us from crucifying him. He will go ahead like a pure, innocent, sacrificial lamb. He'll be the substitute to bear our sins so that we don't have to be punished for them.

An Ugly Beauty

"Surprisingly for a man my age, I ran all the way to the execution site. I knocked on Joseph of Arimathaea's door as I passed it. He was another lawyer who was thinking the same way I was. Together we ran out to Golgotha. It was the ugliest thing we'd ever seen. Jesus had been so beaten, his face was mangled. Soldiers were acting like it was a circus while Jesus' mother stood silently with tears pouring down her face. The ugliest part was knowing he was on that cross because of our sins, not his.

"But there was a beautiful side, too, that I see more clearly as I look back. It was Jesus' love. Just as he had healed one of our Temple servants whose ear was sliced off at Jesus' arrest, he kept on reaching out to people despite his agony. He prayed that the soldiers would be forgiven because they didn't really understand what they were doing. He promised one of the thieves beside him that they'd be together in Paradise later that day. He told John to take care of his mother and for them to look out for each other. After what seemed like an eternity, he screamed: 'It is finished!' and died."

A New Beginning

"At that moment I realized that we were Jesus' people. All we had to do was look up at him and believe. He would save us, give us a new birth, take out our unbelieving hearts of stone that let us crucify him. Silently I prayed, 'Father, forgive me for all my sins, especially this one in sending your Son to the cross. Thank you for your love. I don't understand everything but I want you to change me. Let me be born again like a spiritually new baby so that I can enter your kingdom.'

"My friend Joseph was apparently doing the same thing. We looked at each other and realized we couldn't keep this secret. Joseph and I ran to his family tomb to prepare it for Jesus' body, and then we ran to Pilate to get permission to have the body when they took it down. Pilate looked at us like we were crazy but he granted our request. We quickly gathered burial cloth, perfumes, flower petals, everything we needed. When the soldiers cut the body down, it fell on us like a mountain. It felt as heavy as our grief. We washed his body, wrapped it with layers of potpourri in the folds, and laid him in the tomb before nightfall. Soldiers put the stone in front of the door, sealed it with wax, and began standing guard.

"On Sunday morning, Jesus passed through those two hundred pounds of burial wrappings and stood up. His body was new, fresh, and all-powerful. An angel sent an earthquake to roll the stone away so we could look in and still see these wrapped, collapsed clothes. The guards were terrified. Jesus then spent forty days appearing all over Israel to individuals and groups. Before he went back to heaven, he reminded us on several occasions to go tell others about his death and resurrection. He made it clear to us that the Old Testament is full of predictions about these events as long as our eyes are open to them."

EVANGELISM "IN THE NICK OF TIME"

We are indebted to Nicodemus for his question, "Can a man be born again when he is old?" It forces us rethink the role of evangelism with the elderly and how to give "hope in God" to the dying.

Deathbed Conversions

The pendulum on Nicodemus' question has probably swung to two different extremes during the history of the church. During the Middle Ages, there was an emphasis on "deathbed conversions." Whole rituals developed to reconcile wayward people to the church:

- Call for a priest

- Confess and be absolved of your sins

- Receive the "healing" sacrament of Extreme Unction where seven drops of holy oil are placed on the dying person's eyelids, ears, nostrils, mouth, hands, kidneys, and feet

- Perform last rites, a funeral, and a burial in the church

- Pray and hold mass for the dead to shorten the time needed in purgatory.

This whole emphasis tended to exaggerate the role of the organized church in dispensing God's grace to people. Furthermore, it had its own way of disassociating the person's entire life from "the final short hour." With the majority of modern patients dying in clinical institutions under heavy sedation and with the reformers' deemphasis on priestly intercession, the medieval approach to "deathbed conversions" has waned.

Psychological Autobiography

It is more common in the twentieth century for the question Nicodemus asked to be met with skepticism. With the secularization of theology, even clergy hesitate to mention heaven and hell with any but the obviously faithful. With the emphasis on lifespan development, each individual is treated through the grid of his own perceptions.

The folk expression of this secularized individualism states: "As I age, I become more like myself." The point of such thinking is that one's life is the sum of its parts, the climax of all of its previous tendencies. If one were to "convert" in his final hours or years, it would be an expression of either total regret or an extension of some previous faith commitment.

The Balancing Act

If we were to address the Nicodemus question to the medieval priest, he would probably answer: "Of course a man can be born again when he is old! Regardless of his age, he can even be born again in his final moments on earth. In fact, with the help of the Church, he can be born again even after his death."

The modern cleric might answer differently: "Well, yes, I suppose an elderly person *could* be born again. But it's pretty rare. You know, you can't teach an old dog new tricks—even if they are religious tricks. I think the main goal is to comfort the elders at the time. If their faith is a part of that comfort, then that's great."

Somewhere in between these two extremes is a realistic, biblical balance. There are those like the thief on the cross who make eternally significant decisions just hours before their death. Though this man may not have been chronologically old, he was autobiographically ancient. His life story was almost over. It is encouraging to note that he was apparently ushered into Paradise without so much as a prayer, a baptism, or a church funeral. His example suggests to us that we be willing to minister the gospel in as simple terms as possible and not to emphasize "converting" from one brand of church to another. This new believer reminds us that regardless of our age or our nearness to death, "God is not willing that any should perish. *Today* is the day of salvation!" (see 2 Corinthians 6:2 and 2 Peter 3:9).

Nicodemus, as a well-educated older adult, did have specific questions and objections to the gospel. He needed time to evaluate and weigh the claims of Christ. For him, it took perhaps a couple of years to compare what he already believed with the specific teachings of the Bible. But this pattern of thoughtful evaluation fits nicely with the typical older adult's lifestyle. In general, elders make decisions more slowly than younger adults. But they make them with more accuracy and wisdom. Furthermore, with the leisure time the average elder spends in reading, listening to radio and television, and talking to peers, there is ample room for more to join the Nicodemus Club. Whether the elder's new faith comes as an extension and revision of previous beliefs or as a boldly new idea, this new heir of heaven enters with the same simple faith as that of a child.

Some Guidelines

For any who truly care about sharing the hope-giving gospel with older adults, some principles are in order:

1) The gospel is the same for all people. Learn its simplicity well and share it lovingly and genuinely with people of all ages.

2) Older adults have time to listen. Don't rush into a conversation with a relative stranger and push for an evangelistic "notch on your gun." Allow yourself the time to both talk and listen. Prove that your love is not just "with words or tongue but with actions and in truth" (1 John 3:18). Include them in your life if you expect them to include you in theirs.

3) Show respect for their life, their ideas, and their coping styles. You don't have to call a woman who is old enough to be your grandmother by her first name. You had better not chide her like a child.

4) Avoid being overly identified as the "recruiter" from some formal church. Many older adults have some negative feelings toward a minister or a church in their past. Let them express these feelings without becoming defensive. Emphasize that you care about them, not the money they could give or the formal attendance you would like them to perform at your church.

5) Try to identify and utilize older adult believers who can minister to other older adults. There is nothing like a credible peer-to-peer relationship for evangelism.

6) Keep on hand a generous supply of large-print Bibles, Bibles on cassette, and devotional books by people like Phillip Keller. Be familiar with the best Christian radio and TV programs in your area. Use recreational activities to build loving relationships with seekers: films, concerts, meals, senior trips, etc.

7) Remember that most older adults are concerned about dying. Their anxieties may not be focused on the issue of heaven or hell, but they often wonder about when they'll die, of what, whether there will be pain, whether they will be alone, whether they will run out of money first, and how they will be remembered.

8) Remember that most older adults battle with regrets at times. That's why a leading suicide risk group is white males over

age sixty-five. Don't exaggerate anyone's sense of despair but be sensitive to how the Lord might use it.

9) Discern the difference between "hope" and "denial." "Brittle denial" prevents people from hearing any message about their mortality. "Adaptive denial" causes a person to get off that subject as quickly as possible. "Acceptance" honestly sees what lies ahead, regardless of its unpleasantness. While people who refuse to face reality may be protecting themselves from emotional fallout, this kind of panicky denial should not be confused with "hope." "Hope" says: "I look directly at the reality that lies ahead of me; but I look beyond it to other realities that transcend it."

10) Consider introducing the gospel with a relaxed telling of your own story. Include how you came to know the Lord and what the gospel is. Don't feel you need to confront them with the "bottom line" in that very conversation.

11) Consider introducing the gospel with a familiar elder by saying: "You know, I've been thinking about you a lot lately. I've been concerned that if either you or I died, whether we would see each other again. I know we're both feeling well but I've been thinking about heaven."

12) Consider introducing the gospel by reading or telling the sagely wisdom of King Solomon (Ecclesiastes 12:1-7, 13-14). His point is that the biological clock in our divinely created bodies is running down. As an old man who was one of the wisest in his day and who had his own share of regrets, Solomon advises knowing God.

13) If a person rejects the gospel, don't cut him off. Sometimes elders feel pressured to perform for younger people. Remain in the relationship and look for an opportunity to ask: "Do you remember that time I told you about my faith? I know it didn't seem right for you at the time—do you still feel that way?"

New Hope for Velma

The Lord gives spiritual hope to elders in different ways, in different dosages, and at different times. For Velma, life seemed weary and purposeless. She couldn't live on her own anymore in Johnson, Tennessee. Life kept going downhill until she had to move north to live with her daughter's family.

When cancer struck, it seemed like the end. In fact, during a critical stage in the treatment of her disease at the hospital, her heart stopped. Suddenly she felt freed from her body and floating toward heaven. For her it was relief. But, as she often told, "The Lord had another thing in mind. In an almost audible voice, he said: 'It's not your time. I need you on earth a while longer.'"

She resented being whisked back into her resuscitated body. For a few months, her recovery was blended with curiosity. "What does he want me to do?" Tragically, it was not long before her adult daughter died of a sudden heart attack. Her purpose became clear: "Help raise the children. Keep the house. Be quick to tell others about the Lord. He has a purpose for you." Like the apostle Paul who was "caught up" (2 Corinthians 12:1–6), Velma took hold of the Lord's hope and purpose for living.

Despite her cancer, Velma learned that spiritual hope outlasts physical disease. In the words of one whose body was destroyed by cancer:

> Cancer is so limited . . .
> It cannot cripple love,
> It cannot shatter hope,
> It cannot corrode faith,
> It cannot eat away peace,
> It cannot destroy confidence,
> It cannot kill friendship,
> It cannot shut out memories,
> It cannot silence courage,
> It cannot invade the soul
> It cannot reduce eternal life,
> It cannot quench the Spirit,
> It cannot lessen the power of the resurrection.[3]

The God of Hope taught Velma that our greatest enemy is not disease, it's despair.

To Feel Loved by Others

Building on this foundational need to have hope in God, we suggest that there are two additional spiritual needs: to feel loved by others and to grow through suffering. In an effort to understand the ministry of therapeutic love, we could invite the apostle James, the half-brother of our Lord, to share from his experience (James 5:13–20; Mark 5:22–23, 34, 42; cp. Matthew 21:12–22):

An Eyewitness to Love

"Obviously, I grew up in a very unique home. My mother and aunts spent long hours trying to imagine the full destiny of Jesus, our oldest brother. We knew he was a miracle child—my late father Joseph kept emphasizing that!

"For me, things began to come clear when I saw how Jesus could do miracles at will: healing the blind, the lame, the deaf, the leper . . . outsmarting the rabbis in public teaching . . . fulfilling Old Testament prophecies . . . and his unique kind of love. He had an intense way about him that allowed people to know they were truly loved. People may have disagreed with him; but no one ever accused him of being artificial or phony in his love for them. He struck the right balance of truth and love: he wasn't a brutal truth-only kind of person nor was he a sentimental love-only kind of person. His love had integrity and depth.

"It was common for him when he met a child or a sick person to touch them. He would look them right in the eye. He would ask them penetrating questions. He would look for some sign of their faith in him. He would communicate to them an intense, believable kind of love."

One Day in the Life . . .

"Although I continued to doubt that he really was the Son of God until after his resurrection, I remember some of his special healings. One day our synagogue leader, Jairus, came running up to Jesus. He was out of breath and his dusty face had big tear streaks down it. 'Hurry rabbi,' he begged as he fell down at Jesus' feet. 'My twelve-year-old girl is nearly dead. Will you come and touch her so she can be healed?' It was very interesting to watch this whole scene. Jesus didn't seem anxious about the girl—like he had it all under control. He changed direction and began walking, not running, toward Jairus' house. He seemed considerably more interested in finding out how strong Jairus' faith was than he was in finding out how desperate the daughter's medical condition was.

"Before he ever made it to the house, an older woman almost tackled him in the crowd. She could barely keep up with the men's walking so she dove at his feet from behind. As soon as she touched him, this startled look came over her face. 'I'm healed! The hemorrhage has stopped! I have spent so many years and so much money on different doctors—and none of them could help. Jesus, I'm healed!' Jesus turned around and said instinctively, 'Your faith in me has made you well.' He gave her the most loving look but didn't stop for very long since he was headed to Jairus' house.

"When he arrived at Jairus' house, the mourners were already there. 'She's dead. You're too late!' the family moaned. He didn't even break his pace. He went right to the girl, took hold of her, and spoke her back into life. She stood right up on her feet and looked as healthy as the day she was born. She actually sat down and ate the evening meal with the family right then.

The Big Picture

"More amazing than those two healings was Jesus' warning to the onlookers: 'Don't tell anybody what you have seen here!' It took me a long time to figure that one out. I had assumed he wanted people to accept the idea that he was God's Son, the Messiah. If I had been in his shoes, I would have wanted as much free publicity as I could get. But from my vantage point now, I'm convinced that he didn't want people to get the idea that physical healings were his most important priority. He seemed far more interested in showing love, healing people spiritually through forgiveness, and affirming genuine faith. The physical healings were only a means to an end.

"Now that I am a pastor, I see a lot of people who are hurting and sick. When people ask us for healing, I have to remind them of a few things. First, I tell them we don't have any magical healing power. None of us has the independent power to heal. If there is a healing, it's 'in the name of the Lord.' It's his power; he does the healing. Secondly, we don't have any magical healing place. We don't have a holy shrine or site that makes healing happen. In fact, if a sick person wants us to minister to them, we just go to their bedside in private. Third, we don't have a magical healing person. It's not as if someone in the church is 'the healer.' We go as a team of elders to the sick person. Fourth, we don't have any magical healing ritual. We don't use a special kind of touch or a sacramental oil. We use the best natural medicine we know, regular olive oil, and combine it with the best spiritual medicine we know, prayer. And finally, we remind them of two things: They aren't necessarily sick because of their sin. (Job wasn't. Only they and the Lord know if there is unrepented sin in their life. We'd be glad to help restore them if that is what the Lord shows them; but we don't assume that.) And they won't necessarily be healed simply because they pray. (After all, Jesus unsuccessfully prayed in Gethsemane that he might avoid the cross; but the will of God said, 'no.')

"In our experience, if a sick person requests that the elders of his or her local church come and offer intensive group prayer for his or her healing, we'll come. If he hasn't tried normal medical treatments, we do the best we can with rubbing in olive oil. Many times we have found that when the sick person has the same kind of faith as Jairus or the woman with the hemorrhage, he or she healed."

HELPING PEOPLE BELIEVE THEY ARE LOVED

As ministers of Jesus Christ, we are committed to helping people *know* that they are loved. It is not enough just to love people; we must let them *know* and help them *believe* they are loved.

A Loving Physical Presence

One study in a hospital in Rochester, New York, proved the importance of love. The chaplain regularly spent time in morning prayer for patients who were undergoing surgery that day. But he had two different ways he could communicate his love. The first way was convenient: tell patients when they were admitted that the chaplain would pray for them on the morning of surgery. He could then sit in his office and pray over the list for the day.

The second way took more sacrifice: he could visit patients in their room or in the preoperative waiting area for prayer. For people who were ministered to in the second way, there was a marked difference. Holding hands, listening to the unique concerns of each patient, and praying for them made a medical difference. When the chaplain communicated love in this more believable way, the average patient required only half as much anesthetic as the former group. This loving contact and prayer helped the patient sense the love of God and to rest in his everlasting arms. They could thus rest in the hands of the health care team more fully.[4]

A Loving Body Language

When we are "with" hurting people, our love for them can be shown nonverbally. Patients who felt personally "liked" by their counselors were asked: "What makes you believe you are liked?" Their answers were significant:[5]

- 7 percent said: "They *told* me they liked me."

- 38 percent said: "Their *tone of voice* said they liked me."

- 55 percent said: "Their *facial expression* showed they liked me."

Obviously, nonverbal behavior is a royal route to sending powerful messages. We had better mean what we say or our nonverbal behavior may call us liars. To enhance the nonverbal conversation, we can: face the person squarely, have a relaxed and open posture, maintain good eye contact, and occasionally lean toward them or touch them to reinforce the special concern we have.

Loving Honesty

Truth and trust go hand in hand. When we lie to people, it breaks their trust in us. It makes them wonder if everything we've ever told them was untrue. It distances us and makes them wonder who they can really trust.

Sometimes doctors tell family members that a loved one is going to die; then they all conspire not to tell the patient. However, the patient often begins to suspect. He knows how his body feels. She notices medical procedures changing. The patient begins to notice what is no longer being said about "getting better and going home." At this point, all parties may accept a mutual pretense. The doctor and family may feel they have successfully "protected" (or deceived) the patient from the painful news. The patient, realizing that the family can't handle his medical condition, agrees to "protect" (or withdraw from) the family. Rather than resort to such organized dishonesty, doctors, patients, and family should work toward open awareness to both medical facts and personal feelings.[6]

A Loving Farewell for Smitty

I was just packing my briefcase when the office phone rang. "Pastor, can you come to the hospital?" Smitty's wife asked. "Our brother-in-law has just been brought in and it doesn't look good." As I migrated through Washington rush-hour traffic I began to imagine what I would see when I walked into Greater Southeast Hospital. Smitty's brother-in-law, his best friend, lay semicomatose. A series of health problems and end-stage cancer had climaxed in a congestive heart failure. He lay helplessly exposed in Coronary Care, connected to IV's, a heart monitor, and a machine that breathed for him.

In the hours that followed, it became increasingly clear that Smitty was going to lose his brother-in-law. As the medical prognosis was simplified, the family huddled around the bed to say goodbye: wife, sister, sister-in-law, Smitty, and me. There was a generous supply of loving touch, affectionate words, hymns sung, prayers offered. As the beloved patient began to slip farther and farther away, the family members began to peel away from the bedside.

Beside the bed, Smitty and I spoke quietly, briefly, reassuringly to this weary time-traveler. Loving rubs to the fading patient's hands, arm, forehead, and cheek were all we could offer. The monitor showed the heart slowing down, beating with less strength. Because the "Do-Not-Resuscitate" decision had already been made, there was no rush of activity when the electronic "beep" sounded. The heart had stopped . . . a pilgrim had been welcomed home.

It was hard for Smitty. His brother-in-law/friend didn't really look any different than he had moments before. His chest continued to heave with the modern miracle of a ventilator. A sensitive nurse came and turned it off. A doctor was summoned to pronounce death. And a pastor eased a heartbroken friend away from the bedside. "He's better off now and he had the most loving farewell I've ever seen a family give. You should be proud of yourself. You stayed with him to the end. He knew you were there. . . . He knew you loved him."

To Grow Through Suffering

When we have hope in God and some loving support from others, we can survive almost anything. We can even have a perspective in the midst of suffering that allows us to grow better, not bitter. Because caregivers also suffer while watching their loved ones in pain, we'll seek some perspective from Job's wife. As she tells her story (Job 1–42), we'll have the opportunity to learn from her spiritual hindsight:

"Consider My Servant Job . . ."

"My husband Job and I had an almost fairy tale life together until we hit our sixties. As a strong, faithful man who worked hard in the family businesses, Job took good care of us. He and I began our family in Uz, a city southeast of the Dead Sea. With ten children, seven of whom were boys, we really went after the work. After all, we had 7,000 sheep to graze, 3,000 camels to breed and sell, 500 teams of oxen, 500 donkeys, and a large number of employees working for us. We were probably one of the wealthiest families in the whole eastern Mediterranean area.

"As our children grew up, they all married and set up households within walking distance of the main house. Two of the boys handled the sheep in north and south pastures. The breeding and selling of camels, oxen, and donkeys were managed by the three middle sons. Our youngest boys handled the servants on the estate and the purchasing from merchants. When our grandkids started coming, you couldn't have found a happier set of grandparents."

Family Parties and a Family Priest

"If we had any concerns during those days, it had to do with our children and their walk with God. They partied a lot in the evenings entertaining their friends. We used to be invited but it really wasn't something we enjoyed, especially staying up so late! After a while, we politely excused ourselves from these festivals. But it didn't stop us from worrying about our children.

"The morning after a party, Job would set in motion a spiritual renewal routine. He would write a confessional prayer for the family and send it to everybody. Generally, he confessed sins and praised God in the prayer. But his wording could easily have covered gluttony, drunkenness, immorality, idolatry, or any dark practices—if any of that had happened the night before.

"We don't really know what our children and in-laws thought of the renewal process. They never denied there was a need for it. Job always tossed and turned through those nights. Eventually he'd say, 'I hope they don't curse God!' We believed that sinning against God intentionally risked big judgment. Well, we carried out the renewal process for ourselves as much as for any of them. After the morning prayer was sent, Job would pack up for an atonement trip. He'd load a donkey and head up into the mountains herding seven sheep. Up there he'd pray more and offer the complete number of sacrifices to atone for any known or unknown sin in the family."

The Day We'll Never Forget

"I'll never forget the look on the first ranchhand's face when he came running up to the house. 'The Sabeans attacked! Those nomads murdered all the servants and herded off the oxen and donkeys. I'm the only one who survived!' Because we were so staggered, we had barely begun planning a revenge attack when another runner arrived. This runner had burn marks on his face as he panted out the words, 'Lightning everywhere. All the sheep were standing together because of the rain and wind. The shepherds were among them to keep them from stampeding. Then it happened—like fountains of fire pouring down on us. I was on the edge of the herd and thrown free. What a scene of death! How could God do this to us?'

"It got worse. Within moments, a camel came at top speed. We figured the rider had heard the bad news and was coming up from the camel herd to see if he could help. Instead, he described a three-pronged attack by the Chaldeans. Apparently, they came from three different directions at the signal of a war cry. They ran swords and spears right through our workers. He said it was well planned as they hurried our camels away in long wild caravans.

"Our only relief came in knowing that our own children hadn't been in the fields that day. All ten of them were having a birthday party for one of the grandchildren at our oldest son's house. 'At least we still have them,' we comforted ourselves. Maybe you've heard by now—that was too good to be true. The thunderstorm that had sent the lightning bolts onto the shepherds generated a tornado. That twister made a path and touched down on the house where all the kids were. Someone nearby said it sounded like a huge roaring waterfall. The roof came off partially, making the walls collapse. All twenty-eight were dead in the debris, even the grandkids."

From Dust to Dust

"We were in utter shock. It seemed like a bad dream, but we couldn't wake up. It was real. Our emotions swung the pendulum: numbness, panic, shock, anger, intense sadness. I just fell down weeping—long waves of uncontrollable grief. Job's first instinct was to take charge of things. He said he wanted 'to load up for an atonement sacrifice.' It only took a moment for him to realize that there was no donkey to load, no sheep to offer, and no kids to confess for. 'If this was the judgment of God,' he said, 'it's over! If it isn't from God, atonement sacrifices wouldn't make a difference.'

"We went into mourning, making clothes out of burlap. After Job shaved his head, we collapsed in the ash heap to cry. We felt as hollow as corpses and knew God was reminding us of our own destinies: 'from the dust you were taken . . . to the dust you will return.' We were like the living dead, throwing handfuls of ashes and dust into the air. As the dirt rained down, we pictured ourselves as corpses beginning to decompose. We felt like we had seen the Lord face to face in judgment—it couldn't have been any worse. We felt as helpless as newborn babies—unable to do anything for ourselves. We begged God to finish us off, to give us the last nudge that would put us out of our misery. As confused as we were, we didn't turn to any other god for help. We couldn't reject the Lord. Instead, Job kept saying: 'Blessed is the name of Jehovah. He gives; he takes away.'

How Could It Get Any Worse?

"With all of the devastation we felt, we began to question God. We didn't question whether he existed or accuse him of being evil.

But we did deeply believe that he owed us an explanation. After all, if we had sinned and had not made atonement yet, he ought to point out our fault to us. How else could we correct the matter? And if we hadn't brought on this suffering as a punishment for our sin, then he needed to help us understand why good people were being afflicted. After all, the wicked Sabeans and Chaldeans were prospering from our hard work and we were on the ash heap reading obituaries.

"While we were exploring why this happened to us, things got worse. Job developed some kind of disease of the skin. He had intense itching as this disorder broke out from the sole of his feet up to his forehead. His pain was so constant that he didn't speak to anyone for a week. We tried talking to him but he would just wince and turn away. I think he was afraid if he opened his mouth, he'd say the wrong thing. He was so distressed that his only relief came by gently scraping the pottery fragments from the ash heap over his skin. This allowed him to scratch without gouging himself with worse injuries.

"As the disease worsened, his sores oozed pus continually. A fever came and his bones ached. Insects and worms had to be swatted off of his painful body. Some areas of his skin darkened and turned a dry, crusty texture. According to our customs, I had to withdraw from him in case it was contagious. Any conversations we had were from at least five feet away."

The Wounded Helper

"I don't know; in some ways I think I had the hardest job. I had all of the same losses my husband had but I was supposed to take care of him. I know he was the one with the disease but sometimes that allowed him to think only about himself. It took all of the energy I had to just survive one day at a time.

"I had just about given up hope of encouraging him when some friends arrived. Eliphaz, Bildad, and Zophar had traveled a great distance to see if they could help. As soon as they caught sight of his hunched appearance, they began to cry. They spent their first week with us simply listening, watching, and sharing our grief.

"Eventually Job spoke openly to them, including them in the very struggle he was having with God—demanding that God either name his sin or stop his pain. They pressed him, insisting that Job could name his own sin if he were honest. You can imagine how angry that made Job! He pushed back, demanding that they should name his sin if they were so brilliant. If they couldn't, he reasoned, they should shut up.

"Day after day was spent in these painful arguments. Then Elihu arrived and further incited the dialogue. One day after what seemed like years of hostile debating, I shouted to my husband: 'So just curse God and die!' All five of them turned deathly silent. Their jaws dropped open and they waited to see what would come out of my mouth next. Nothing came next. I just felt that if sin was the issue and God was trying to nudge us toward the edge in judgment, we might as well get it over with. Give up on a God like that or help him do what he seems like he is going to do anyway. What we had tried so far certainly hadn't brought any relief."

"Thus Sayeth the Lord"—Eventually

"Eventually the Lord spoke, He chided our four friends and me for presuming that Job was being punished because he had sinned. God's ways are a lot more complex than simply prospering the good and punishing the bad. He asked Job to pray for all of us that we could learn this lesson. Then he chided Job, not for sin but for ignorance. After all, if God could create and maintain a majestic universe with gems, mysterious weather, and esoteric animals, who was Job to demand simple answers? Even if God did give him a direct audience and felt obliged to justify his actions to Job, there's no guarantee that Job would understand God's wiser designs. Whether we get an explanation or not about our suffering, we are to maintain our spiritual integrity. The Lord gave him a big lesson in humility.

"Only later did we learn that the Lord had allowed this whole catastrophe as an example to Satan and others of Job's faithfulness. In time, the Lord also proved his own faithfulness. He restored my husband's health, allowed us to have double the herds we had before, and gave us ten more children. Before my husband died at 140 years old, he was able to enjoy grandchildren again."

The Problem of Pain

The story of Job and his family proves that even the best of us will suffer, though perhaps to varying degrees. It also shows us that caregivers, like Job's wife and friends, must bear their own unique burdens while trying to care for another. Furthermore, suffering tends to exhaust our optimism as other losses pile up and as the pain is prolonged.

A chaplain spoke to a suffering veteran about the death of Christ. "Don't tell me about your man on the cross," the patient responded sharply. "He suffered only a few hours and then it was all over. I've been in this hospital more than fifteen years and never had a day without pain."[7] Whether this suffering soldier had biblical faith or not, he was one for whom Christ died. He was worthy of loving spiritual care. From that day on, his pain was partially shared by the caregiver who was trying to reach out to him.

Why Does It Happen?

As people like Job and his wife suffer, they ask "why?" It is an instinct for self-preservation. If we can figure out why our suffering has happened, we will at least have some measure of rational control over it. Ideally, we can prevent it from happening again and perhaps place some responsibility where we feel it is due.

In the Book of Job, the main theory about what caused his suffering was "punishment" for sin (Job 4:7). While this theory isn't always wrong, it was wrong in Job's case. If Job had been Jonah, the disobedient prophet (Jonah 1–4), or if Job was a drunk driver being prosecuted in our day, some measure of his punishment would have been due to his personal sin.

A second theory is briefly exposed to the light (Job 5:7). It suggests that Job's suffering was simply a fact of "nature," a part of living in a sin-cursed world. If Job had been one of the Galileans killed in a construction accident (Luke 13:4–5) or a woman hurting from childbirth (Genesis 3:16), some share of his lot could have been chalked up simply to nature.

A third theory based on Job's life is sometimes presented: his suffering was sent to make him "grow" (Job 42:1–6; cp. 38:3). We, like Job, must always anticipate what the Lord would teach us as we suffer (James 1:2–4; 2 Corinthians 12:1–10). But while Job did learn some new lessons in humility, these lessons were the beneficial effect of his suffering, not the cause.

According to the prologue and epilogue of the book (Job 1:8–12; 42:7–10), a fourth theory fits his experience best: God used him as an "example." He served a purpose in teaching Satan a lesson, not to mention lessons taught to Job's own wife, friends, and subsequent readers.

What Do We Do During Silence?

Although it is easy for us to weigh Job's experience against these four theories, we have the benefit of hearing the dialogue in the heavenly throne room. We are *told* God's purpose. Remember, however, Job was never told God's purpose throughout the ordeal.

In fact, he was chided for demanding to know. All Job could do initially was to search himself for any known sin that should be confessed. Then he had to hold on to his integrity despite the pressure to quit.

If we were to absorb these four models of suffering into our experience, we would pray during times of God's silence: "Lord, correct my integrity if that's needed [punishment]. Help me maintain my integrity despite the pressure [nature]. Further build my integrity through this experience [growth]. And use my integrity for your glory [example]." In the maelstrom of pain, we can remember the words of the Lord of sufferers: ". . . I know the thoughts that I think toward you . . . thoughts of peace, and not of evil, to give you a hopeful end" (Jeremiah 29:11).

What Can We Do to Help?

The first challenge caregivers must hurdle is apathy. To ignore the "Jobs" in our lives is to preserve an artificial calm. But the Lord will not ignore our apathy: ". . . If you refuse to help those who are nearing death . . . If you say, 'I didn't know!,' doesn't the Lord look right down into your heart? Isn't he going to treat you according to how you treat those in need?" (Proverbs 24:11–12, author's paraphrase).

As we truly care for sufferers, we must remember the blessed paradox: ". . . though outwardly we are wasting away, yet inwardly we are being renewed day by day . . . our light and momentary troubles are achieving for us an eternal glory that far outweighs them all . . . we fix our eyes not on what is seen, but on what is not seen. For what is seen is temporary; but what is not seen is eternal" (2 Corinthians 4:16–18). The caregiver's spiritual perspective must not merely be rooted in monitoring physical conditions and temporary circumstances. If it were, we could be moved, as was Job's wife, to a kind of "hypervigilance" for putting our loved one "out of his misery." Instead, our calling to care reaches its ultimate heights in patiently attending to inward spiritual conditions and consequent eternal glory.

Those who deeply engage in the spiritual care of sufferers are commended by our Lord. When he praised those who would ". . . visit the sick" (Matthew 25:36), he described their visiting ministry with the Greek word *episkope* ("to inspect, to look over diligently, to oversee"). His choice of words implies that we should responsively study the whole panorama of a person's needs: body, soul, and spirit.[8] Ultimately we can do no less than spiritually serve the suffering person whom, at death, angels will carry into the loving embrace of heaven (Luke 16:22).

Here Am I, Lord. Choose Me

By the time her pancreas was eaten through with cancer, Rowena had been a fruitful believer for many years. From diagnosis to death, she had but several months to finish out her life. In one of her last hospital conversations with her husband, she said: "Now, William, I'm worried about you. With us having no kids and with you being so dependent on me, you're going feel like marrying someone very quickly. Promise me, for your sake, you'll wait at least one year? And honey, stop worrying about why this has happened to us. Years ago when I had cancer, I pictured the Lord walking to and fro in the earth. He was asking, 'Who can I trust like Job to use as an example?' He said, 'I need an eye.' So I volunteered and gave him mine. That's why I lost my eye to cancer. And now I feel like he's saying, 'Who can I trust now? I need a life.' And again I gladly said, 'Lord, use me.' And he is. . . . Someday, we'll be together again and we'll understand how he used us." With accepting sadness, William laid his own head beside his wife's on the pillow. They wept and said good-bye.

SUMMARY

1. Everyone, sick or well, old or young, has three deep spiritual needs: "to have hope in God" (i.e. to be spiritually born again), "to feel loved by others" (i.e. to know someone cares), and "to grow through suffering" (i.e. to learn something from our hardships).

2. As we seek to share the gospel with older adults, we might see some "deathbed conversions" (like the thief on the cross) or some gradual faith developments (like Nicodemus). While the gospel is the same for all people, there are some healthy guidelines for witnessing to senior adults.

3. As we seek to demonstrate love to people, we can utilize physical presence, body language, and truthful conversation.

4. As we seek to model growth through suffering, we can prayerfully meditate on the different possible reasons for our suffering and remember the Lord's priority on our inward spiritual condition.

9

Tough Decisions: Cultivating the Art of Ethical Decision-Making

J. P. Moreland, Ph.D.

It was a cold day in January as Jane drove away from the nursing home. Her mother and father had entered the home in September as they neared the age of seventy. It was a hard decision for them, but they had been adjusting nicely, that is, until Jane's father died suddenly on November 6 of a stroke.

Her mother, who had been on kidney dialysis for three years, had often remarked that only two things mattered to her: her life with Jane's father and her love for playing the concert piano. When her father died, Jane's mother never really grieved publicly, but, instead, concentrated all her efforts on preparing for a Christmas performance of Handel's *Messiah*. This had been her way of coping.

J. P. MORELAND received his Th. M. in theology from Dallas Theological Seminary, his M. A. in philosophy from the University of California-Riverside, and his Ph. D. in philosophy from the University of Southern California. He is the author of numerous articles and four books, including *Scaling the Secular City* (Baker, 1987), *Christianity and the Nature of Science* (Baker, 1989), and *Does God Exist? The Great Debate* (with Kai Nielsen, Thomas Nelson Publishing, 1990). He was on the staff of Campus Crusade for Christ for ten years, has lectured and debated on more than 100 university campuses, and has planted three churches. He is currently a Professor of Philosophy of Religion at the Talbot School of Theology, Biola University, La Mirada, California. Dr. Moreland is married to his wife Hope, and they have two young daughters, Ashley and Allison.

Two days after the performance Jane's mother experienced a stroke herself. She was in no pain, was recuperating well, and could lead a fairly productive personal and social life in the nursing home, but the stroke had paralyzed her hands to the extent that she could no longer play the piano. Three days ago Jane had visited the nursing home only to have her mother announce that she wanted to quit taking her dialysis treatments and be allowed to die. Jane had repeatedly attempted to talk her mother out of the decision, but to no avail.

Jane felt pulled in two directions. On the one hand, her mother had clearly and repeatedly expressed her wishes and Jane did not want to disrespect her mother and become coercive and paternalistic toward her. On the other, she could not bring herself to believe that what her mother was doing was right. In her opinion, her mother was committing suicide and she did not want to remember her mother in light of a suicidal death. As she drove away from the home that day, confused, upset, and with a sense of urgency, she wondered—*what is the right thing to do?*

As followers of Jesus of Nazareth, there are many aspects of life that matter to us. We deeply desire to be a caring, loving presence in the world. We want to respect other people, their lives, their thoughts, and their needs. And we believe with C. S. Lewis that right and wrong are clues to the meaning of universe. Caring about morality and doing what is right are part of the very essence of life. Morality matters a great deal to us. Deep within us we know that the things we often give our time to—television, obtaining possessions, gaining recognition, and social prestige—do not matter all that much in comparison to the great task of becoming virtuous people who live exemplary lives from the moral point of view to the glory of the Father who made and loves us. We know that part of what it means to respect others and ourselves is to try our best to do what is morally right.

Nowhere is the importance of morality more relevant than in caring for an elderly person. For one thing, issues of life and death are serious—perhaps the most serious—matters, from a moral point of view. And when we ourselves or our loved ones approach late adulthood, we know that living in the shadow of the valley of death has become an imminent reality.

Second, the way one dies is very important. A dignified and morally virtuous death can underscore a life well lived and leave behind a final legacy that enhances the memory of the life of the person who has departed. Conversely, if someone, for example, commits suicide, such an act can be so painful that it hinders those left behind from remembering the good things about a person's life.

Third, a dignified and morally virtuous death can be the last—and perhaps the only—thing a dying person can contribute to the community he or she leaves. If part of our responsibility to our family members and broader community is to teach them how to face life, then one's death need not be in vain. One can, by morally preparing for death, teach others how to face this universal event.

Finally, by showing moral concern and respect for end-of-life decisions regarding the elderly, we can help to correct a broad cultural perception, reinforced by advertising, that elderly people as a group are not valuable. Thus, we proclaim to a youth-oriented culture that all persons, made in God's image, are appropriate objects of concern and care, including moral concern and care.

This is not to suggest that moral decision-making regarding the elderly should focus exclusively on end-of-life issues. But as one reaches the winter of life, one becomes more vulnerable and dependent on others. Nowhere is this more evident than in issues of life and death. As Christians, we desire to honor Christ by caring for elderly loved ones in a morally sensitive way.

There is a problem, however. Clear moral thinking is hard to find these days, and there is very little training in the church or elsewhere about how to think morally. All too often we approach moral issues by relying on a "gut feeling," an intuition or hunch about what is the right thing to do. We all agree that if someone is going to become a good lawyer, doctor, or automobile mechanic, then one needs training in how to think about that area of involvement. But when it comes to morality, we have a tendency to think that we become good moral decision-makers by osmosis. If we go to church or function as respectable citizens, then we have all we need to think clearly about moral dilemmas.

Nothing could be further from the truth. It is certainly true that a virtuous life will help a person behave morally. But one needs more than a good life and a set of virtuous feelings if one is going to face difficult moral decisions like those which arise at the end of life. Such decisions are complicated by the advances of medical technology which enable us to sustain life in ways not possible a generation ago. And such decisions are often made in the heat of the moment, when a loved one is facing death. What is needed is good moral forethought so that issues are anticipated and proper, and pure principles are considered in the decision-making process when one is in a position to think clearly.

The purpose of this and the next chapter is to discuss some important moral considerations involved in ethical decision-making. In this chapter, we will investigate the nature of moral decision-making in a pluralistic culture, the general structure of moral reasoning, and some key ethical principles relevant to end-of-life situations. Finally, we will look at a grid which offers a set of questions you should ask if you are faced with a serious ethical dilemma.

MORAL VALUES IN A PLURALISTIC CULTURE

How should a Christian approach moral issues in a pluralistic culture? This question is important for several reasons. For one thing, you may be a Christian who is involved as a volunteer or in a vocation providing long-term care. You will most likely give care to those who do not share your religious views. Or you may have an elderly parent or other loved one who is not known to be a believer and who does not accept the authority of the Bible. Or you may simply be a Christian who wants to be involved in promoting social justice and respect for life in the culture generally, and you do not know how to do this in a predominantly secular setting. In cases like these, how is one to approach moral issues when others do not share a Christian view of reality?

Throughout the history of Christianity, most Christian thinkers have acknowledged that there is something called natural moral law or general revelation. Simply put, an advocate of natural moral law believes that there are certain moral laws or norms which are true and which can be discerned by all men as men. These moral norms may, in fact, come from God, but one does not need to believe in God or appeal to Holy Scripture to know that certain basic moral precepts are genuine moral absolutes.[1] These basic principles of moral obligation are absolutes which are true, unchanging, and universal. Furthermore, they are knowable by all men everywhere without the aid of Scripture.

Belief in a natural moral law seems to square with the Scriptures themselves. For example, one often finds the Old Testament prophets pronouncing judgments on Gentile nations who did not have the Law of Moses. The pronouncements of judgment often appeal to the fact that these nations have violated fundamental principles of morality which they know to be true—breaking promises, lying, murdering, stealing, and oppressing the poor and weak (cf. Amos 1–2). These nations do not know the God of Israel nor do they possess Holy Scripture, but they are culpable for violating basic moral principles which they should know to be true simply because they are human beings.

In the New Testament, texts like Romans 1–2 indicate that Paul believed in a natural moral law. In this passage, Paul teaches that there is a universal knowledge of God and his moral will available to all men apart from the special revelation of God in the Bible. Humans, he tells us, can sin against nature (Romans 1:26, 27), that is, against natural obligations that they should know are right. Furthermore, Paul candidly observes that "when Gentiles, who do not have the law, do by nature things required by the Law, they are a law for themselves, since they show that the requirements of the law are written on their hearts" (Romans 2:14–15). In other words, Gentiles have a knowledge of right and wrong even though they have no access to Scripture.

The existence of a natural moral law also squares with what we observe in life. For example, in moral debates it is usually possible to appeal to fundamental principles of justice, fairness, and human dignity regardless of the religious orientation of the disputants, provided, of course, they are sincere people of good will who are trying to discover what is right. C. S. Lewis studied a number of ancient and modern civilizations and summarized his findings by stating that the great majority of people throughout history have believed in "the doctrine of objective value, the belief that certain attitudes are really true, and others really false, to the kind of thing the universe is and the kind of things we are."[2]

The existence of a natural moral law offers us two important applications. First, when we are trying to make moral decisions in a religiously pluralistic situation, we do not need to get everyone to accept the Bible before we can find a point of common ground and agreement. We can be confident that everyone should have access to some basic moral principles which they know deep down are true. Later in this chapter, we will look at some of those principles which are relevant to the morality of end-of-life decisions.

Natural moral law theory does not imply that we should be naive about moral agreement. Some ethical decisions can be very difficult and no clear moral option may present itself. In addition, present-day American culture does not really foster the development of people who care passionately about doing what is morally right. We are a pragmatic and individualistic society. Often, our sense of moral clarity is covered over by layer after layer of moral rationalizations, self-centered living, an emphasis on personal comfort and prosperity, and so on. When people habitually live this way, they can lose their moral sensibilities. This often makes moral agreement difficult. But if there really is a natural moral law, as Scripture and common sense tell us, we can be confident that deep within most people there is a basic awareness of right and wrong. This gives us hope for common ground when it comes to moral decision-making.

A second application is this. Natural moral law theory assures us that there are moral absolutes. A moral absolute has three important features. For one thing, a moral absolute is objective. It is true regardless of whether or not anyone believes it to be true. We discover moral truths, we do not create or invent them. They are not subjective. When someone is trying to decide what to do in a difficult moral situation, it may be very difficult to discover what the right alternative (or alternatives) is/are. But there is at least a moral option waiting to be found, and believing that one is right is not sufficient to make one right. For example, a dying patient may request that some beneficial treatment should be discontinued. It may be difficult to know whether it is morally correct to honor the patient's own wishes or to continue the treatment. But sincerely believing that one alternative is the right one is not enough. After all, someone can be sincerely wrong.

Another feature of an absolute is that it is universalizable. Moral considerations apply equally to all cases which are relevantly similar. In other words, if two people are in the same moral situation, then all of the moral factors relevant to the first person are relevant to the second person. Rightness or wrongness is not relative to particular individuals or cultures. If something is morally obligatory for me, then it would be obligatory for anyone in the same situation. If two people are equally guilty of murder, then each person should receive the same punishment.

There is one further aspect of a moral absolute that has been misunderstood by a number of people. If some moral principle is an absolute, that does not mean it cannot be overridden by a weightier absolute if the two come into conflict. Sometimes, one absolute can be more important than another. Just as a king can trump a ten in a card game, so one absolute can trump another in a moral dilemma. Jesus himself taught that there were "weightier provisions of the Law," but he did not thereby imply that lesser matters of the Law were false and subjective.

Consider an example that a nurse shared with me recently. She was taking a thirty-five-year-old man to the hospital in an ambulance. He had just had a mild heart attack which she could see by reading certain instruments in the ambulance. He was extremely nervous and asked her point blank if he had just undergone a heart attack. Based on her experience, she knew that if she told him the truth, it could easily upset him to the point of precipitating another heart attack. She tried to change the subject, but the patient would not let her. He let it be known that no answer would imply to him that he *had* suffered a heart attack. She was caught in a moral dilemma involving a conflict between two moral absolutes—one ought to tell the truth, and one has a duty to benefit a patient and not harm him. She decided that the second absolute was weightier than the first one and told him a lie to avoid seriously harming his health.[3]

Regardless of whether or not you agree with her decision, this case illustrates that it is possible to have two absolutes come into conflict and one of those absolutes can override the other. When this happens, it does not transform the less weighty principle into a nonabsolute by somehow making it "relative" or a matter of private, subjective opinion. The nurse's decision cited above does not mean the principle, "Do not lie," is only a subjective one that expresses the private opinions of most people. The principle expresses a truth, even if it can be overridden by a weightier moral truth.

In summary, natural moral law theory accords with the teachings of the Bible and rationally informed common sense. Natural moral law theory teaches us that there are absolute moral principles knowable to all men apart from the Bible. These principles are objectively true and universal. Thus, one can appeal to broad moral principles in a pluralistic culture without first having to get everyone to accept Holy Scripture. At this point, we should face a problem. Even if there are moral absolutes available to all men, how do we use these principles in trying to decide what is right in a specific moral dilemma? And just what are some of these moral principles, anyway? The next two sections of this chapter will attempt to answer these questions.

MORAL THEORIES AND MORAL REASONING

In a certain sense we all know the difference between right and wrong. What Mother Teresa does to the sick is right and what Hitler did to the Jews was wrong. Many of the things we encounter in daily life are morally straightforward. Often, our problem is not deciding what is right; rather, our problem is doing what we decide.

Other situations, however, are not so easy to decide. What if someone who is terminally ill enters the hospital, continues to deteriorate, and further treatment becomes pointless? If that person has only a few weeks to live and is in excruciating pain, should a doctor give the patient pain medication, say morphine, which will alleviate suffering but shorten the prospect of living for more than a week? If your elderly parent is hospitalized, enters a coma which appears to be irreversible, and is being kept alive by artificial food and water, should these be withdrawn so your parent can die in peace? Cases like these must be faced with ethical sensitivity and forethought, but they are not as straightforward as we would like. By learning certain concepts in moral theory, you can make informed decisions in these difficult situations instead of relying solely on your feelings.

Moral theory cannot make the difficulties totally disappear, but it can help to clarify issues and bring assurance to us that we have done our moral best in making our decisions. Moral theory should do three things for us. *First*, in those straightforward cases where we already know what is right, moral theory should clarify why one choice is right and the other wrong. *Second*, moral theory ought to shed light on difficult, borderline ethical decisions by clarifying what moral issues are relevant to the decisions. *Third*, moral theory ought to help us be more consistent in our moral views. For example, some have argued that it is inconsistent to be prolife regarding abortion and also be an advocate of capital punishment. Others respond that they are not being inconsistent. They believe that one ought not take innocent human life, and the unborn baby is innocent human life, but the murderer on death row is not. The point here is not to argue one side or the other, but to point out how a moral principle (one ought not take innocent human life) can clarify a person's moral views and bring consistency to them.

But just what is a moral theory and how do we reason morally? To answer this, let us first look at a nonmoral situation. Suppose you were trying to decide whether you should buy an expensive spring outfit. Suppose further that you decided in this particular case to go ahead and buy the outfit. You might cite the following rule to assure yourself that it was all right to make the purchase: If I have the money to buy a piece of clothing, and if that piece of clothing will cause people to notice me positively, then I should buy that piece of clothing. Now, you may still wonder to yourself if this rule is a good one. To justify the rule, you may embrace this principle: If being noticed makes my self-image better, then I ought to try to be noticed. Still, you may wonder, is this principle a good one? How does it fit into my life in general? To answer this question to yourself (by now the people in line behind you are getting impatient!) you may remind yourself of your general theory of possessions, clothing included: possessions are things I own for the sake of making a statement about who I am and how I want to be viewed.

What would happen if you had a different general theory about possessions? What if you believed this theory: possessions have only functional value and I get them to save time and money for more important things? If you believed this theory, you may also believe this principle: money should be spent on other priorities besides clothing, and clothing is not a factor in how I feel about myself. This may, in turn, imply the following rule: Don't buy an item of clothing unless your other clothes are wearing out. Finally, on the basis of this rule, you may decide to go without the expensive spring outfit.

In the cases above, four levels of thinking may be discerned: a specific action or judgment, a rule, a principle, and a general theory. These levels are also involved in moral decision-making as can be seen in the following chart:

Level 4	Ethical theories	Bodies of principles/ rules systematically related	Ex: Utilitarian or Deontological Theories
Level 3	Principles	Statements which are more general and fundamental than rules and which justify rules	Ex: Respect the rights of patients. Ex: Life is sacred.
Level 2	Rules	Statements which assert that actions of a certain kind ought/ought not be done because they are right/wrong	Ex: It is wrong to intentionally kill an innocent patient. Ex: It is wrong to lie to patients.
Level 1	Particular actions/judgments	A decision or judgment in a particular case	Ex: Dr. Jones will not lie to Mrs. Smith now.

Suppose Dr. Jones is trying to decide whether to tell Mrs. Smith about a bad diagnosis or to withhold this information or lie to her. Perhaps Dr. Jones fears that the truth will harm her. If he decides not to lie to her, he may cite the rule: It is wrong to lie to patients. To justify this rule, he may cite the principle: Patients' rights should be respected and lying does not respect their rights. This principle may, in turn, be part of a general ethical theory that Dr. Jones believes to be true. The details of this illustration need not concern us. What is of concern is the type of reasoning going on. In general, our moral reasoning is done in this way: we justify particular actions and decisions by appealing to rules; we justify rules by appealing to principles which are broader than rules; and we justify principles by embracing a general ethical theory which contains those principles. Level 2 justifies level 1, level 3 justifies level 2, and level 4 justifies level 3. Broad ethical theories are justified by their clarity, their ability to explain our most fundamental ethical intuitions, and their ability to shed light on problem cases.

In the next chapter, we will discuss specific types of cases like withdrawing life support or withdrawing food and water, so we do not need to look at these issues here. Furthermore, we will not discuss moral rules for two reasons. First, there are so many of them that we do not have the space to discuss them in a helpful way. But more importantly, moral theories and moral principles are the most important things about the chart. Why? Because most people do not know anything about them and because they are the levels of moral reasoning that justify rules and decisions. So to help you grow in your understanding of moral decision-making, let us look at moral theories and moral principles in that order.

Moral Theories

There are two major types of ethical theories: teleological theories and deontological theories. The word "teleology" comes from the Greek word "telos" which means goal or outcome, and according to a teleological theory, the rightness or wrongness of an act is a matter of the goal or outcome of that act. The major version of teleological ethical theories is utilitarianism. So for all practical purposes, the major competing ethical theories are utilitarianism and deontological views of moral action. These are compared in the following chart:

Deontological	Utilitarian
Command	Consequences
Duty is intrinsic	Duty is instrumental
Moral value performed	Nonmoral value produced
Regulations	Results

First, let us look at utilitarianism (also called consequentialism). Utilitarianism is a moral theory developed and refined in the modern world in the writings of Jeremy Bentham (1748–1832) and John Stuart Mill (1806–1873). There are several varieties of utilitarianism, but basically, a utilitarian approach to morality implies that there is nothing intrinsically right or wrong. Rather, the rightness or wrongness of an action is solely a matter of the consequences produced by that action.[4] This is sometimes popularly expressed by saying that the end justifies the means. More specifically, utilitarianism can be stated as follows:

An act is right if and only if that act produces as much overall utility as any other act open to the agent.

Three observations will help to clarify what this principle means. First, what is meant by utility? Various utilitarians answer this question differently, but all are agreed that utility is some nonmoral good which can result from some moral action. For example, *hedonistic* utilitarians define utility as the amount or type of pleasure vs. pain produced by an action. *Pluralistic* utilitarians define utility as the amount of friendship, health, knowledge, individual freedom, peace and security, love, courage, etc. that an act produces. *Subjective preference* utilitarians claim it is presumptuous and impossible to specify things that all people will agree have intrinsic nonmoral worth. So, they claim, utility ought to be defined as that which is subjectively desired or wanted. According to them an act is right only if it maximizes the satisfaction of individual preferences or wants.

The common denominator for all three views of utility is this: utility is not a moral good but a nonmoral good. An act is not good because it is morally right; rather, an act is morally right because it produces nonmoral good as its consequence. For example, friendship, pleasure, beauty, and so on are not things which have intrinsic *moral* value. Nevertheless, they are intrinsic nonmoral goods; they are things that morality should seek to produce.

A second observation about utilitarianism is this: The amount of utility an act should produce is not just the utility for the moral agent himself, but the total utility. An example may help to clarify this point. Suppose we identify utility as the amount of pleasure vs. pain that an act produces. Now suppose that Tim Roberts is trying to decide whether or not he should steal a tape recorder in a store. If he does not get caught, the act would produce more utility (pleasure vs. pain) for him than would the act of buying the tape. If he steals it, he can then purchase something else and increase his own pleasure. However, such an act would hurt the store owner, it would hurt shoppers in general because shoplifting increases the price of consumer goods, and so on. Thus, according to utilitarianism, the act is wrong because when all the utilitarian considerations are taken into account, the net amount of utility would be lower for the act of stealing the recorder vs. the act of buying it, even though Tim Roberts himself would gain in utility by stealing the tape.

There is a third observation we should make about utilitarianism. Utilitarianism is not a version of moral relativism. According to utilitarianism, it may be difficult in a given situation to calculate the net amount of utility a given act will produce. There is, however, an amount, say, of pleasure vs. pain that an action will generate as consequences. And other actions that one could perform will also produce a specific amount of utility. Thus, the alternative which produces as much utility as any other alternative action is the morally right one to do.

In sum, utilitarianism views morality as an instrumental means for the production of positive consequences. No motives or moral actions like breaking promises are intrinsically right or wrong. The moral correctness of a motive or an action is solely a matter of the results or consequences produced by that action.

What shall we say about utilitarianism? The vast majority of Christian thinkers have rejected utilitarianism as an inadequate moral theory because it conflicts with a biblical view of morality and with common sense intuitions about what is right and wrong. Two examples will illustrate the problematic nature of utilitarianism. Suppose a serial killer has murdered ten women in New York City and the police have not caught him. Suppose further that they have caught a homeless drunk off the street. Should they claim that this innocent man was the murderer and punish him for the crimes while secretly continuing to look for the real criminal? According to utilitarianism, such an act may be the morally correct thing to do. Why? If they punish the innocent man (assuming they could keep this a secret to avoid a lot of bad utility in the form of social chaos resulting from a loss of respect for the police department), they could present themselves as efficient and hard on crime. This could, in turn, deter other killers and actually save lives. Further, millions of women are worried about the killer (they suffer emotional pain from fear and a few in New York City have actually suffered divorce or heart failure from the stress) for no reason, since only a few will be killed by the real killer before he is caught, and the police are going to continue to look for the real killer. These women are needlessly worrying, so if they think that the police have caught the real killer, it will remove a lot of negative utility (emotional stress and its effects). Now, if punishing the innocent man would maximize utility, then it would be the morally correct thing to do according to utilitarianism. But it certainly seems that we ought not punish an innocent person regardless of the consequences of doing so. Indeed, any theory which justifies such an act must be defective.

Consider a second example. Suppose there are two philanthropists, Beck and Roth, and each gives a sum of money to charity. Beck gives a million dollars to cancer research and his motives are terrible. He does it to make his wealthy friends jealous, and he also wants the social prestige that will accrue to him from this act. He could care less about the dying children who will be helped by the money, although he publicly acts as if he cares.

Roth gives the same amount of money to the same charity and his gift produces the same amount of utility as does Beck's gift. However, Roth does it out of a deep sense of moral duty and good will. Which act was morally better? According to utilitarianism, the two acts are morally the same because each produced the same amount of utility. But surely Roth's act was better than Beck's because Roth had good motives and reasons for his action while Beck had terrible motives and reasons.

Utilitarians respond to this example by claiming that we should praise Roth's motives and blame Beck's because such acts of praising and blaming will themselves produce good utility. But shouldn't we praise Roth's and blame Beck's motives because the former are intrinsically right and the latter are intrinsically wrong? It would surely seem so. We do not just praise good motives and blame bad ones because these acts of praise and blame will themselves produce more pleasure and less pain than acts of praising bad motives and blaming good ones. Rather, we praise and blame motives because of their intrinsic moral value. Thus, utilitarianism is an inadequate moral theory.

A second moral theory, deontological ethics, is more in keeping with common sense morality and with a biblical version of right and wrong. Deontological ethics is associated with divine command theories of right and wrong (right and wrong are ultimately a matter of what God commands as being right and wrong regardless of whether those commands are found in the natural law or in the Scriptures). A major modern exponent of deontological ethics was the philosopher Immanuel Kant (1724–1804). The word "deontological" comes from the Greek word "deon" which means "binding duty."

A deontological ethical theory has three important features. First, duty should be done for duty's sake. The rightness or wrongness of an act is, at least in part, a matter of the intrinsic moral features of that kind of act. For example, acts of lying, promise breaking, murder, and so on are intrinsically wrong from a moral point of view and we have a moral duty not to do these things.

This does not mean that consequences of acts are not relevant for assessing those acts. For example, we may have a duty to benefit a patient, and we may need to know what medical consequences would result from various treatments in order to determine what would and would not benefit the patient. But consequences are not what make the act right as is the case with utilitarianism. Rather, at best, consequences help us determine which action is more in keeping with what is already our duty. Consequences help us find what is our duty, they are not what make something our duty. We intervene with a certain medical treatment because we have a duty to benefit someone, and this treatment has beneficial consequences.

Second, people should be treated as objects of intrinsic moral value, that is, as ends in themselves and never as a mere means to some other end. We often treat each other as means to an end. For example, students may treat their teacher not specifically as a person, but as a means to an education. There is nothing wrong with this, according to deontological ethics, but a person should never be treated merely as a means to an end, because this would dehumanize a person by treating that person as a thing, an instrument for some end. This principle is what rules out punishing an innocent person even if such an act would produce better consequences than not punishing him. Such acts are wrong because they treat the innocent person as a mere means to some end.

Third, a moral principle is a categorical imperative which must be applicable for everyone who is in the same moral situation. Moral statements do not say, "If you want to maximize pleasure vs. pain in this instance, then do such and such." Rather, moral statements are imperatives or commands which hold for all examples of the type of act in consideration, such as truth telling. Moral statements say, "If anyone is faced with a situation where that person can tell the truth, then that person must be honest and not lie."

In sum, a deontological ethical theory holds that duties, principles, and commands have intrinsic moral value. Thus, duty should be done for duty's sake. People ought to be treated as ends in themselves and never merely as a means to some end. And moral statements confront us as universalizable commands which define our intrinsic moral responsibilities.

This completes our brief comparison of utilitarianism and deontological ethics which are involved at level 4 of the chart on page 171. To make ethical decisions in the real world we need much more than broad ethical theories. We also need some specific ethical principles which are relevant to bioethical decision-making.

Key Bioethical Principles

There are a number of ethical principles which are part of the natural moral law and which are especially relevant to the kinds of dilemmas that occur in medical contexts.[5] Some of the major ones will now be discussed.

1) *The Principle of Autonomy:* A competent person has the right to determine his or her own course of action in accordance with a plan he or she chooses. We have a duty to respect the wishes and desires expressed by a competent person.

The principle of autonomy captures the rightness of treating persons as self-governors when it comes to their own lives. It recognizes a person's right to self-determination. Two related issues are important for a proper understanding of autonomy. First, a person's wishes should be respected if the person is competent. The moral notion of competence is hard to make precise, largely because someone can be competent in one area, such as knowing his name, the date, and where he is, but incompetent in another area, i.e., in feeding himself. Competence is task specific and judgments about competence require asking the question, "competent to do what?" This is especially important to remember in dealing with the elderly because we tend to treat the entire class of elderly people as incompetent children. And we tend to make decisions for them whether it is appropriate or not. The basic idea of competence involves an ability to effectively deliberate about one's own individual goals, medical ones included, to understand medical options and their consequences, and to choose a specific medical option in a rational way.

The second issue involves decisions made regarding incompetent patients. While there should be a presumption that a person is competent unless proven otherwise, sometimes a person reaches an incompetent state and a medical decision needs to be made. I will leave to the next chapter a discussion of advanced directives (e.g., living wills and durable power of attorney) and the selection of a proxy decision-maker. But for now, it should be pointed out that if someone, e.g., a family member, must decide about a medical intervention for an incompetent loved one, there are two types of proxy decision-making functions. A *best interest* standard for proxy decision-makers requires the proxy to act for the best interests of the incompetent loved one, with a presumption being that the continuation of life is obligatory unless clear, overriding reasons are present. A *substituted judgment* standard for proxy decision-makers requires one to act as the incompetent loved one would have acted in this situation. The substituted judgment standard attempts to capture the importance of preserving the autonomous wishes of the patient, while the best interests standard tries to capture the importance of the next two principles to be discussed, the principle of beneficence and the principle of nonmaleficence.

2) *The Principle of Beneficence:* One should act to further the welfare or benefits of another and to prevent evil or harm to that person. Beneficence requires me to *do* something for someone else.

3) *The Principle of Nonmaleficence:* One should refrain from inflicting harm (or unduly risking the infliction of harm) on another.

Nonmaleficence requires me to *refrain* from doing something to someone else.

Beneficence and nonmaleficence are closely related. Beneficence requires me actively to provide something for another person and it is correlated with that person's positive right to have a benefit provided for him or her. Nonmaleficence requires me to refrain from doing something harmful to another, and it is correlated with that person's negative right to be protected from harm.

Beneficence and nonmaleficence can be used to morally justify paternalism. Paternalism is the interference with a person's liberty of action justified by reasons referring exclusively to the welfare, good, happiness, needs, and values of the person whose liberty is being limited. Laws which require motorcycle helmets are paternalistic in nature and are often justified on the basis of beneficence and nonmaleficence: helmets benefit motorcycle riders (and others) and keep them from harming themselves (and others). *Weak paternalism* is the view that paternalistic interventions are morally justified in these two cases: a) to keep persons with severely diminished autonomy from doing themselves serious, irrevocable harm, or b) to constrain persons temporarily from acting to bring about presumably irrational self-harming ends until it can be determined whether the individuals are acting in a competent, autonomous way. *Strong paternalism* is the view that paternalistic intervention is sometimes justified even when these two cases do not pertain.

4) *The Principle of Justice*: Everyone should be treated fairly and receive the benefits and burdens due them. We have a duty not to discriminate unfairly against a person.

5) *The Principle of Honesty*: We have a duty to deal honestly with others.

These principles are among the most important ones which surface time and again in ethical dilemmas at the end of life. In fact, an ethical dilemma often results when two or more of these principles appear to conflict with each other. For example, a person may desire to have some medical treatment withheld or withdrawn, say kidney dialysis, but the physician, family, (and even the person himself) has a duty to benefit and not harm the patient. Here autonomy and beneficence/nonmaleficence conflict. Or a nurse may be monitoring the vital signs of a person who has just had a heart attack. If the person asks the nurse if he has in fact had a heart attack, should the nurse tell him? What if that information itself might seriously risk the precipitation of another heart attack? Here the principle of honesty conflicts with beneficence/nonmaleficence.

Cases like these bring to mind our earlier discussion about greater and lesser absolutes. The principles listed above are objectively true but they may not express absolute duties, if by "absolute duty" we mean a duty that can never be trumped or overridden by another duty. These principles express *prima facie* duties. A *prima facie* duty is an objectively true moral duty which can be overridden by a more stringent duty in a given case. When two duties conflict and one duty overrides another, the less stringent duty does not disappear completely, but it is still present in a morally relevant way.

An illustration may help to clarify how a principle can function as a *prima facie* duty. Consider again the heart attack victim mentioned above. Suppose that, given the patient's condition and relevant medical information, it would seriously threaten a second, life-threatening heart attack if he were informed that he had just undergone a heart attack. It would seem that in this case, the principle of honesty is overridden by the principles of beneficence and nonmaleficence. But that does not mean that the principle of honesty evaporates entirely. Its presence is still felt. We are not entitled to lie to the patient to whatever extent we please. First we should try to withhold information altogether, e.g., by changing the subject. However, as was mentioned earlier in the chapter, a nurse I know was in this situation and the patient would not let her do this (he claimed that her avoidance would be interpreted as telling him he had undergone a heart attack). Next, we should disclose partial information which, while not false in itself, is misleading. For example, we might say, "You had an episode that is stabilizing nicely." Only as a last resort should we disclose false information.

The point here is not whether you agree with the specifics of the case. Clearly, there appears to be a conflict of principles. The point is that if the principle of honesty is overridden, it still makes its presence felt by requiring of us that we first withhold information, then disclose partial information, and finally disclose false information. Each one of these three alternatives violates the patient's right to know what happened, but they do so in an increasingly more serious way. Thus, the principle of honesty is a *prima facie* duty. It is objectively true, it can be overridden, and when it is overridden, its presence is still relevant to the morality of the situation.

These principles can be immensely valuable in helping you to reach good ethical decisions when a medical difficulty arises. While there is no step-by-step procedure which guarantees that one will make a good ethical decision in a given situation, there are helpful questions one can ask to facilitate good decision-making. Let us now look at a grid which can be used to surface questions for ethical decision-making. This grid is no cure-all, but it does show how ethical principles fit into an overall framework for making tough moral decisions.

As the grid indicates, when you are confronted with an ethical dilemma, the first thing you should try to do is get clear on the factual circumstances involved in the dilemma.[6] What are the medical facts of the situation? What is the diagnosis/prognosis, and how urgent is the case? Is there a need for further tests or a second opinion? What treatment options are available, and what is the probable result of not treating the situation at all? What are the values of all the persons involved in the situation (the patient himself, the family members, the doctor or nursing staff)?

Next, one should try to examine and apply the relevant moral principles and rules involved in the dilemma. What are they, do they conflict, and how should we weight them in this particular situation?

Finally, what are the consequences for each available option? What are the factual consequences? These can be medical consequences (for example, what are the medical results of each alternative?), they can be economic consequences (for example, are there less expensive alternatives that are morally acceptable?), and they can be social consequences (what impact will this option have on the family, the other people in the nursing home, the friends of the patient?). What are the moral consequences of each alternative? For example, will this alternative weaken respect for human life?

These questions are not exhaustive nor am I suggesting that one needs to go through every detail of this grid each time one faces a moral dilemma. But these questions and the grid of which they

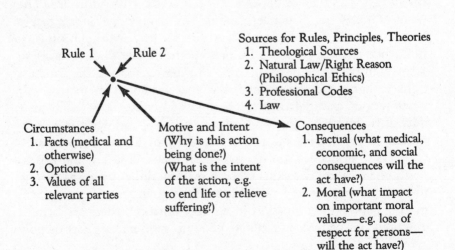

Rule 1   Rule 2

Sources for Rules, Principles, Theories
1. Theological Sources
2. Natural Law/Right Reason (Philosophical Ethics)
3. Professional Codes
4. Law

Circumstances
1. Facts (medical and otherwise)
2. Options
3. Values of all relevant parties

Motive and Intent
(Why is this action being done?)
(What is the intent of the action, e.g. to end life or relieve suffering?)

Consequences
1. Factual (what medical, economic, and social consequences will the act have?)
2. Moral (what impact on important moral values—e.g. loss of respect for persons—will the act have?)

are a part can help you to order your thoughts, gather appropriate information, and clarify just what the issues are in making a good, rational moral decision.

SUMMARY

We show love and respect toward ourselves and others when we treat people in an ethically sensitive way. We also bring honor to our Father who is himself holy and good. We have seen that there is a natural moral law which can provide common ground for ethical decision-making in a pluralistic culture. We have looked at the structure of moral theories and moral reasoning, and in the process, we clarified certain moral principles which are relevant to most ethical dilemmas arising in medical contexts. Finally, we sketched a grid which is useful for surfacing questions that ought to be asked in the process of actually making an ethical decision. But what we need now is a discussion of some of the specific problems that arise when someone approaches the end of life. What is euthanasia and is it morally permissible? What is a living will? To these and related issues we now turn.

10

Ethical Issues at the End of Life
J. P. Moreland, Ph.D.

If we allow ourselves to feel and think about certain images, they can be very painful and haunting. We are often used to seeing our parents as those who nurture us, love us, and make the world safe for us. But when our parents grow old, these roles can be awkwardly reversed. We are often used to seeing our parents as great boulders ahead of us in the stream of life who bear the brunt of the waters of time. As long as they are alive, we think, death will not pour over us because we are downstream. Thus, it can be very painful to think about the death of a parent. This is especially true today, because our society sanitizes death and keeps it away from us. Our primary exposure to the grim reaper is on television, not in real life. People used to die at home surrounded by family; today, they die in institutions surrounded by health care professionals.

For these and other reasons, it is important that we do not wait until we are in a crisis situation to think about the ethical issues involved in end-of-life situations. If we do, the pressure of the moment and the cacophony of emotions can blur our thinking and prevent us from loving our parents and ourselves in making good ethical decisions. The purpose of this chapter is to help you think more clearly about ethical issues at the end of life so you can be in a better position to show ethical respect to yourself and your loved ones. We will briefly look at life-threatening situations that you may

face and we will investigate some important moral distinctions relevant to end-of-life decision-making. After this, we will discuss the
morality of euthanasia and the decision to forego artificial food and
water. Finally, we will look at the importance of a Christian worldview for making tough ethical decisions at the end of life.

LIFE-THREATENING SITUATIONS AMONG THE ELDERLY

The elderly population is a heterogeneous group and should
not be stereotyped in a demeaning way. Nevertheless, members of
this population are at greater risk of dying than younger members
of the population. Thus, the elderly are more vulnerable in a number of ways. The elderly often encounter severe chronic conditions
associated with old age, they frequently suffer from dementing illness, and they can require life-sustaining technologies—medical interventions (drugs, procedures)—which keep individuals alive who
would otherwise die in a foreseeable time period. Five specific life-
sustaining technologies are widely used to manage life-threatening
situations:[1]

1. *Cardiopulmonary Resuscitation* (CPR): refers to a range of
interventions that restore heartbeat and maintain blood flow and
breathing following a cardiac or respiratory arrest. CPR methods
include manual cardiac massage and mouth-to-mouth activity all the
way to prescription drugs and electrical devices which seek to restore the heart to its normal pacing.

2. *Mechanical Ventilation:* refers to the use of a machine to
assist in breathing and in regulating the exchange of gases in the
blood.

3. *Renal Dialysis:* refers to an artificial method of sustaining
the chemical balance of the blood when the kidneys have failed.

4. *Nutritional Support and Hydration:* refers to artificial methods of providing nourishment and fluids. It usually involves the in-
sertion of a feeding tube which delivers nutrition directly into the
digestive tract or intravenous feeding which delivers nourishment
directly into the bloodstream. Later in the chapter, we will see why
artificial nutrition and hydration should not be classified as medical
treatments.

5. *Antibiotics:* refers to a number of drugs used to protect a
patient from various types of life-threatening infections.

If you or a loved one enter a life-threatening situation and require life-sustaining treatment, a point can be reached where difficult
ethical decisions arise. Should such treatments be withheld or withdrawn? If so, why and when is such an action morally permissible?

Who should make such a decision? Theologians and other ethicists have wrestled with these questions and offered a number of crucial moral distinctions which can help us get a handle on how to think through these issues. Let us look at some of these distinctions.

IMPORTANT MORAL DISTINCTIONS

The Principle of Double Effect

When we evaluate the morality of someone's action, we take into account the intention of the person who acted. For example, if a person drives recklessly through a residential area and kills someone, he or she is morally culpable. We charge such people with manslaughter. But if a person drove through the same residential area and intentionally ran over someone, we would consider him or her even more culpable from a moral point of view. He or she would be guilty of murder. Morally speaking, our intentions or lack thereof make a difference.

When we evaluate the morality of someone's action, we also take into account whether or not that person uses an immoral means to accomplish some end which may be either good or neutral from a moral point of view. For example, suppose your next door neighbor was a self-centered egotist who constantly bothered the rest of the neighborhood with excessively loud noise, lewd behavior, and physical intimidation. Now suppose you knew that your neighbor hated children and would move if you put a swingset in your back yard. Two situations could arise. First, you could put the swingset up with the sole intention of harassing and harming your neighbor. If you followed through with the swingset, you would accomplish a good result—the neighbor would move and peace would be restored to the community. But you would accomplish this result by means of an evil, namely, a malicious intent.

A second possibility could obtain, however. Suppose you put up the swingset solely for the purpose of providing a place for your children to play, even though you could foresee that such an action would cause your neighbor to move. Morally speaking, the second situation would be better because the good result was not obtained by means of an evil action, but by means of a good action (providing a place for your children to play).

These two moral insights—the importance of intentions and the avoidance of using a bad means to accomplish a good or neutral end—were discussed long ago by Catholic and Protestant moral theologians. They captured these and other insights in what is called the principle of double effect. This principle states that when an action has good and bad consequences, then the action may be performed under the following circumstances: 1) the act is good or at least indifferent regarding the end that one directly intends; 2) the good and evil effects follow immediately from the act—that is, the good effect is not obtained by means of the evil effect; 3) one only intends the good effect but merely tolerates the bad effect, even if that bad effect was foreseen prior to the act; 4) there is a proportion between the good and bad effects, that is, the good must be at least equal to the bad.

An illustration may help to clarify these four conditions. Suppose someone were terminally ill with only a few weeks to live. Suppose further that they were in terrible pain, wanted to die, and there was no hope for recovery. Finally, suppose that an injection of morphine would alleviate the suffering but also shorten life from a few weeks to, say, a few days. The first condition states that one should not inject the morphine with the express intent of killing the patient. Such an act would have death as its intended end and would amount to the intentional taking of innocent human life. But suppose a person really intended to alleviate suffering by bringing about the death of the person through the morphine injection. Here the intent is different. Condition two forbids this action as well. Why? Because it accomplishes a good effect (the alleviation of suffering) by means of an evil effect (directly causing the death of the patient). But a third option would be available. One could honestly intend only to treat the suffering by the injection even though death could be a foreseen, but unintended and tolerated result. Here, suffering is not alleviated by means of an evil (i.e., death), but by means of a good (the intentional use of a pain medication). The principle of double effect says that such an action is permissible because death is not intended nor is suffering alleviated by means of an evil.

This example may make you think that the principle of double effect is unduly nitpicky with its emphasis on intentions and means to ends. After all, you may reason, the results are the same in each case, so who cares about intentions?

Because our society is so pragmatic and results oriented, we often feel impatient with finely tuned discussions of topics, moral ones included. We want to press on to the bottom line and not "waste" time with minute distinctions. Nevertheless, the principle of double effect is extremely important because it captures the centrality of intentions and means to ends which figure crucially in moral actions.

Another example may help to illustrate the importance of intentions and means to ends. Suppose that Patty, Sally, and Beth each has a grandmother who will leave behind a large inheritance. Each visits her grandmother on a Saturday afternoon and brings a cherry pie to her. Patty, motivated by respect for a relative, intends to love her grandmother by staying with her for the afternoon and by giving her a cherry pie. Sally, motivated by greed, intends to secure a place in the will by being with her grandmother for the afternoon and by giving her a cherry pie. Beth, motivated by hate for her grandmother, intends to secure a place in the will by giving her grandmother a cherry pie with poison in it.

Each woman had a motive, an intent, and a means to accomplish that intent. A motive is why one acts, an intent is what one is intending to do, and a means is a step one takes to accomplish that intent. Patty had a good motive (respect for a relative), a good intent (to love her grandmother), and a good means to accomplish that intent (spending time with her grandmother and giving her a pie). Sally had a bad motive (greed), a bad intent (selfishly securing a place in the will), and a good means to that end which was the same means that Patty used. Beth had a bad motive (hate), a bad intent (the same as Sally's), and a bad means to that end (killing her grandmother). This illustration shows that motives, intents, and means to ends, far from being irrelevant and nitpicky, are all crucial to assessing a moral action, and the principle of double effect tries to capture these important notions.

Withholding vs. Withdrawing Treatment

This distinction is fairly straightforward. If one withholds a treatment, then one does not start that course of action. If one withdraws a treatment, then one stops what has already begun. Emotionally, some people feel that it is morally preferable to withhold a treatment rather than withdraw it, perhaps because it seems more dramatic to stop something than it is not to start it in the first place. But ethically speaking, it is hard to see any relevant difference between the two. If it is morally permissible to withdraw a treatment, e.g., because the patient requests such a withdrawal or because the treatment is pointless and excessively burdensome, then it would have been permissible to withhold the treatment and vice versa. The issue is not starting or stopping a treatment per se, but whether the treatment, considered in itself, is appropriate or inappropriate. Thus, there is no important moral distinction between withholding vs. withdrawing a treatment.

The Ordinary/Extraordinary Distinction

Ethicists frequently distinguish ordinary means of treating an illness from extraordinary means. Ordinary means are all medicines, treatments, and operations that offer a reasonable hope of benefit for the patient without placing undue burdens on him or her (e.g., pain or other inconvenience). Extraordinary means are those which are not ordinary, i.e., those that involve excessive burdens on the patient and do not offer reasonable hope of benefit.

The distinction between ordinary and extraordinary treatment should not be made for kinds of medical treatments in general, but should be made in terms of specific persons in specific situations. The idea here is that what is excessively burdensome and offers little hope for one patient may be less burdensome and more hopeful for a second patient in a different situation. The distinction between ordinary and extraordinary means of treatment for a given person attempts to express the moral intuition that a treatment is not obligatory, and thus can be withheld or withdrawn if it is excessively burdensome and offers little benefit. But an ordinary treatment should not be withheld or withdrawn. The line between ordinary and extraordinary is not always easy to draw, and such judgments should be made on a case-by-case basis. They should involve the patient himself (if possible), the family, and the attending physician.

The distinctions listed above are extremely important and they play a central role in moral decision-making. This will become clearer as we turn to consider the morality of euthanasia.

EUTHANASIA

The term "euthanasia" comes from the Greek language and literally means "good death" or "easy death." More broadly, euthanasia refers to the ending of a person's life regardless of whether such an act is active or passive or whether it is voluntary or involuntary. Since these latter distinctions—active/passive and voluntary/involuntary—are important but still unclear, we need to spell them out in more detail.

The active/passive distinction amounts to this: Passive euthanasia refers to the withholding or withdrawing of life-sustaining treatment in certain justifiable circumstances and allowing a patient to die. Active euthanasia, also called mercy killing, refers to the intentional, direct killing of an innocent human being. The distinction between voluntary/involuntary is also important. Voluntary euthanasia proceeds with the informed, autonomous consent of the person involved. Involuntary euthanasia proceeds without this consent, that is, the person involved is incapable of informed consent.

With these distinctions in mind, we can now understand the major debate currently raging between two schools of thought regarding the morality of euthanasia—the traditional and the radical approach. Presently, the traditional approach is embraced by most people and has been held by the vast majority of Christian ethicists and theologians. According to this view, there is an important distinction between active and passive euthanasia. Active euthanasia is morally forbidden but passive euthanasia is morally permissible in certain circumstances. What are these circumstances?

First, a life-sustaining treatment can be withheld or withdrawn if this is requested by a competent, informed, and autonomous person. We may think that the person is wrong to request such an action, and he may actually be morally wrong to do so, but it is often morally worse to force someone to continue a treatment that he does not desire. Thus, in most cases, if a person requests that a treatment be withheld or withdrawn, then honoring that request is morally permissible.

Second, treatment may be withheld or withdrawn (provided, of course, that such an act is not against the wishes of the patient) if the patient is terminal (a prognosis has determined that death is certain and the dying process is irreversible), death is imminent, treatment is extraordinary (it is excessively burdensome and offers little benefit), and death is not directly intended.

Recently, a more radical view has been growing in popularity, largely through the influence of groups like the Hemlock Society and the Society for the Right to Die.[2] The radical view sees no distinction between active and passive euthanasia and it implies that the intentional and/or direct killing of an innocent human being is morally permissible, in certain circumstances (e.g., the patient requests death or the patient is in terrible agony and death is allegedly the only merciful option). For example, active euthanasia can occur in cases of autonomously chosen suicide, where a doctor assists a patient to commit active euthanasia against himself, e.g., by prescribing sleeping pills to a hopelessly ill patient with knowledge of their intended use. Or, if a patient cannot carry out suicide plans, the physician himself may perform a medical procedure that directly causes death. Either way, these acts are examples of active euthanasia, directly performed by the patient himself or by the doctor.[3]

The radical view is morally inadequate for at least four reasons. First, a mistaken diagnosis can be reversed in passive euthanasia. If treatment is withdrawn or withheld and the patient was not as severely diseased as was thought, he or she will get well. Obviously, no such possibility exists if active euthanasia is allowed.

Second, advocates of the radical view justify active euthanasia on the grounds that it is often the only merciful way to alleviate suffering and pain. But this is not the case. For one thing, if proper medical care is administered, then cases will be very rare where medication cannot manage pain and suffering and keep it within acceptable limits. This would not degrade or inappropriately distress the sufferer. Second, even in cases where pain cannot be so easily managed, a doctor can offer medication which is not intended to bring about death even if death is a foreseen consequence of the medication. In such cases, medication is given to contain pain and not to kill, even if the dosage required will shorten life as a foreseeable result. Finally, though this can be abused, suffering and pain are not without meaning and purpose and should not be avoided at all costs. If the goal of life was to avoid suffering and pain at all costs, even at the expense of what is morally right, then human life itself would be radically devalued. More will be said about this at the end of the chapter.

Third, active euthanasia violates the special duties that health care professionals have to patients, namely to preserve their lives and "Be present to them" in a caring way when a cure is not possible. If we allowed active euthanasia as a medical practice, it would seriously alter our trust and respect for the health care profession, and it would cause an overall weakening in our value of and respect for human life.

Fourth, and most importantly, active euthanasia is wrong because it involves the direct, intentional killing of an innocent human being. Such an act is an act of murder and it treats the person as a means to some end, even if that end is an appropriate one (the removal of pain). Remember, often this end can be reached without directly intending it, and we have already found reason in the previous chapter for rejecting the notion that a good end can justify an evil means.

The discussion above is no mere exercise in academic, moral theory. The issues above are currently being debated throughout our society, and the two schools of thought represent radically different pictures of the nature of morality, persons, and the kind of community we wish to have. For anyone who respects human life as having intrinsic value, active euthanasia is not an option. If we wish to respect ourselves and our loved ones, then we must care for people ethically as well as medically. This means that passive euthanasia can express good moral concern, but active euthanasia cannot.

If a loved one has requested that a treatment be withdrawn or withheld, then such a request may be granted. If you think your loved one is wrong in this request, then you should try to reason with him or her, provide comfort and support, and try to find out why your loved one wishes to die.

For example, if a person wants to die just because he can no longer engage in a favorite activity, such as playing a musical instrument or going for walks, then he is actually trivializing his own life. His value in living goes far beyond these activities. Since the point of life was not playing an instrument in the first place, the absence of this opportunity is not a sufficient moral reason to die. Nevertheless, if one has tried moral persuasion, emotional support, and, perhaps, professional counseling, then a person's requests should most likely be granted. Why? Because moral coercion at this point would be worse than granting the request.

If a loved one has been diagnosed as terminal, death is imminent, and treatments are extraordinary, then such treatments may be appropriately withdrawn or withheld on the grounds that they are unduly burdensome and/or are merely delaying the dying process and not preserving life. But even here caution must be exercised. In such cases, an extraordinary treatment can be withheld or withdrawn (i.e., a mechanical ventilator), but it would not be permissible to withhold or withdraw some ordinary drug, such as a simple antibiotic used to treat a mild infection. To withdraw such an ordinary treatment would be to fail in our duty to provide normal care to the dying in their time of need.

We have seen how different moral considerations can help us to provide ethical care to ourselves and others in situations at the end of life. In the process, we have seen how important it is to determine the desires and wishes of the dying person himself or herself. But it often happens that a person is unconscious or incompetent and cannot express his or her own views in the moment of medical crisis. In light of this, it is important to understand the use of advanced directives.

An advanced directive is a set of instructions from a competent, autonomous, informed person regarding decisions about future medical treatment in the event that the person becomes incapable of making a decision at a future time. An advanced directive expresses the person's desires regarding medical treatments that the person will consent to or refuse, and it can designate a surrogate decision-maker who can speak for the person when and if the need arises.

There are two main types of advanced directives.[4] The first is called a living will. Different states have different specifications regarding the legal acceptability of a living will and the precise form that a living will should take (thus you should consult a lawyer in your state for more information about this). Basically, however, a living will expresses an individual's preferences for treatment to a physician in advance of the onset of serious illness wherein a person loses the capacity to express his wishes. A living will often contains a statement like this: "In case of serious illness from which I am unlikely to recover, I do not wish to be kept alive by heroic or extraordinary measures." Alternatively, it may contain this type of statement: "I want my life to be prolonged to the greatest extent possible without regard to my condition, the chances I have for recovery, or the cost of the procedures."

Living wills can be a very good idea. They help to preserve the dignity of our loved ones by giving them the chance to autonomously express their own desires for medical treatment and to select a proxy decision-maker in the event that one is needed. They also help the family and elderly person face the reality of death and plan accordingly. The appendix contains a sample living will.

However, two things regarding living wills should be kept in mind. First, even after signing a living will, a person still has the right to make health care decisions for himself as long as he is able to do so. Thus, an oral statement by a competent person (and there should always be a presumption of competence) made after signing a living will takes precedence over that will. A person reserves the right to revoke a living will through an oral or written expression of a change of desires.

Second, by the very nature of the case, living wills are somewhat vague.[5] For one thing, one cannot anticipate all the things that would happen in the future. For another, terms like "heroic" or "extraordinary treatment" and "hope of recovery" are vague. Finally, it often happens that a person would change his or her mind about medical treatment but not be able to express that change of opinion because of incompetence. Living wills are made while death or severe illness are distant, and one can have a change of heart as death or illness draws near. For these reasons, many people favor the selection of a proxy decision-maker or durable power of attorney.

A proxy decision-maker is the second main form of advance directive. A person, perhaps in the living will itself, can appoint a durable power of attorney. This is a legal instrument which empowers a designated person to act on another's behalf, including the making of medical decisions. Unlike the traditional power of attorney, the durable power of attorney is not revoked when the person who executed it becomes incompetent and incapable of making decisions.

The durable power of attorney is recognized in the vast majority of states, and it is more flexible than the living will. A living person can be more sensitive to changing circumstances and can clarify the meanings of his own words. By contrast, a document is less flexible and interpretation is sometimes difficult.

On the other hand, the proxy decision-maker is not an infallible guide to the present desires of the living person, and this point should remind us that there should always be a presumption toward sustaining life unless clear reasons override this presumption. One of two positions may be taken by the proxy decision-maker. A "best interests" standpoint implies that decisions should be made in the best interests of the patient. A "substituted judgment" standpoint implies that decisions should be made in light of what the person thinks the patient would want in this situation. Either way, a presumption toward life should be adopted.

In case a person has not designated a durable power of attorney, it is still often necessary to consult a proxy decision-maker when a medical emergency arises regarding an incompetent person. If no one has been designated, then the following order for a proxy is usually followed: a spouse, a son or daughter twenty-one years old or older, a parent, a brother or sister twenty-one years old or older, or a close friend.

In sum, living wills and proxy decision-makers can help to protect patient dignity and autonomy, they can aid in anticipating and processing the likelihood of death, and they can help to assure all parties concerned that the best ethical care possible was given.

So far we have discussed situations where passive euthanasia is morally permissible—most cases where it is autonomously requested and cases where the person is terminal, death is imminent and is not directly intended or caused, and treatment is extraordinary. This last point about treatment provides a fitting transition to a discussion of the morality of withholding or withdrawing artificial nutrition and water. This particular topic requires separate treatment.

FOREGOING ARTIFICIAL NUTRITION AND HYDRATION

Recently a woman in my church called me about a bioethical dilemma she was facing. Her grandmother was very close to death and she was being kept alive by artificial food and water. The grandmother was not conscious, she was in no pain, and the food and water were not burdensome. Nevertheless, several of the relatives wished to have the food and water removed on the grounds that their grandmother's life was over, for all practical purposes, because she would probably not regain consciousness again. What kind of advice should be given to this family? How should we view this situation?[6]

We have already seen that respect for human life is our most fundamental duty. This means that the burden of proof is on any decision to end life. Even if such a decision is reached, there are certain conditions that must be present before it is morally permissible to withhold or withdraw a life-sustaining treatment.

Ethically speaking, artificial food and water are in a category different from life-sustaining medical treatments. The latter clearly function to treat some specific disease or to assist some diseased bodily function. Drugs treat infections, and mechanical ventilation assists normal respiratory functions. If they are withdrawn or withheld, death may result, but death need not be directly intended as a final end for the person or as a means to some end (a painless state which death brings). Furthermore, it is the disease itself that actually brings about death when a life-sustaining treatment is withheld or withdrawn.

Artificial food and water do not have as their direct or immediate intention the cure of any pathological condition whatever. They are not therapeutic treatments at all. Rather, food and water are means used to meet basic human needs for life and to provide comfort. Furthermore, if food and water are withdrawn or withheld, then death is intentionally brought about directly and immediately by that act itself. Disease does not directly kill; the act of foregoing treatment kills. The fact that the food and water are administered by an artificial means is not morally relevant. If a criminal kills his victim with a gun, he is just as morally culpable as he would be if he used his bare hands, even though the former involves an artificial instrument (the gun) whereas the latter does not. The artificiality of an instrument used to accomplish some intention does not seem to be morally relevant.

Thus, food and water should not be withheld or withdrawn because 1) they are not extraordinary treatments where burdens outweigh benefits, but are basic resources which provide care and which express our duty to preserve life; and 2), if an extraordinary treatment is foregone, the disease itself brings on death, but if food and water are withdrawn, the only immediate and direct intention or effect is the death of the person which the act itself accomplishes. Put another way, if one foregoes a life-sustaining treatment in certain circumstances, then this would be a permissible example of passive euthanasia. But if one foregoes food and water, this would be an impermissible example of active euthanasia.

Artificial food and water are different from, say, a mechanical respirator. Respirators assist the breathing functions of the body, but artificial nutrition and hydration replace the natural bodily functions. Thus, when a respirator is withdrawn, a person usually goes on breathing. If the person does die, the removal of the respirator merely permits a previously existing pathology to run its natural course. However, when food and water are withdrawn, this act itself brings about a new and lethal situation for the person, namely, a starvation or dehydration situation. The removal of food and water is morally identical to placing a plastic bag over a patient's head (they both directly and immediately bring about death in a very short time).

There is another reason why food and water are morally different from an extraordinary life-sustaining treatment. If we withhold or withdraw an extraordinary life-sustaining treatment, we are focusing on the quality of the treatment itself, and one intends to spare a person an unduly burdensome means of medical intervention. On the other hand, if we withdraw or withhold food and water, we are focusing on the quality of the patient's life itself, not the treatment. We are not considering ordinary/extraordinary *treatments*, but ordinary/ extraordinary *patients*. In the latter case, we make a judgment that a person who is in a certain situation is no longer morally valuable, and we violate our duty to respect human life itself. Food and water should not be considered useless because they sustain a human life and protect the dignity of human life, even if they do not cure. Their point is not to cure, but to provide basic human resources necessary for the preservation of life.

Does this mean that there are no cases where it would be morally permissible to forego food and water? No, it does not. The only ethically justifiable reasons for withholding or withdrawing food and water would be 1) if they would not prolong life perceptibly (the person would die in a short time span whether or not he had nutrition or hydration); or 2) the means of administering the food and water was itself excessively burdensome. In this latter case, if the means used to give food or water is itself excessively burdensome (i.e., excessively painful or dangerous), then it places an undue burden on the patient and can be foregone for that reason. These situations are in the minority, but they do arise.

If you have grappled with the reasoning in this chapter, you may be convinced that passive euthanasia is permissible in certain circumstances, active euthanasia is forbidden, and that food and water should be provided in the vast majority of situations. But this information may appear to be cold and abstract. If you are faced with a dying mother or father who has irreversibly lost consciousness, then every emotion within you may make you feel that giving food and water is really pointless after all. Why, you may feel, should I keep my parent alive if there is no prospect of him recovering and enjoying life again? Why should I continue to watch my parent deteriorate?

These are certainly normal feelings and no amount of ethical theory, no argument about what is right will, by itself, remove these types of feelings if you are in a difficult situation like this. All that can be offered is an overall perspective about the point of life, suffering, and human dignity, and it is at this point that the resources of a Christian worldview become especially precious.

A CHRISTIAN WORLDVIEW OR MINIMALISTIC ETHICS

A worldview is a person's overall philosophy of life. It includes a person's beliefs about what is real and true, what is right and wrong, what the purpose of life is, and whether or not there is a God and an afterlife. As our culture has become increasingly secular, our worldview has changed. Even Christians have been impacted by the secularization of society due to the things we read, the programs we watch, the jobs we perform, and the ways we spend our leisure time. It is very difficult not to let the world "squeeze us into its mold" as the apostle Paul put it (Romans 12:2). When it comes to our worldview, it is very difficult to avoid being affected by a secular way of seeing the world. Regarding end-of-life decisions, the problem is that we approach those decisions with the mental glasses we are wearing, and we evaluate things in light of the worldview we have knowingly or unknowingly internalized.

While there are exceptions to the rule, most modern adherents of a secular worldview look at the world in the following way.[7] First, we live in a pluralistic society and we cannot agree about the good life, that is, about our view of what is important, what is morally right, and what is the point of life. Thus, the most important function of ethics and laws is to keep us from harming one another. The most important ethical principle is the principle of autonomy. If a person has certain wishes regarding his or her life, then those desires should be honored unless they significantly harm another. We have no moral right to tell others how to live.

Second, I do not exist for morality, rather, morality exists for me. The whole point of morality is to protect my individual rights, preserve my individual happiness, and maintain a well ordered society within which I can seek happiness in whatever way I define happiness (provided, of course, that I do not infringe on the rights of others). The main purpose of life is happiness, and pain and suffering are to be avoided whenever possible. My own goals and purposes are what give my life meaning, and when I cannot pursue those goals and purposes, my life is no longer meaningful.

Third, my loyalty to my community is a much lower priority than is my loyalty to myself. Communities exist for the individual, not vice versa, and when community loyalties require me to sacrifice personal pleasures in a way which is not in my own self interest, then I have no obligation to the community.

Fourth, the time and manner of my death is basically my own business and others have little right to intervene when it comes to my decisions in this area. My life is my own, death is an act that I must undergo alone, and I have the moral right to end my life in whatever way I rationally and autonomously choose.

In a number of ways, a Christian worldview differs from the secular one just presented. *First,* there are moral principles that all men ought to know, and there are duties that we have to live by morally even when we don't want to do so. The principle of autonomy is an important moral principle, but it is not the only or most important one in all cases. A person can autonomously choose to treat himself in a trivial and dehumanizing way. If a person wants to cease an ordinary life-sustaining treatment because he or she can no longer play the piano or do some activity that used to be his or her primary source of satisfaction, then that person may still be making a moral mistake. Why? Because the person should never have received his or her whole meaning in life through engaging in that activity in the first place.

Second, while happiness is important, it is not the point of life. The main point of life is to glorify, enjoy, and serve the living God, and a main aspect of a life well lived is morality. Morality does not merely exist to make me happy. Rather, part of the very meaning of life is that I should seek to become a virtuous person who models a morally sensitive life.

Furthermore, while we should not glorify pain and suffering, they can have a point. I can grow through them and I can teach others to value life, as well as give them hope by my example of appropriately coping with pain and suffering. Thus, when I am trying to decide what to do with a painful situation, my only consideration should not be trying to avoid the pain. I should also try to consider the opportunity pain gives me to grow, teach others, trust God, and model a concern for a virtuous, moral life.

Third, while I am certainly an individual with rights, I am equally a member of my community, and I have duties and responsibilities to that community. I must make my individual moral decisions in light of how they will affect those around me—my family, church, and larger community.

Finally, my life is not my own to do with as I please. Rather, my life is a gift from God, and I should face my own death as I believe He would have me face it. That may be difficult to determine, but I should at least raise these considerations when deliberating about when and how I wish to die. I should die in such a way that I bring honor to my Lord, I teach others in the community to trust him, maintain hope in the midst of suffering, and face death with dignity. In death, I should model my belief that life itself is sacred and it is not valuable simply because of its present quality.

Further, I should seek to die in a morally appropriate, dignified way. Otherwise, I trivialize myself in my death, e.g., by actively committing suicide or by allowing myself to die for morally trivial reasons, and I make it difficult for those left behind to remember me in a morally helpful way. Sometimes, the only thing a person has left to contribute to others is a morally appropriate, dignified death.

What does all this have to do with end-of-life decisions? Simply this. When one is trying to decide what to put on one's living will, or when one is serving as a proxy decision-maker for an incompetent relative, inevitably, one can only approach these decisions by weighing worldview judgments about the purpose and ownership of life, the importance of morality, the meaning of suffering and death, sanctity vs. quality-of-life judgments, and the responsibility I have to consider community needs in the way I live and die.

These worldview considerations and the ethical topics discussed in this chapter are of immense importance in helping us face end-of-life decisions in a Christ-honoring and morally appropriate way. By themselves, they will not solve all moral problems nor will they always point unambiguously to a specific moral decision. But they can help us bring ethically sensitive care and respect to ourselves and others. They can also help to assure us that we have done our best in reaching our decisions. And they can be an expression of our conviction that whether and how we live or die, we are the Lord's.

SUMMARY

In this chapter, we have surveyed a number of life-sustaining technologies which illustrate the vulnerability of the elderly. This vulnerability raises important moral questions about euthanasia. We have seen that several important distinctions (e.g., the principle of double effect, the ordinary/extraordinary distinction) can be very helpful in sorting out the different ethical and medical aspects of end-of-life situations. We have also seen that there is an important difference between active and passive euthanasia. Reasons were given for judging the former to be morally impermissible and the latter morally permissible in certain cases. Next, artificial nutrition and hydration were discussed, and it was concluded that these should not be viewed as treatments, but as means to meet basic human needs for life. Thus, it is morally wrong to withhold artificial nutrition and hydration which function in this way. Finally, we saw how important one's overall worldview is to making judgments about the good life and the meaning and significance of death.

11

Talking with Your Elderly Parents
James W. Duncan, Jr.

The Value of Discussing Important Issues with Your Parents

You are reading this book because as a caring daughter or son, you recognize that there are important issues relating to your parent's well-being that will need to be acted upon. It may be obvious to you that the discussion of these matters could be difficult to initiate and sustain. Even for those of us who are professionals working with the elderly, discussions about important matters with our own parents is often a wholly different matter. These topics are never discussed in some families, sometimes with unpleasant or disastrous results. In other families, these discussions do take place.

It takes courage to wade into the potentially turbulent waters of a discussion with your parent about his or her health, housing, financial, or legal matters. There is no guarantee that your overtures will be well received—but it is possible that you'll discover your loved one also wanted to talk about these concerns. He or she just didn't know how to start the conversation. While it is seldom easy

JAMES W. DUNCAN, JR. is a founder and Co-Chairman of PersonaCare, Inc., a provider of nursing home and assisted living services to the elderly. Mr. Duncan is a graduate of Wheaton College and The University of Maryland School of Law. He is responsible for PersonaCare's financial and development activities and its Bioethics Committee.

and sometimes painful, important information and feelings can be shared in these discussions. If they are properly handled, misunderstandings and uncertainties are less likely to get in the way of the good of everyone in the family. How we communicate with our parents will also have an impact on how we feel about ourselves for having made the effort to care in a Christ-honoring way.

Helen and Jim had both turned 80, and Helen's health was deteriorating to the point that she could walk only with Jim's help. He was an able caregiver, but the responsibilities of caring for Helen tired him quickly. They both knew that only one bad fall and Jim's sustained health separated her from a nursing home. Helen's daughter, Katherine, and her husband, John, came cross-country to visit one weekend. They were struck by the reality of Helen's infirmity and both parents' vulnerability. Katherine and John quickly agreed that somehow, someway, they would initiate a discussion that weekend with Katherine's parents. John pulled Jim aside and asked what he had thought about if Helen's condition worsened or if his health were to suddenly fail. Jim had been considering the situation, and for over a year had been thinking that they should sell their home and move into a life care community while they were still well enough to qualify for admission. But he quickly added, "Helen will never hear of it."

Katherine had taken her mother shopping and posed a similar question, only to learn that Helen was fearful about the future, too. She knew that another fall would make it impossible for Jim to take care of her. And if something happened to Jim. . . . She, too, thought a retirement community might offer continuity if anything happened to either her or Jim.

Katherine and John realized that neither parent had wanted to broach the discussion of selling their home and moving into a life care community; each thought such a move would be best for them. When the four of them were at dinner that evening, Katherine took a deep breath and shared about her discussion with her mother. Both Jim and Helen were astonished that the other thought a move to a retirement community—soon—would be best for them; each had been silenced by the fear the other would recoil at the mere suggestion that they consider it. A thoughtful discussion of issues, options, and timing lasted well into the night.

Katherine and John's experience with her parents illustrates the value of starting the discussion of important matters like housing before a crisis occurs and limits one's options. Had Helen fallen and become wheelchair bound, it is doubtful that they could have gained admittance to a retirement community; had Jim's health failed, Helen would not have been able to stay in her home. Fortunately, Katherine and John made the most of the opportunity to voice their concern.

In this chapter we will share some thoughts about the process of communication concerning these matters that may aid an understanding of why these topics can be so painful to discuss. It is to be hoped that the discussion will reinforce your resolve to initiate the conversation accordingly. We will also share some ideas that may make it easier to initiate and sustain such discussions. Throughout, we will identify some of the issues that might form part of your agenda. In much of this discussion we are indebted to Mark Edinberg, who in his book, *Talking with Your Aging Parents*, offers a wealth of useful strategies and skills for communicating with older relatives.

It is never too early to begin the discussion of topics that may one day present themselves in the midst of crisis—at a time when thoughtful interaction may be difficult or impossible. Our natural tendency is to ignore such issues, for a host of reasons. Some issues do go away or never materialize. But the ones that first emerge as the result of a crisis can wreak havoc in your life and in the life of your parent. Even if they don't, you may regret that you didn't deal with your parent's situation more forthrightly.

The primary goal in opening the discussion with your parent is to help him or her make a decision about issues you recognize are or will become important. "Parenting your parent" is a metaphor some use to describe the role reversal that often accompanies a parent's aging. Like most metaphors, it conceals as well as discloses. As revealing as this allusion to childrearing may be in some instances, it fails to identify one of the most significant differences between parenting a child and caring for older adults—their expectations about making their own decisions. When you raise a child, your goal is to encourage independence within a context of dependency; with your parents, your aim is to help them adapt to change and loss within the context of long-established independence and autonomy. Unless you are ready to take legal measures (such as applying for guardianship), you will need your parents' cooperation in all these matters.

An approach that might best be characterized by "asking questions" will generally yield better results with parents than a "telling" style. If your overtures are rebuffed, try to leave the door open to have another discussion later. One way to accomplish this is to acknowledge the disagreement but say that you would like to talk about these things again at a later time. Determine if there are any points of agreement—even if it's only an agreement that the topic is worth discussing. You might also try to identify the potential consequences of alternatives taken (or not taken) and use other strategies and skills for handling difficult situations.

Why Discussions Can Be Difficult

While you may readily recognize that the discussion of these topics could be difficult, the reasons for the difficulty is seldom apparent. The difficulties can lie on both sides of the discussion—for your parent and for you.

First, generations are not used to making decisions together. Each family develops its own norms and rules for handling various matters. "Mom always handled the money," or "Parents never talk about money with their kids," or "Dad has the final word." In almost all respects since you were a child, your parents have handled their own affairs. It is a new idea that children might want or be entitled to say anything about them. These are some of the "rules" that are often unrecognized but that inhibit our flexibility in discussions with a parent. An attempt to break from these rules, as you may now need to do, may be met with suspicion about motives.

Second, in many parent-child relationships, there is some (or much) emotional scar tissue that has developed over the years. These wounds from prior emotional battles may stand as barriers to any discussion devoid of a strong suspicion of motives. If trust is low between you and your parent, the decisions will be made by the one with the power to make them. You must work to separate the present issue from unresolved issues of the past. Although it is never too late to stimulate some repair in the relationship, we cannot ignore how the past will impact on the present attempt to make decisions together. It may even be necessary to resolve old wars before dealing with the issues at hand.

Third, the topics themselves are not easy to contemplate or deal with. The anticipation of possibilities that may never occur raises a number of issues that tend to represent a loss of independence: going "senile," "nearing the end," or "being with all those old folks." The very ideas of separation, dependency, or helplessness are fearsome ones to face. And some of the practical topics that may need to be discussed hold immense symbolic value over and above their considerable substance. The sale of the family home can signal the loss of independence and the trappings of status in the family or in the community. The loss of a driver's license can mean a loss of identity as well as independence, especially for men. A frank discussion of treatment options in the event of serious illness raises the "what-ifs" of medical technologies and institutionalization that everyone prays they will never experience.

Fourth, both the elderly and their children harbor inaccurate perceptions about older people. These myths of aging flavor our expectations for the outcome of discussions with our parents. First, there is the myth that as people become older they become more set in their ways, or rigid. Research in this area does not support this myth. Then there is the myth that older people are emotionally fragile: cranky and easily upset, or the opposite: sad, passive, and dependent. In actuality, emotional patterns are rather consistent throughout life. The result of believing this myth is that we can tend to dismiss or minimize a parent's reactions. A third myth is that the elderly are incompetent, that they cannot manage their own affairs, or make decisions that are in their own best interest. The opposite is much more likely. As has been mentioned before, older persons who need others to manage their affairs are a minority, and only 5 percent of the elderly live in nursing homes.

A fourth myth is that older persons are senile—that they are losing their minds. This belief leads to great fear among the elderly and their children alike. This fear immobilizes both generations from a frank discussion of the early signs of memory loss because everyone feels that this is the beginning of senility: soon the parent will not recognize who he or she is, or who we (the children) are.

Another reason these discussions are difficult to initiate is that we fear the discussion will "hurt" Mom. If we talk about these things, she will think we are aware of and thinking about "the end," and this will hurt her. You may find comfort in knowing that the elderly think about these matters a good bit, and they sometimes wonder why younger persons act as if the end of life is not a reality. They also wonder why we seem to ignore the loss or change our elders are coping with.

There are also those, both elderly and their children alike, who superstitiously believe that talking about unpleasant things will make them happen. For them, a frank discussion runs a serious risk of becoming a self-fulfilling prophecy. Your recognition of this dynamic, if it emerges, will allow you to address it head on, thereby lessening it as an obstacle to a frank discussion.

Another obstacle to initiating a discussion may be that there are no apparent options to the current situation. In fact, there may not be any options, but such a conclusion is best reached after considerable research and conversation between you and your parent. Often there are incremental decisions that can be reached and changes made, with great benefit to your parent. The earlier the discussion, the greater the number of options that may be or become available.

Older parents sometimes don't think their children will listen to them. By now their children have established a life of their own and it may have been a long time since they sought out or accepted their parents' opinions. Some parents infer from this that their children just won't listen to them, so they hesitate to raise the topics themselves.

Your Purposes for Discussions

There may be many reasons for talking to your parents, each of them worthy ones. We may assume we know why we are talking with our elderly parents, but I would like to suggest that it can be beneficial to more consciously acknowledge the reason for particular conversations. A clearer picture of your purpose in the discussion will help you communicate that purpose to your parent, thereby allaying misperceptions about your intentions. It will also help you stick to the point and guide you in pressing the matter to resolution. Of the many reasons for talking with your elderly parent, I will focus on just three of them here—Decision-making, Warding Off Harm, and Clarifying Your Role.[1] These three purposes for communicating can be summarized as follows:

• Decision-making—The focus of your conversation with your parent is on aiding her to make her own decision on how to care for herself. Decision-making can take time on both sides. If discussions focus on decision-making you may have to reassure your parent of your collaborative role. Different generations are not used to making decisions together.

• Warding Off Harm—When you seek to ward off harm, it means you anticipate a potential problem that your parent is ignoring, consciously or unconsciously. Your opinion may be unwelcomed, denied, or even incorrect. For all intents and purposes, this type of discussion is a "confrontation"—your view may well not be your parent's view, but you are going to air it anyway. There are two goals: 1) to get your parent to believe or accept the possibility of danger of one type or another, or 2) to help him or her become an active decision-maker with you, so as to prevent harm to him or her. These goals are not easy to achieve.

• Clarifying Your Role—The nature of conditions faced by older persons is such that, over time, the roles of children may need to change as the physical and emotional dependency of their elders increase. Help from the outside may be needed. Other family obligations may mean altering the types of assistance given. As we illustrated in Chapter 8, at times the demands for care of older parents may go beyond the resources, financial as well as human, of the children, who would be relegated to denying their own children and themselves in order to "give care." Clarifying your role means setting limits. It may mean substituting paid services for care by family members, or it may mean functioning in a new role—including that of "casemanager"—to coordinate services for older parents. As you make these changes, it would be wise to talk about them with your parent. You may need to ensure that clarification is not perceived as a question of love. In addition, role clarification needs to be accomplished in a way that includes the needs of everyone, including your parent, you, and your family.

Armed with a better understanding of your purposes in talking with your parent, you may be able to cut down on miscommunication and misunderstanding of your motives.

Discussing Housing and Legal and Financial Matters

In earlier chapters we have described the various services that can be provided to your parent in the home, the kinds of noninstitutional housing that may be available in your area, nursing home care, and the medical treatment issues that can accompany the end of life. From time to time, each of these may form the agenda for a discussion with your parent. In the balance of this chapter we want to focus specifically on the topics of *discussing* housing, and legal and financial matters. We will use these topics as a basis for exploring how to approach discussions of other important matters. We will then conclude with some suggestions on ways to be helpful to your parent in starting and sustaining the discussions.

Talking about Housing

Sally was the daughter of Ella, 77. Ella's husband had died in the last year. They had owned their own home, but Ella was beginning to feel the house was too big for her to handle. Sally thought Ella wanted to move in with her and her family. She felt guilty because she did not want her mother to live in their already overcrowded home. She would avoid discussing the topic with her mother by saying things like, "Oh, Mom, you can do it. Dad would want you to stay in the house."

Finally, after almost a year, Sally decided that she would have to come clean with her mother and tell her that there was no room for her at her house. Fearing the worst, she waited until her mother made another remark about the house being too much for her. Then Sally asked, "Have you considered living somewhere else?" Her mother replied, "Yes, I have considered moving into an apartment or senior housing, but I thought you wanted me to stay in the house where you were raised."

Sally was as surprised as she was delighted at this outcome and was able to help her mother decide to apply for senior housing, although this took another year to accomplish.

Your concern about your parent's housing may well arise in connection with a noticeable decline in your parent's health or mobility. Since housing options for the elderly are in particularly short supply and services provided to their homes require a good bit of coordination, this is an area of concern where advance planning can really pay off. Unfortunately, even considering changes in housing is often one of the last things an elderly person wants to contemplate. One's home has immense symbolic value. It denotes independence and control over one's environment. Often many pleasant family memories are closely associated with the home. It may be where your parent raised her family or shared some of the best years with her husband. It may also be a measure of one's social attainment and status. To an elderly person, leaving home can signal the loss of independence and the beginning of the "inevitable" road to a nursing home.

These obstacles to considering a change in housing are not insignificant. Just getting your parent to fill out the application forms that would get them on waiting lists and keep options open means these emotions and perceptions must be addressed. All this is "simply" to prepare for events that will take place in the future, if at all.

Many elderly persons who have waited until they had a current need for alternative housing arrangements have found that the most desirable options have waiting lists that are years long. Waiting periods at established subsidized housing or retirement centers can be as long as three to five years. During such a wait, your parent's health and ability to care for herself may deteriorate to such a degree that she will not qualify for admission when the opening occurs.

There are other reasons to consider housing options before a current need forces the issue. For instance, a move to a retirement center while a couple is still mobile and socially active can mean the establishment of friendships and a social network that will remain in place in the event one of them dies. It can also be a current comfort to know that if the health of one of them fails, the other will not be "stranded."

Your purpose, then, in initiating the discussion about housing might constitute long-range planning in an effort to aid their decision-making. Or your purpose may be to ward off harm and therefore it may be more urgent—to drive home the reality that Mom cannot safely maintain herself at home, for instance, or that physical changes in the environment may need to be made to accommodate her needs. Your purpose may be to intervene after a crisis—due to your parent's fall, hospitalization, or the fact that he or she left the gas on.

Talking about Financial and Legal Matters

Martha was 72 when she had a stroke which left her significantly debilitated and in a nursing home. It was hard for her to communicate verbally or in writing. Her children thought it would be wise for them to have control over her bank accounts not only to facilitate her payment of on-going expenses, but also in case she became totally unable to write checks. But her children did nothing for fear that raising the issue with her would signal that they had given up on her and were anticipating her death.

Several months later, Martha suffered a second stroke which left her barely conscious and unable to write. Without intervention by the courts, they were unable to access her accounts to pay her expenses and had to use their own money, which necessitated a bank loan.

Martha's situation is but one example of the legal and financial entanglements in which you might find yourself when crisis strikes. Talking about these matters will help anticipate problems and develop strategies to deal with them if the need arises. In Martha's case, it is obvious that her children wish they had taken action earlier and had found a way to communicate, in the process, that they were not giving up on her.

Legal and financial matters are no easier to talk about than housing matters. For one thing, the impact of either planning or failing to plan falls primarily on the children, not the parent. Discussion of estate planning (wills, trusts, etc.) can raise suspicions about motives, particularly if there is a low level of trust in your relationship with your parent. Secondly, legal and financial planning is based largely on uncertainty—not only uncertainty about *when* such a plan would go into effect (such as a will), but also *whether* such a plan will go into effect (such as a plan to handle assets if your parent is incapacitated).

There may be no good way to raise the issue, even if there is a high level of trust on both sides. No one, regardless of age, likes to be told that he or she is not handling finances appropriately. Nonetheless, you can decide what you will and will not talk about, and some ways of raising the topic may be better than others. You can minimize the frustration by dealing with the issues directly. Or you may choose not to talk about certain topics and pay the price later, both emotionally and financially.

There are several purposes for discussing financial and legal matters. One is to avoid fraud. There seems to be no shortage of con artists who prey on the elderly. Schemes range from talking them into withdrawing funds from their savings for "bank examiners," to selling them services and products (roofing and siding, for instance) they don't need. Other schemes are even more insidious, such as those by housekeepers who have glowing resumés but who leave a trail of theft or abuse. It is important for your parent to know that phony I.D.'s can be obtained, that information can be found about them and used to support a fraud's credibility, that deals too good to be true, aren't—and that it is nearly impossible in an interview or a short encounter to recognize a pathological liar. Your goal is to encourage your parent to consult you before undertaking major transactions or purchases of these types.

Another reason to discuss financial and legal matters is to explore for leading indicators of future problems: Do your parents have enough resources to live on? How are they managing things? What's going on in their thought process? Are bills getting paid on time? What are they paying the housekeeper?

Often this involves subtle probing; other times direct questions need to be asked.

Some of the useful topics to explore are the following:

• Where are assets held, in what name, and who has legal access to them? If your parent becomes partially or totally incapacitated, who should have access to her assets to facilitate payment for her care and how will they get access? Most states permit people to give authorization in advance to another in case they are later unable to manage their own affairs. Such an authorization is generally known as a durable power of attorney. What this type of power of attorney contains is crucial to its later effectiveness. The requirements can vary from state to state so it is best to consult a lawyer about this. Most bank accounts and other financial accounts permit the accounts to be in "joint names" so that more than one person has access to them. If your parent trusts you, she could make you a joint owner of the accounts, thereby permitting you to access them in the event of her incapacity. Since such joint ownership may entail tax issues, it is best to consult a lawyer about doing this if the accounts are substantial.

• Has a will been prepared? The effectiveness of a will depends almost entirely on its precise compliance with legal requirements in your state. Since the consequences of not having a will or having a defective will can be disastrous, it is important to have a lawyer involved in its preparation. All states have stringent requirements about how a will's execution is witnessed, how many witnesses are required, and who qualifies as acceptable witnesses. Legal counsel is a must. If your parent has a sizable estate, good tax planning can save significantly on the estate taxes due and is well worth the legal expense involved. Since the tax laws affecting estates and trusts tend to change fairly frequently, a will should be reviewed periodically.[2]

• Who would be appointed as your parent's conservator or guardian if one ever needs to be appointed? A conservator (or guardian) is someone who has legal power to make decisions for another in the event that person is unable to do so for himself. Such matters could include decisions about financial and legal concerns as well as judgments about institutionalization and medical treatments. In states that do not permit the use of a durable medical power of attorney for medical decisions, this is the only formal mechanism for giving another such power. The appointment of a conservator involves a petition to the court, which has the power to appoint anyone it feels will appropriately manage the person's affairs. A person can ask the court to appoint someone as a conservator over herself, but this rarely takes place. Most often the appointment of a conservator is sought because the person is already incapacitated. The courts are more likely to appoint as a conservator someone who the older person has previously indicated he or she desires. Such a preference can be expressed in any number of ways, but it helps if it's in writing executed by the person. The senior may even want to include a statement to that effect in his or her will.

• Is your parent taking full advantage of the several federal, state, and local entitlement programs available to the elderly? Four major federal programs provide financial help to the elderly:

1) Social Security is intended to provide older persons with a supplemental income. The amount of money to which a person is entitled depends on her or her spouse's prior work history, and it is paid after retirement.

2) Supplemental Security Income is designed for the poor elderly to provide a minimum income. States often subsidize this program, and eligibility depends on satisfying a financial means test.

3) Medicare is the federal medical insurance program for which everyone over age 65 is qualified if they are eligible for social security. Medicare has two parts, called Part A and Part B. Part A pays for in-hospital services, certain home health care services, and some nursing home stays (up to 180 days if it follows a hospital stay). Part B is elective and requires a monthly payment by the recipient. It is wise for you and your parent to become familiar with the precise extent of Medicare's coverage (as well as having a clear understanding of what Medicare doesn't cover). Coverage is less than most people assume.

4) Medicaid is a federal medical insurance program subsidized and administered by each state. It is much more comprehensive in its coverage than Medicare, but it is available only for the indigent. Eligibility requirements focus on the recipient's own ability to pay for his or her own health care, and in some states there is a prior residency test. Medicaid pays for extended nursing home care as well as most typical medical expenses. In some states Medicaid pays for drugs, dental care, and mental health care. Payments are made directly to the provider of services, although the rates of reimbursement are generally lower than the true costs of providing the care. This makes many fine providers reluctant to admit very many Medicaid recipients (that portion of the cost of care which is not covered by Medicaid must be shifted to those residents who are paying for their own care).

Other programs exist in various areas to help the elderly. Some states provide property tax credits, and some utility companies grant heating fuel subsidies. There are so-called "Golden Age" cards that qualify the holder for discounts on transportation, admission costs, and shopping. Many merchants and restaurants have certain days or times of each day when costs to the elderly are discounted. The requirements of each varies, so some research in your particular area will be necessary.

Ways to Be Helpful

Whatever your purpose in initiating a discussion with your parent, and whatever the topic, here are some ways to be helpful:

• *Do some initial research,* even if it's only to find out where to get information. If you do too much work before talking to your parents, you risk being perceived as meddlesome or trying to run their lives. In earlier chapters we discussed the various sources of information and assistance that may be available. With that information you can begin to determine what possibilities exist in your area that address your particular circumstances.

• *Be emotionally prepared.* Try to anticipate your parent's likely reaction and the concerns that underlie her negative feelings. Avoid getting caught up in your own unresolved feeling about the issue (such as how bad Sally might have felt about her father's death), or you may inadvertently get pulled into the ties that keep your parent in undesirable living arrangements. Consider the fears and myths your parent may have, such as "They want me to move in" (Ella's concern), or "They really don't want me to move in," or "I really don't like X or Y," or "They don't really want to help me." Also consider the fears and myths you may have, such as "She wants to move in and won't consider anything else" (which was Sally's concern), or "She won't listen," or "She doesn't care what I think," or "She is a typical stubborn old person." These myths will make things worse unless dispelled or addressed head-on.

• *Determine, in fact, what are your parent's needs.* What, in actuality, are the changes that suggest she should consider a change in housing or needs help with her finances? What are her physical needs, need for security, need for convenience and independence, need for access to desired activities, preference for familiar surroundings, or desire to socialize with others her own age?

• Appreciate the role her current housing has played in your parent's life: it represents territory, identity, independence, and autonomy. Many moves come as a result of adaptation to loss, and a move represents the physical giving up of power, prestige, and so forth.

• Appreciate the role that control over her own finances plays in your parent's sense of independence. Many elderly persons fear that they will not have enough to take care of them through their old age, so they control what they do have very tightly. For others, the ability to give to others, especially to loved ones, means that they still have something to contribute to life. Losing that control can be a fearsome prospect.

• Have your parent be a critical part of the process from the beginning. People are much more likely to follow through on a decision in which they have participated than they are on a decision made for them. Encourage a frank discussion of wishes and preferences.

• Appreciate the several roles you can play, ranging from researcher to sounding board, from judge to landlord. Some roles may be necessary, although at times either you or your parent may not want you to play those roles.

• As much as you can, directly air your specific feelings about how you are working together.

• Decisions are not usually made suddenly, or once and for all. Allow time (weeks or months) to sort out and decide, for both you and your parent.

• Present information for your parent, not conclusions. With some prior approval by your parent, you can serve a valuable function as a diligent researcher rather than judge and jury.

• Expect emotional reactions from your parent and yourself. Emotional reactions are likely to surface indirectly. For example, in an endeavor to consider options rationally, your parent may identify all the "problems" with each, telescoping the problems into a seemingly insurmountable mountain to be conquered all in one climb. Or she may march a perceived "parade of horrors" past you, as if all of them will surely come to pass in their worst form.

• Try to enlist a trusted "outsider" such as an old friend who is a lawyer or an accountant. Sometimes the advice of a friend with nothing to gain from a decision can be helpful, particularly if the trusted friend knows how to be subtle in his initiation with your parent.

• Above all, let your parent know repeatedly that you care, that you will be there to help, and that not all decisions need to be made at one time.

To be sure, simply starting the discussion of important matters with your parent holds no guarantee of the outcome. But the implications of reacting to the impact of aging instead of planning carefully can be devastating to your parent and the entire family. Your willingness to initiate such dialog speaks volumes about your care. Regardless of the outcome of the talks, you will be confident that you did your best to honor your parent by helping her in this way to live her life to the fullest.

SUMMARY

There can be tremendous value in initiating a discussion with your elderly parent before a crisis intervenes and limits your options.

The primary goal of such discussions is to help your parent make his or her own decisions about issues which you recognize are or will become important. But discussions of such issues can be difficult; generations are not used to making decisions together; there may be a low level of trust in your relationship; the topics to be discussed may be uncomfortable; and both you and your parent may harbor misconceptions about aging and the elderly.

Identifying your role and your purposes for discussions with your parent can lead to better communication and understanding.

Your purpose may be to help in decision-making, warding off harm and clarifying your role.

Housing concerns are often a major issue to be discussed with your elderly parent. Longer range planning often pays significant dividends. Legal and financial matters are another common topic, since the consequences of poor planning can be disastrous to the family.

Ways to be helpful to your elderly parent include gathering information, being emotionally prepared yourself, carefully assessing your parent's actual needs and appreciating the roles housing, independence and finances play in his or her life.

Appendices

1. STATUTORY FORM FOR LIVING WILL
(Conn. Gen. Stat. § 19a-575)

<u>STATEMENT OF (NAME)</u>

If the time comes when I am incapacitated to the point where I can no longer actively take part in decisions for my own life, and am unable to direct my physician as to my own medical care, I wish this statement to stand as a testament of my wishes. I, ____(name)____, request that I be allowed to die and not be kept alive through life support systems if my condition is deemed terminal. I do not intend any direct taking of my life, but only that my dying not be unreasonably prolonged. This request is made, after careful reflection, while I am of sound mind.

_____
(Name)

_____
(Date)

_____
(Witness)

_____
(Witness)

2. EXAMPLE OF LIVING WILL

To my family, my physician, my lawyer, and all others whom it may concern:

Death is as much a reality as birth, growth, maturity, and old age; it is the one certainty of life. If the time comes when I can no longer take part in decisions for my own future, let this statement stand as an expression of my wishes and directions, while I am still of sound mind.

If at such a time the situation should arise in which there is no reasonable expectation of my recovery from extreme physical or mental disability, I direct that I be allowed to die and not be kept alive by medications, artificial means, or "heroic measures." I do, however, ask that medication be mercifully administered to me to alleviate suffering, even though this may shorten my remaining life.

This statement is made after careful consideration and is in accordance with my strong convictions and beliefs. I want the wishes and directions here expressed carried out to the extent permitted by law. Insofar as they are not legally enforceable, I hope that those to whom this Will is addressed will regard themselves as morally bound by these provisions.

Signed _____

Date _____

Witness _____

Witness _____

Copies of this request have been given to _____

_____

_____

_____

3. DECLARATION

If at any time I should have an incurable injury, disease, or illness certified to be a terminal condition by two (2) physicians who have personally examined me, one (1) of whom shall be my attending physician, and the physicians have determined that my death is imminent and will occur whether or not life-sustaining procedures are utilized and where the application of such procedures would serve only to artificially prolong the dying process, I direct that such procedures be withheld or withdrawn, and that I be permitted to die naturally with only the administration of medication, the administration of food and water, and the performance of any medical procedure that is necessary to provide comfort care or alleviate pain. In the absence of my ability to give directions regarding the use of such life-sustaining procedures, it is my intention that this declaration shall be honored by my family and physician(s) as the final expression of my right to control my medical care and treatment.

Declaration made this _____ day of _____ (*month, year*).

I, _____ , being of sound mind, willfully and voluntarily direct that my dying shall not be artificially prolonged under the circumstances set forth in this declaration.

Other instructions:

I am legally competent to make this declaration, and I understand its full import.

Signed _____

Address _____

     Under penalty of perjury, we state that this declaration was signed by _____ in the presence of the undersigned who, at his/her request, in his/her presence, and in the presence of each other, have hereunto signed our names and witnessed this _____ day of _____ , 19 ___ , and declare: The declarant is personally known to me, and I believe the declarant to be of sound mind. I did not sign the declarant's signature to this declaration. Based upon information and belief, I am not related to the declarant by blood or marriage, a creditor of the declarant, entitled to any portion of the estate of the declarant under any existing testamentary instrument of the declarant, financially or otherwise responsible for the declarant's medical care, or an employee of any such person or institution.

_____   Address _____

                               _____

_____   Address _____

                               _____

Study Guide

Chapter 1.   The Sandwiched Generation

1. As a result of the huge number of "baby boomers" entering their senior years in the next couple of decades, what sociological, political, and attitudinal changes do you forecast for our society?

2. How does your perception of close family relatives in their senior years differ from your perception of the elderly in general? Why?

3. Describe your fears about growing old. What childhood incident reinforces for you the dread of growing old?

4. How does the media depict the elderly and what role do you think it plays in our understanding or misunderstanding of the aging process?

5. Why is caregiving socially sanctioned for females? With the ever-increasing presence of females in vital roles in today's work force, what changes do you see for tomorrow's caregivers?

6. Erma Bombeck describes guilt as the "gift that keeps on giving." How has guilt played a role in your caring for a loved one? What feelings did this guilt provoke?

7. Clearly, the family member who lives out of town can feel rather awkward about his or her role in the caregiving process. What do you feel is the most effective way for the out-of-town family member to participate in the caregiving of a senior relative?

Chapter 2.   When Someone in the Family Is Sick

1. Following the author's example, describe two or three of your closest experiences with eldercare. What happened? Was it home-based or institutionally based? How long did it last? What was your role? What "do's and don'ts" did you learn from your experience?

2. How would you like to be cared for in the event that you became a dependent elder? What are you doing now to create the best scenario for yourself in that situation? What are you doing to

create the best scenario for other loved ones who may come into this situation?

3. What thoughts or feelings did you have as you read the story of Jacob, Joseph, and Asenath? If you could have rewritten the story or read between the lines, what would you have imagined?

4. In what ways are eldercare and childcare similar? Different? Please explain.

5. How do you feel about the balance of "nurturance" and "assertiveness"? Do you agree with the author's approach to equal emphasis? Do you tend to emphasize one aspect over the other? Why?

6. How do you feel about the female "kin-keeper" role in America?

7. Have you ever seen a relationship where a caregiver went to either extreme of irresponsibility or hyperresponsibility? What happened? How could you tell it was extreme?

8. Give at least one illustration of a need you have today that represents human needs in the "basement, the first floor, and the upstairs." How are you doing with the developmental task of achieving "integrity" rather than "despair"? What are you doing to prevent preoccupation with your body, your work, and your ego?

9. How well does your church do in caring for the elderly? Is there ministry "to" and "by" the elderly? Could it be improved? Does your church minister to the adult caregivers? Please describe. What would you consider an ideal church-based helping model?

10. If the oldest member in your immediate family became immediately disabled and could never return to work, what would happen? What is the financial status of the family? What are the family dynamics that might enter into the decision-making and caregiving process?

11. What thoughts and feelings did you have about the modern "Joseph" and his wife, Irv and Francis? Who do you admire for their excellence in eldercare or for a "ministry of maturity"?

Chapter 3. The Age of Loss

1. How do Carol's concerns and feelings, as depicted in the anecdote in Chapter 1, differ from those expressed by her mother in Chapter 3? What conflict might these differences cause in their relationship?

2. How might our knowledge of the sensory losses experienced by many seniors guide our:

- communication with them?
- our selection of gifts of clothing, furnishings, and appliances for them?
- preparation of meals for them?
- our provision of safety devices for them?

3. Think of a time when you were hospitalized or remained at home for an extended time as a result of an accident or illness. How did this temporary loss of physical well-being impact you emotionally? How much more difficult would it have been for you to deal with your infirmity if you had no hope of regaining your strength or complete health?

4. Why do you think the agonizingly slow process of "losing" a loved one to Alzheimer's is such a torturous and grievous event for close family members?

5. What hints do a person's personality and social abilities in his or her young adult years offer you for predicting how a senior will cope with the dynamics of growing old?

6. How can men, who derive considerable esteem from their careers, prepare themselves for a successful retirement from those careers?

Chapter 4. Getting Assistance for the Caregiver

1. What are the apparent advantages of caring for a parent in your home? Do these advantages primarily favor the senior parent or are there significant advantages to other family members as well?

2. What are some of the interview questions you might use in selecting home health care assistance? What qualities would you look for in the course of the interview that might not be apparent in a review of the candidate's work history, educational background, or licensure?

3. How do you feel about the prospects that your parents' estate (your inheritance) could be exhausted by the high costs of providing their long-term care? How do you think your parents feel about the erosion of their estate?

4. What feelings do you think you will experience once you relinquish much of the hands-on care you had provided for a parent to a professional caregiver? How do you think your parent will feel about this change?

Chapter 5.   Housing and Healthcare Alternatives for the Elderly

1. Why are many seniors reluctant to live with their children as a solution to a health or financial problem?

2. Most seniors do not want to move from their homes. These desires are understandable when you consider the fact that they are distancing themselves from friends, leaving familiar surroundings, and most often relinquishing furniture and possessions that won't fit into their new accommodations. What is the emotional cost for seniors who find it necessary to move from their own homes?

3. Life-care communities often require a substantial entrance fee which is usually refundable in part if a resident should leave or pass away. What reluctance do you feel you and your parent would have in committing such a large amount of money? What is the reason for that reluctance?

4. Nursing homes are often the dreaded last resort for seniors in need of long-term health care. In fact, nursing homes undeservedly suffer a shabby image. What negative impressions do you have about nursing homes and how were those impressions derived?

5. Long-term care is very expensive. Many seniors do not have the assets to afford the cost of nursing home care for more than a few years and soon become reliant on the Medical Assistance program to fund the cost of their care. What reluctance do you perceive the general public will have to financing long-term care costs of the rapidly growing sector of indigent seniors?

6. Is it socially acceptable among your friends to place a parent in a nursing home? If not, why not?

Chapter 6.   Selecting a Nursing Home

1. What do you believe will be the primary objection to overcome when you "sell" a parent on the virtues of the nursing home you have determined to be the best suited for your parent?

2. What is the most important criteria you will use in selecting a nursing home?

3. What criteria are negotiable? That is, it would be nice if the facility offered these features or services, however, they are not critical to either you or your parent.

4. Most consumers do not base purchase decisions on objectivity alone. In fact, most purchase decisions are based on the subjective feelings a product or service invokes within us (i.e., the purchase of a new car is often based more on image than the mere need for a mode of transportation). When you purchase the services of a

nursing home, what are the feelings you hope will result from that purchase?

5. What objections will your family members have to making regular visits to a nursing home to visit your parent?

6. What do you imagine are your parent's worse fears about living in a nursing home? What are your greatest fears about placing a parent in a nursing home?

7. Children of institutionalized seniors play an important role in the overall care their parent receives when they visit regularly, are vigilant to lapses in quality care, and vocalize their concern about these service shortcomings in an appropriate manner. Which parts of this role make you uncomfortable? How might you augment your efforts in any of these areas with the assistance of another family member?

Chapter 7. The Eldercare Connection

1. After reading the story of The Shepherd's Center in Kansas City, what reactions did you have? What potential do you see in your area for such a ministry? Which home and center services seemed most important to you? What kinds of obstacles stand in your way from implementing such a ministry in your neighborhood?

2. Is it possible to prevent or delay "premature" nursing home admissions? Is it desirable?

3. Why do retirees make good volunteers for ministry? Are they being used in your church? Why or why not?

4. How do the specific qualifications laid down for the Greek Widows Food Ministry fit the task? Are they the same today?

5. Why might the priest and Levite have walked past the wounded man on the Jericho Road? Why might the Samaritan have stopped?

6. What are the key principles for working with volunteers?

7. How do you feel about adult daycare such as at The Fellowship Club of University Church? Would your feelings differ if you were the staff member? The elder? The caregiver?

8. How many people in your church are involved in eldercare right now? How many have been at some point? How many are likely to be in the future?

9. If you had a Barnabas Ministry, would you allow anyone to serve in that capacity? If so, why? If not, what kind of person would not qualify?

10. Which is the greater problem in your experience that hinders quality eldercare: deficiencies in clergy leadership? in volunteer ownership?

11. Which group do you feel the greatest burden for: the elder at home? the elder in an institution? the elder's caregiver? Why?

12. Have you ever seen elder abuse in any form? If so, please describe what you saw. How did you feel? What did you do? When did you come closest to committing elder abuse in some form? What can we do to prevent and to intervene in elder abuse?

Chapter 8.   When the Going Gets Tough

1. How did you feel about Adolph and Klara Hitler's experience? Did your feelings change after you knew the eighteen-year-old caregiver was Adolph Hitler? Why? Do you believe it is possible for an infected grief wound to turn into pathological mourning and push an unstable person "over the edge"? Have you ever had "anniversary reactions," such as Hitler's Christmas depressions? Please describe them and whether their intensity and frequency has decreased over the years.

2. Have you ever witnessed to an elderly person? What happened? Were they more like Nicodemus or the thief on the cross? How much do you believe the thief on the cross understood about the Lord and his work?

3. Have you ever had an OBE/NDE (Out-of-Body Experience/Near-Death Experience) like Velma? Have you known someone who did? What was it like? What effect(s) did it leave?

4. How do you understand James 5:13–20 (". . . the prayer of faith shall save the sick . . .") functioning in the twentieth century? Do you believe the faith of the sick person is a part of the healing process? How do you understand the healing of Jairus' daughter or the woman with the hemorrhage? How do you understand Jesus' words: "your faith has made you well?" (Mark 5:22–43; Matthew 21:12–22).

5. How did you feel about Smitty's farewell to his brother-in-law? Have you ever been with a person when he or she died? Please describe the experience and the reactions of the people around you. How did you react at the time and in the hours that followed?

6. How did you feel as you thought about Job's experiences? What was your reaction to the mourning rituals (the ash heap, etc.)? To Job's friends? To Job's wife? To the Lord's eventual words?

7. Can you name at least one experience in your lifetime when you suffered because of punishment? Nature? Growth? Example? Have you ever seen these meanings overlap in some cases? Have you ever seen two different people interpret the same loss in two different ways? How do you explain that? How do you feel

about the Lord leaving us "in the dark" sometimes about why we are suffering?

8. What bearing does Proverbs 24:11-12 have on preventing you from bystander apathy? Name some people in need who are "near death": the suicidal person, the unborn baby at risk of abortion, drunk drivers, the physically or mentally handicapped, cancer patients, police officers, AIDS patients. Should you help? How can you help?

9. What reaction did you have to Rowena's attitude of willingness to give up her eye? To give up her life? To be especially usable to the Lord? To be caring for her husband's needs while she was dying?

Chapter 9.   Tough Decisions

1. Define "natural moral law" and state how you think this approach to morality helps or hinders moral discussion and decision-making in a pluralistic culture.

2. How do the following passages inform the Bible's own view about natural moral law: Genesis 18:16-33; Amos 1 and 2; Romans 1:18-32; Romans 2:1-16?

3. What is a moral absolute and how does absolutism differ from moral relativism? Give examples, biblical or otherwise, that illustrate the fact some moral absolutes can be weightier than others. What is your view of how this fact helps to solve cases where there appear to be moral principles in conflict?

4. Use the chart on page 171 and try to surface the moral rules and principles involved in some moral conviction that you hold.

5. Compare and contrast utilitarian and deontological moral theories. Can you give biblical support for the idea that one of these systems is to be preferred to the other?

6. A woman and her husband were admitted to a nursing home at age 70 and 75, respectively. Three months later, the husband died suddenly, and shortly thereafter, the woman had a stroke that kept her from playing the piano, the only thing she felt she had left. She requested to be permitted to forego kidney dialysis, knowing that she would die in a few days. What should be done in this case and why? What ethical principles listed in the chapter are involved here?

7. Which principle do you believe is more important in conflict situations, the principle of autonomy or the principles of beneficence and nonmaleficence? Give reasons for your answer.

8. Take the chart on page 171 and use it to analyze the ethical case given at the beginning of the chapter. What issues does the chart help you to surface?

9. Repeat question 8, but this time focus on an ethical dilemma you are presently facing.

Chapter 10.   Ethical Issues at the End of Life

1. State the principle of double effect and discuss how it tries to capture the importance of intentions and means-to-ends in moral actions. Do you agree with the principle of double effect? Why or why not?

2. List the various distinctions (e.g. withholding/withdrawing) associated with the traditional view of euthanasia. What are the advantages and limitations of each distinction?

3. What are the differences between active and passive euthanasia? Do you think that the differences are morally significant? Why or why not?

4. How would you use this chapter to argue against a growing trend in this country: physician-assisted suicide (where a physician gives drugs to a patient knowing that the patient will use the drugs to commit suicide)?

5. Do you or your loved ones have a living will? What do you think of them? Use the example in the appendix to write a living will for yourself.

6. Who would you appoint as a proxy decision-maker for you in case you ever needed one? What instructions would you give that person?

7. Discuss your view of foregoing nutrition and hydration. Do you agree that these should not be viewed as treatments? How does your answer to this question influence the morality of your views about nutrition and hydration?

8. Discuss your view of the good life and include in your discussion a statement of what a meaningful death means to you. How does the chapter treatment of a Christian worldview vs. a minimalistic ethic inform your views about these issues?

Chapter 11.   Talking to Your Elderly Parents

1. Recall a time in the recent past when you tried to talk with your parent about issues concerning their well-being that were important to you. What happened? What might you have done or said differently that could have taken the discussion in a different direction?

2. What possible fears or concerns might your parent be dealing with that are not immediately obvious and which he or she has not chosen to disclose to you?

3. You may feel that in your caregiving role you are in some sense "parenting your own parent"; how might you be communicating this attitude to your parent? Do you think that he or she would perceive this in positive or negative terms?

4. How high is the level of trust between you and your parent? Is there emotional scar tissue in the relationship that stands as a barrier to your discussions? What might you do to initiate resolve and healing?

5. Can you identify each of your purposes for wanting to talk with your parent? What outcome do you hope to achieve? What, short of this, can you live with? What are the potential consequences of not addressing the issues? Is it worth ignoring?

6. Imagine that roles were reversed—that you were the elderly loved one. If your children had a particular concern about your well-being, how would your like them to approach you about it?

7. How do you understand your role(s) in the relationship with your elderly parent? In what ways do you predict that your role(s) will change in the future?

Endnotes

Chapter 1. The Sandwiched Generation

1. For more discussion on aging trends, see Ken Dychtwald, Ph.D., and Joe Flower, *Age Wave—The Challenges and Opportunities of an Aging America* (Los Angeles: Jeremy P. Tarcher, 1989), 1–23; Alan Pifer and Lydia Bronte, eds., *Our Aging Society—Paradox and Promises* (New York: W. W. Norton & Co., 1986), 3–110.
2. John Wood, "Labors of Love," *Modern Maturity* (August-September 1987), 28.
3. Nicky Marone, *How to Father a Successful Daughter* (New York: Fawcett Crest, 1988), 97–98.
4. "America's Aged: Longer Lives, Heavier Burdens," *Newsweek on Health* (Winter 1985).
5. Wood, "Labors of Love," 31.
6. Barbara Silverstone and Helen Kandel Hyman, *You and Your Aging Parent* (New York: Pantheon Books, 1976), 38–58.
7. "How Do Family Members Share Caregiving Tasks?" *Parent Care*, 4, no. 3 (March/April 1989) (published by the University of Kansas Gerontology Center).
8. "Caregiving Approach Differs for Husbands and Wives," *Parent Care*, 3, no. 3 (March/April 1988).

Chapter 2. When Someone in the Family Is Sick

1. This ratio of noninstitutional to institutional eldercare is based on private research by Andrew Hofer, M.A. who serves as the Executive Director of the National Association for Families Caring for Their Elders (P.O. Box 3441, Silver Spring, MD 20901).
2. Alan Pifer and Lydia Bronte, *Our Aging Society—Paradox and Promise* (New York: Norton, 1986), 150–51, 154, 156.
3. This analogy of the two-story house with a basement is original but adapts Maslow's "Hierarchy of Human Needs" (1954) toward aging-related needs as illustrated by Stephanie Pollack, Coordinator for the Center on Aging, University of Maryland.
4. Erik Erikson, *The Life Cycle Completed* (New York: Norton, 1982).
5. Barbara F. Okun, *Working with Adults: Individual, Family, and Career Development* (Monterey, CA: Brooks/Cole, 1984), 328–329; cp. David A.

Peterson, "A History of Education for Older Learners," in D. Barry Lumsden, *The Older Adult As Learner* (Washington, D.C.: Hemisphere, 1985), 3, 6.

6. This average length of the eldercare career at home is based on private research by Andrew Hofer, M.A., who is the Executive Director of the National Association for Families Caring for Their Elders (P.O. Box 3441, Silver Spring, MD 20901).

7. Richard A. Kalish, *Death, Grief, and Caring Relationships*, 2d ed. (Monterey, CA: Brooks/Cole, 1985), 143-153.

8. Robert C. Tate, Jr., "The Identification of Emotional Stress and Spiritual Needs of Senior Citizens in an Institutional Setting" (Ann Arbor, MI: Xerox University Microfilms, 1976), 111-113.

9. Jon Hendricks and C. Davis Hendricks, *Aging in Mass Society—Myths and Realities* (Boston, MA: Little, Brown, & Co., 1986), 41.

Chapter 3.   The Age of Loss

1. Barbara Silverstone and Helen Kandel Hyman, *You and Your Aging Parent* (New York: Pantheon Books, 1976), 61.

2. Ibid., 65; Lissy Jarvik, M.D., Ph.D. and Gary Small, M.D., *Parentcare—A Commonsense Guide for Adult Children* (New York: Crown Publishers, 1988), 248-249.

3. Florence D. Shelley, *When Your Parents Grow Old* (New York: Harper & Row, 1988), 222-239.

4. Ibid., 284-294.

5. Ibid., 298-317.

Chapter 4.   Getting Assistance for the Caregiver

1. Pamela J. Bayless, *Caring for Dependent Parents* (New York: Research Institute of America, 1986), 48.

2. "Who's Taking Care of Our Parents," *Newsweek*, May 6, 1985.

3. Barbara Silverstone and Helen Kandel Hyman, *You and Your Aging Parent* (New York: Pantheon Books, 1982), 189.

4. "In-Home Personal Care and Homemaker Chore Service Standards," Missouri Department of Social Service of the Division of Aging; P.O. Box 1337, Jefferson City, MO 65102.

Chapter 5.   Housing and Health Care Alternatives for the Elderly

1. Margaret Gold, Ph.D., *Guide to Housing Alternatives for Older Citizens* (Mount Vernon, NY: Consumer Reports Books, 1985), 10-11.

2. AARP, "Understanding Senior Housing," 1987; and Sumichrast et al., "Planning Your Retirement Housing," 1984.

3. AARP, "Understanding Senior Housing."

4. HRM Update, Alexander and Alexander, *Group Long-Term Health Care Insurance: The Next Employee Benefit?* (Newburyport, MA: The Alexander Consulting Group, December 9, 1989).

5. Ibid.

Chapter 6. Selecting a Nursing Home

1. R. Barker Bausel, Ph.D.; Michael A. Rooney, M.P.A.; and Charles B. Inlander, *How to Evaluate and Select a Nursing Home* (Reading, MA: Addison-Wesley, 1988), 28-29.
2. Nancy Fox, *You, Your Parent, and the Nursing Home* (Buffalo, NY: Prometheus Books: 1986), 46-51.

Chapter 7. The Eldercare Connection

1. Elbert C. Cole, "Lay Ministries with Older Adults," in William M. Clements, ed., *Ministry with the Aging—Designs, Challenges, and Foundations* (New York: Harper & Row, 1981), 250-265.
2. James Williams, "How to Minister to Senior Adults," an audiocassette (Nashville, TN: Broadman Records, 1975).
3. "National Survey of Caregivers—A Summary of Findings Conducted for The American Association of Retired Persons and The Travelers Companies" (Washington, DC: AARP Stock No. D13203, Oct. 1988), 3, 8, 14, 18, 21, 31-32.
4. Robert C. Tate, Jr., "The Identification of Emotional Stress and Spiritual Needs of Senior Citizens in an Institutional Setting" (Ann Arbor, MI: Xerox University Microfilms, 1976), 111-113.
5. "Coping with Eldercare: A Growing Challenge in the Workplace"—*A Hearing Before a Subcommittee of the Committee on Government Operations for the House of Representatives, One Hundredth Congress* (Washington, DC: U.S. Government Printing Office, 1989).
6. Richard L. Douglass, *Domestic Mistreatment of the Elderly—Towards Prevention* (Washington, DC: Criminal Justice Services of the American Association of Retired Persons, 1987), 3-4.

Chapter 8. When the Going Gets Tough

1. John Toland, *Adolf Hitler*, vol. 1 (Garden City, NY: Doubleday & Co., 1976), 10-11, 24, 26-29, 140-41, 295-96, 326, 345.
2. These three spiritual goals parallel the "transcendence" needs described in chapter 4: ego-transcendence/hope in God (i.e. "there is more to life than just me"), work-transcendence/love by others (i.e. "there is more to me than just what I do"), and body-transcendence/growth through suffering (i.e. "there is more to me than just how my body feels or looks"). These three goals are both *needs* that we should seek to meet for one another as well as *tasks* that we should seek to meet for ourselves. In the apostle Paul's words, "The goal of my ministry is love: sourced in a pure heart, a clean conscience, and an unhypocritical faith" (1 Timothy 1:5, author's paraphrase). These sources describe the "heart" purified through suffering, the "conscience" kept clean in our loving relationships to one another, and the "faith" that seeks to genuinely know and please God. As such, we seek to fulfill the chief commandment: "To love God with everything that is in us

and to love our neighbor as we wish others to love us" (Matthew 22:36–40, author's paraphrase).

3. Words by Dan Richardson who died of cancer in *Our Daily Bread* (Grand Rapids, MI: Radio Bible Class, 1989), Feb. 7.

4. Joseph H. Fichter, *Religion and Pain* (New York: Crossroads, 1981), 58, 63, 91–92.

5. Gerald Egan, *The Skilled Helper* (Belmont, CA: Wadsworth, 1986), 75–82.

6. Richard A. Kalish, *Death, Grief, and Caring Relationships* (Monterey, CA: Brooks/Cole, 1985), 145–149.

7. Joseph Fichter, *Religion and Pain* (New York: Crossroads, 1981), 63.

8. J. Epperly, "The Cell and the Celestial: Spiritual Needs of Cancer Patients" in *Journal of the Medical Association of Georgia* 72:5 (1983), 374.

Chapter 9. Tough Decisions

1. For more on natural law theories of ethics, see Alan J. Johnson, "Is There a Biblical Warrant for Natural-Law Theories?" *Journal of the Evangelical Theological Society* 25 (June 1982): 185–99; A. P. d'Entreves, *Natural Law* (London: Hutchinson, 2d. ed., 1970); Martin D. O'Keefe, *Known from the Things That Are* (Houston: Center for Thomistic Studies, 1987); Josef Fuchs, *Natural Law* (New York: Sheed and Ward, 1965); John Finnis, *Natural Law and Natural Rights* (Oxford: Clarendon, 1980).

2. C. S. Lewis, *The Abolition of Man* (New York: Macmillan, 1947), 29. Cf. John Warwick Montgomery, *Human Rights and Human Dignity* (Grand Rapids: Zondervan, 1986).

3. For more on the nature of ethical absolutes and ethical conflict, see W. D. Ross, *The Right and the Good* (Oxford: Oxford University Press, 1930); Norman Geisler, *Options in Contemporary Christian Ethics* (Grand Rapids: Baker, 1981). A brief overview of these issues can be found in Thomas A. Mappes, Jane S. Zembaty, *Biomedical Ethics* (New York: McGraw-Hill, 1981), 5–43.

4. Actually, there are two main types of utilitarianism, act utilitarianism and rule utilitarianism. The former focuses on the utility produced by specific, individual acts and the latter focuses on general kinds of acts (e.g. acts of promise keeping, acts of stealing). According to rule utilitarianism, an act is morally justified if and only if it falls under a correct moral rule. A correct moral rule is a rule which would maximize utility if everyone followed that rule as opposed to alternative rules. Thus, rule utilitarians directly compare the alternative utilities produced by different rules or sets of rules and act utilitarians directly compare the utility of specific actions and see moral rules as mere rules of thumb telling us how past actions have produced utility. What is important for both forms of utilitarianism is their agreement that no moral rule is intrinsically correct. What ultimately counts is the utility that is maximized. Introductory overviews of utilitarianism can be found in Fred Feldman,

Introductory Ethics (Englewood Cliffs, NJ: Prentice Hall, 1978), 16–79; Tom L. Beauchamp, *Philosophical Ethics* (New York: McGraw-Hill, 1982), 71–105.

5. It should be pointed out that both utilitarians and deontological ethicists can embrace these principles. The former will do so because these principles maximize utility when acted upon, the latter do so because these principles are intrinsically right. For more on these principles, see Tom L. Beauchamp, James F. Childress, *Principles of Biomedical Ethics* (Oxford: Oxford University Press, 1979).

6. I am indebted to Martha Elliot for suggesting to me a number of these questions.

Chapter 10.   Ethical Issues at the End of Life

1. For more information on this, see *Life-Sustaining Technologies and the Elderly* (Washington, DC, Congress of the United States), 166–354.

2. See James Rachels, *The End of Life* (Oxford: Oxford University Press, 1986). For a criticism of Rachels, see J. P. Moreland, "James Rachels and the Active Euthanasia Debate," *Journal of the Evangelical Theological Society* 31 (March 1988), 81–90.

3. Cf. Sidney H. Wanzer, et al., "The Physician's Responsibility Toward Hopelessly Ill Patients," *The New England Journal of Medicine* 320 (30 March 1989), 844–849. This article makes a distinction between assisted suicide on the one hand and active euthanasia on the other. But this does not seem to be correct. Assisted suicide still is an example of active euthanasia if for no other reason than the fact that the patient himself directly intends and causes his own death. Thus, assisted suicide is active euthanasia done by the patient, and what the article calls "active euthanasia" is that done directly by the physician. Thus, in assisted suicide, the physician is an accomplice to an immoral act, since he willingly participates and contributes to a suicide.

4. For more on advanced directives, see Paul Hofmann, ed., *Values in Conflict* (Chicago: American Hospital Association, 1985); Albert Johnson, Mark Siegler, William J. Winslade, *Clinical Ethics* (New York: Macmillan, 1986), 47–99; John F. Monagle, David C. Thomasma, eds., *Medical Ethics* (Rockville, MD: Aspen Publishers, 1988), 165–258.

5. For a brief, recent treatment of these issues by an evangelical Protestant, see John M. Frame, *Medical Ethics* (Grand Rapids: Baker, 1988), 58–73.

6. Cf. Joanne Lynn, editor, *By No Extraordinary Means: The Choice to Forego Life-Sustaining Food and Water* (Bloomington, IN: Indiana University Press, 1986). Also of value are several articles in *Issues in Law & Medicine,* 2 no. 2 (1986), especially the articles by Robert Barry and John R. Connery.

7. Cf. Daniel Callahan, "Minimalistic Ethics," *Hastings Center Report* 11 (Oct. 1981), 19–25; Stanley Hauerwas, *Suffering Presence: Theological Reflections on Medicine, the Mentally Handicapped, and the Church* (Notre Dame: University of Notre Dame Press, 1986).

Chapter 11.   Talking to Your Elderly Parents

1. Mark Edinberg, in his book *Talking with Your Aging Parents*, explores these kinds of communication in a more extended way and also explores three other kinds of communication: Sharing, Socializing, and Straightening out the past.

2. A useful and readily available paperback book entitled *You and Your Will* by Paul Ashley, Mentor Books, is helpful in preparing a client to make maximum and economical use of an attorney to do estate planning.

Bibliography

1. The Sandwiched Generation

Jo Horne, *Caregiving: Helping an Aged Loved One* (Des Plaines, IL: AARP Books/ Scott Foresman, 1985). Offers extensive coverage on resources, decision-making, caregiver stress, health problems, and home care. Also offers suggestions for advocacy.

Jamia Jacobson, Ph.D., *Help! I'm Parenting My Parents* (Indianapolis: Benchmark Press, 1988). Offers extensive coverage on wellness, medications, legal issues, financial issues, pets, crime and safety, elder abuse, and insurance.

Lissy Jarvik, M.D. Ph.D. and Gary Small, Ph.D., *Parentcare: A Commonsense Guide for Grown-Up Children* (New York: Crown Publishers, 1988). Offers extensive coverage of resources, communication, caregiver stress, wellness, health problems, death and dying. Also has helpful section on sexual health in aging.

James Kenny, Ph.D. and Stephen Spicer, M.D., *Eldercare: Coping with Late-Life Crisis* (Buffalo, NY: Prometheus Books, 1989). Offers extensive coverage of decision-making, and death and dying.

Nora Jean Levin, *How to Care for Your Parents: A Handbook for Adult Children* (Washington, DC: Storm King Press, 1987). Offers extensive coverage on legal and financial issues.

Helene MacLean, *Caring for Your Parents: A Sourcebook of Options and Solutions* (Garden City, New York: Doubleday, 1987). Offers extensive coverage of available resources, medications, insurance, community service, and nursing homes. Also lists state-by-state resources.

Bernard Shulman, M.D. and Raeann Berman, *How to Survive Your Aging Parents* (Chicago: Surrey Books, 1988). Offers extensive coverage on communication, caregiver stress, and tips on discussing difficult topics.

Barbara Silverstone and Helen Hyman, *You and Your Aging Parent* (New York: Pantheon Books, 1982). Offers extensive coverage on decision-making, communication, nursing homes, and death and dying. Also has good section on marriage and widowhood.

The University of Kansas Gerontology Center publishes every two months an excellent periodical called *Parent Care (Resources To Assist Family Caregivers)*. This is an excellent and practical publication specifically designed to meet the needs of the caregiver at home. To subscribe, write: Parent Care, Gerontology Center, 316 Strong Hall, The University of Kansas, Lawrence, KS 66045.

Children of Aging Parents is a group that offers lists of support groups for some states, a long distance directory of case management workers and caregiving booklets. The group can be reached at Children of Aging Parents, 2761 Trenton Road, Levittown, PA 19056.

2. When Someone in the Family Is Sick

John Claypool, *Tracks of a Fellow Struggler* (Waco: Word, 1974). A pastor wrestles with the death of his daughter.

Norman Cousins, *Anatomy of an Illness* (New York: Bantam, 1979). This bestseller explores the connection between mental outlook and medical recovery.

Billy Graham, *Facing Death and the Life After* (Waco: Word, 1987). A landmark book on the realities of death and preparing to meet God.

C. S. Lewis, *The Problem of Pain* (New York: Macmillan, 1962). A classic discussion of human suffering and the powerful questions it raises.

Gail Sheehy, *Pathfinders—Overcoming the Crises of Adult Life and Finding Your Own Path to Well-Being* (New York: Bantam, 1981). Why do some adults thrive during life's stresses while others wither?

Gary Smalley and John Trent, *The Blessing* (Nashville: Nelson, 1986). An excellent guide for healing conflicted family interactions.

Paul Tournier, *Learn to Grow Old* (San Francisco: Harper & Row, 1972). A Christian psychiatrist reveals the inner world of the older adult.

John W. Wenham, *The Goodness of God* (Downer's Grove: InterVarsity, 1974). How can God be good and allow suffering?

3. The Age of Loss

Collette Brown and Robert Onzuka-Anderson (editors), *Our Aging Parents: A Practical Guide to Eldercare* (Honolulu: University of Hawaii Press, 1985). Offers extensive coverage on wellness, health problems, home care, and nursing homes. Contains a helpful glossary of terms.

Elwood N. Chapman, *The Unfinished Business of Living: Helping Aging Parents Help Themselves* (Los Altos, CA: Crisp Publications, 1988). Offers extensive coverage on decision-making, communication, caregiver stress, and death and dying. Also offers excellent communication exercises.

John Deedy, *Your Aging Parents* (Chicago: Thomas More Press, 1984). Offers extensive coverage on religion and crime and safety and adequate coverage on a wide range of senior-oriented issues.

James Halpern, Ph.D., *Helping Your Aging Parents* (New York: Fawcett Crest, 1987).

Florence D. Shelley, *When Your Parents Grow Old* (New York: Harper & Row, 1988). Offers extensive coverage on health problems, housing possibilities, behavioral changes, and strategies for successful aging.

David A. Tomb, M.D., *Growing Old: A Handbook for You and Your Aging Parent* (New York: Viking Penguin, 1984). Offers extensive coverage of wellness, health problems, and insurance.

For those families with loved ones afflicted with Alzheimer's disease, there is a toll-free number for the Alzheimer's Disease and Related Disorders Association. The number is (800) 572-6037. The organization has more than 160 chapters and 1,000 support groups nationwide to help caregivers.

4. Getting Assistance for the Caregiver

Nora Jean Levin, *How to Care for Your Parents* (Washington, DC: Storm King Press, 1986).

Helene MacLean, *Caring for Your Parents: A Sourcebook of Options and Solutions* (Garden City, NY: Doubleday, 1987). Offers extensive coverage on home care options, medications, insurance, community service, and nursing homes. Also lists state-by-state resources.

The National Association for Home Care is a national clearing house of information regarding home care agencies. Available from these agencies are helpful pamphlets such as *All About Home Care: Consumer's Guide* ($2.00), *How to Select a Home Care Agency* (free) and reprints of *Caring Magazine's ABC's of Home Care* issue ($7.50). The National Association of Home Care's address is 519 C Street, N.E., Stanton Park, Washington, DC 20002.

5. Housing and Healthcare Alternatives for the Elderly

Margaret Gold, Ph.D., *Guide to Housing Alternatives for Older Citizens* (Mount Vernon, NY: Consumers Union of United States, Inc. 1985). Offers an in-depth discussion of the distinguishing features of the many types of senior housing, both traditional and innovative, available in the country.

Free information on housing options for seniors is available from the American Association of Homes for the Aging, 1129 20th Street, N.W., Suite 400, Washington, DC 20036.

6. Selecting a Nursing Home

R. Barker Bausell, Ph.D., Michael A. Rooney, M.P.A., and Charles B. Inlander, *How to Evaluate and Select a Nursing Home* (Reading, MA: Addison-Wesley, 1988). Offers a comprehensive, well-organized approach to identifying an appropriate nursing home as well as a glossary and numerous lists of evaluatory questions.

Nancy Fox, *You, Your Parent, and the Nursing Home* (Buffalo, NY: Prometheus Books, 1986). Offers a sensitive and empathy-filled discussion on life for both the patient and his family in the nursing home. One of the few works that departs from endless lists to discuss the finer distinctions on how care is delivered.

Ted Rossi, *Step by Step: How to Actively Ensure the Best Possible Care for Your Aging Relative* (New York: Warner Books, 1987). Offers adequate discussion on nursing home selection process and a good practical discussion on enriching the life of a nursing home patient.

7. The Eldercare Connection

William M. Clements, ed. *Ministry with the Aging* (San Francisco: Harper & Row, 1983). Creative ideas and proven programs for ministering with the elderly.

Edward F. Dobihal, Jr. and Charles William Stewart, *When a Friend Is Dying* (Nashville: Abingdon, 1984). A guide to caring for the terminally ill and bereaved.

Joseph H. Fichter, *Religion and Pain* (New York: Crossroads, 1981). The spiritual aspects of health care.

Robert M. Gray and David O. Moberg, *The Church and the Older Person* (Grand Rapids: Eerdmans, 1977). What the church can do for the older adult and what the older adult can do for the church.

Ruth Kopp, *When Someone You Love Is Dying* (Grand Rapids: Zondervan, 1980). A physician gives practical counsel to those who care for the very sick.

Larry Richards and Paul Johnson, *Death and the Caring Community* (Portland: Multnomah, 1980). A guide for developing excellent church visitation ministries.

Samuel Southard, *Training Church Members for Pastoral Care* (Valley Forge: Judson, 1982). Enlarging your pastoral staff with lay caregivers.

Howard W. Stone, *The Caring Church* (San Francisco: Harper & Row, 1983). Training lay ministers for strategic hospital and shut-in ministry.

Frank R. Tillapaugh, *The Church Unleashed* (Ventura: Regal, 1982). Getting God's people out where the needs are.

8. When the Going Gets Tough

Barry K. Estadt, *Pastoral Counseling* (Englewood Cliffs, NJ: Prentice-Hall, 1983). An excellent introduction to pastoral counseling.

Heye Faber, *Striking Sails* (Nashville: Abingdon, 1984). A pastoral-psychological view of growing older in our society.

E. Brooks Holifield, *A History of Pastoral Care in America —From Salvation to Self-Realization* (Nashville: Abingdon, 1983). How expectations about clergy ministry have changed from the colonial period to the present.

Lawrence E. Holst, ed. *Hospital Ministry* (New York: Crossroad, 1985). The role of the chaplain today.

Richard A. Kalish, *Death, Grief, and Caring Relationships* (Belmont: Brooks/Cole, 1985). An outstanding introduction to the psychosocial aspects of loss.

Patrick L. McKee, *Philosophical Foundations of Gerontology* (New York: Human Sciences, 1982). Competent essays on the most poignant questions and answers about aging given since ancient times.

Therese A. Rando, *Grief, Dying and Death* (Champaign: Research, 1984). Clinical interventions for professional caregivers.

R. Scott Sullender, *Grief and Growth* (New York: Paulist, 1985). Pastoral resources for emotional and spiritual growth.

Robert J. Wicks, ed. *Clinical Handbook of Pastoral Counseling* (New York: Paulist, 1985). The complexities and techniques of delivering pastoral care in a clinical setting.

9. Tough Decisions: Cultivating the Art of Ethical Decision-Making

1. General Introduction to Ethics

Tom Beauchamp and LeRoy Walters, *Contemporary Issues in Bioethics* (2nd edition, Belmont, CA: Wadsworth, 1982). Pages 1–43 are the first place to begin for a brief overview of ethics and bioethics (Basic).

Tom Beauchamp, *Philosophical Ethics* (New York: McGraw-Hill, 1982). This book contains a set of readings by various thinkers on the nature of morality, utilitarianism, deontological theories, virtue ethics, rights, justice, and the nature of moral justification (Advanced).

Fred Feldman, *Introductory Ethics* (Englewood Cliffs, NJ: Prentice-Hall, 1978). This work is an introduction to both normative and metaethics. It is well done and helpful, especially in metaethics (Intermediate).

Thomas Mappes and Jane Zembaty, *Biomedical Ethics* (2nd edition, New York: McGraw-Hill, 1986). Pages 1–46 rival Beauchamp and Walters (see above) as the best introduction to basic concepts in ethics and bioethics (Basic).

2. General Introduction to Bioethics

Tom Beauchamp and James Childress, *Principles of Biomedical Ethics*, 2nd edition, (New York: Oxford, 1983). This is a detailed treatment of autonomy, nonmaleficence, beneficence, and justice. It also includes discussions on utilitarianism, deontological theories, and virtue theories (Advanced).

Stanley Hauerwas, *Suffering Presence: Theological Reflections on Medicine, the Mentally Handicapped, and the Church* (Notre Dame: University of Notre Dame Press, 1986). Hauerwas argues that a Christian worldview and virtue ethics are essential in approaching ethical decision-making. He has an excellent chapter on the morality of suicide.

Paul B. Hofman (Chairman, Special Committee on Biomedical Ethics), *Values in Conflict* (Chicago: American Hospital Association, 1985). This is a very helpful introduction (117 pages) to issues which arise in the context of hospital bioethics committees. It includes useful material on DNR orders, Living Will/Natural Death Acts, and materials for further study (Basic).

Albert Jonsen, Mark Siegler, and William Winslade, *Clinical Ethics*, 2nd edition, (New York: Macmillan, 1986). This work is written for nurses, doctors, and medical students but it is still a helpful tool for those without medical training. It offers a good overview of ethical issues which arise in acute care, but Chapter 2 (Patient Preferences), Chapter 3 (Quality of Life Issues), and Chapter 4 (Socioeconomic Factors) are relevant to the Long Term Health Care setting (Intermediate).

Edmund D. Pellegrino and David C. Thomasma, *For the Patient's Good* (New York: Oxford, 1988). An excellent treatment of how to approach medical ethics which emphasizes beneficence and does not overstate the value of autonomy (Intermediate).

3. Works on Ethics from Different Religious Traditions

A. Catholic

Benedict Ashley and Kevin O-Rourke, *Health Care Ethics* (St. Louis, MO: The Catholic Health Association of the United States, 1982). This is a massive, detailed treatment of health care issues (Advanced).

Richard M. Gula, *What Are They Saying about Moral Norms?* (New York: Paulist Press, 1982). The most helpful introduction to Catholic moral philosophy I have seen. It is very helpful and easy to read (Basic).

B. Evangelical Protestant

John Jefferson Davis, *Evangelical Ethics* (Phillipsburg, PA: Presbyterian and Reformed, 1985). Davis' work is broad and touches on issues not directly relevant to Health Care (war, divorce, civil disobedience). But there is much of value here for health care providers and the book is a good example of how articulate evangelicals use the Bible in moral reasoning (Intermediate).

Norman L. Geisler, *Christian Ethics: Options and Issues* (Grand Rapids: Baker Book House, 1989). This is a completely revised and updated version of Geisler's earlier work *Ethics: Alternatives and Issues*. The first half covers alternative approaches to ethics and the second half discusses different topics in ethics. It is written in a very readable way and is an excellent resource (Basic or Intermediate).

C. *Mainline Protestant*

Paul D. Simmons, *Birth and Death: Biomedical Decision-Making* (Philadelphia: Westminster Press, 1983). Simmons models the use of the Bible in moral decision-making from a moderate protestant perspective by focusing on abortion, euthanasia, biotechnical parenting, and genetics (Intermediate).

D. *Jewish*

David Feldman and Fred Rosner, *Compendium on Medical Ethics*, 6th edition, (New York: Federation of Jewish Philanthropies of New York, Inc. 1984). This is a very helpful survey of Jewish moral, ethical, and religious principles in medical practice (Intermediate).

10. Ethical Issues at the End of Life

1. Case Studies in Euthanasia

Robert M. Veatch, *Case Studies in Medical Ethics* (Cambridge: Harvard University Press, 1977). Chapter 13 contains helpful case studies in euthanasia (Intermediate).

2. Works Focusing on Life-sustaining Technologies

John W. Rowe, chairperson, *Life-Sustaining Technologies and the Elderly* (Washington: U.S. Government Printing Office, 1987). This is a standard resource for information about the nature of various life-sustaining interventions (Basic).

Robert M. Veatch, ed., *Life Span: Values and Life-Extending Technologies* (San Francisco: Harper & Row, 1979). This is a collection of essays on topics surrounding life-extending technologies and the ethical issues involved in using them. One section is devoted to natural death and aging (Advanced).

3. General Works on Medical Ethics Which Contain Sections on Euthanasia

John Arras and Robert Hunt, *Ethical Issues in Modern Medicine* (Palo Alto: Mayfield Publishing Company, 1983). This contains a section devoted to euthanasia and caring for dying patients. It is written from a variety of points of view (Advanced).

Benedict M. Ashley and Kevin D. O'Rourke, *Health Care Ethics* (St. Louis: The Catholic Health Association of America, 1982). This is a very thorough work written by Catholic moral theologians which includes helpful treatments of euthanasia (Intermediate to Advanced).

Tom L. Beauchamp and LeRoy Walters, *Contemporary Issues in Bioethics* (Belmont: Wadsworth Publishing Company, 1982). This work is a standard resource in medical ethics and features a helpful section of euthanasia (Intermediate to Advanced).

Stanley Hauerwas, *Suffering Presence* (Notre Dame: University of Notre Dame Press, 1986). Hauerwas is one of the leading Christian ethicists writing today and his approach to end-of-life questions is from within a virtue theory of ethics. This book is must reading for anyone trying to get insight into how Christianity relates to medical ethics (Intermediate).

Albert R. Jonsen, Mark Siegler and William J. Winslade, *Clinical Ethics* (New York: Macmillan, 1986). This is a handbook on ethical issues. It covers a number of issues in clear fashion, but the discussions are too brief (Basic).

Thomas A. Mappes and Jane S. Zembaty, *Biomedical Ethics* (New York: McGraw-Hill, 1986). This work contains an entire section on euthanasia from several points of view and rivals Beauchamp and Walters above as the best text currently available (Intermediate to Advanced).

Tom Regan, ed., *Matters of Life and Death* (New York: Random House, 1980). This book is a popular anthology of articles on several issues involved at the end of life (Intermediate to Advanced).

Andrew C. Varga, *The Main Issues in Bioethics* (New York: Paulist Press, 1980). Varga has written a very helpful brief introduction to bioethics. It is written from a conservative Catholic point of view (Basic).

4. Works Which Largely Focus on Euthanasia

Morris B. Abram, chairman, *Deciding to Forego Life-Sustaining Treatment* (Washington: U.S. Government Printing Office, 1983). This is a book which includes various legal, moral, and medical aspects of euthanasia (Basic to Intermediate).

Germain Grisez and Joseph M. Boyle, Jr., *Life and Death with Liberty and Justice* (Notre Dame: University of Notre Dame Press, 1979). This is a classic, conservative treatment of euthanasia and other ethical issues written by Catholic thinkers (Advanced).

James Rachels, *The End of Life* (Oxford: Oxford University Press, 1986). Rachels is the main defender of the libertarian view that active euthanasia is no different from passive euthanasia (Intermediate).

Paul Ramsey, *Ethics at the Edges of Life* (New Haven: Yale University Press, 1978). Ramsey's book is written from the perspective of a Protestant thinker with traditional views about euthanasia (Advanced).

5. Works Discussing Artificial Nutrition and Hydration

Joanne Lynn, ed., *By No Extraordinary Means* (Bloomington: Indiana University Press, 1986). This book covers several issues involved in nutrition and hydration from several moral points of view (Advanced).

11. Talking with Your Elderly Parents

Malcolm Cowley, *The View from Eighty* (New York: The Viking Press, 1980).

Mark A. Eidenberg, *Talking with Your Aging Parents* (Boston: Shambhala Publications, Inc., 1987).

Carol C. Flax, Ph.D. and Earl Ubell, *Getting Your Way—The Nice Way* (New York: Wideview Books, 1980).

John Gillies, *A Guide to Caring for and Coping with Aging Parents* (Nashville: Thomas Nelson Publishers, 1981).

Lissy Jarvik, M.D., Ph.D. and Gary Small, M.D., *Parentcare: A Commonsense Guide For Adult Children* (New York: Crown Publishers, 1988).

Arthur N. Schwartz, M.D., *Survival Handbook for Children of Aging Parents* (Chicago: Follett Publishing Company, 1977).